STATUTE MILES

Drawn by Irvin E. Alleman,
National Geographic Staff

© National Geographic Society

Atlantic Ocean

Godthaab

Narssaq
Julianehaab
Cape Farewell

...ait

Cumberland Sound
Frobisher Bay
Loks Land
Lower Savage Islands
Resolution Island
Button Islands
Cape Chidley
Bowdoin Harbour
Nachvak Fiord
Hebron
Okak
Kiglapait Mts.
Nain
Hopedale
Cape Mugford
Port Manvers
Assawaban River
Davis Inlet
Turnavik Islands
Makkovik

Hawke Harbour
Battle Harbour
St. Anthony

NEWFOUNDLAND
Bay of Islands
Port aux Basques
Cabot Strait
St. John's

Cape Breton Island
Bras d'Or Lakes
Sydney
St. Peters Locks

LABRADOR

Strait of Belle Isle
Cape Anguille
Gulf of St. Lawrence
St. Paul's I.
Big Harbour
Beinn Breagh
NOVA SCOTIA
Halifax
Cape Sable

Q U E B E C

Sept Îles

St. Lawrence River

Quebec
Montreal
Ottawa
St. Lawrence R.

MAINE
Bay of Fundy
Boothbay Harbor
Casco Bay
Provincetown
Boston
New York

UNITED STATES

Washington

Harbour
Hudson Strait
McLelan Strait
Port Burwell
Button Islands

Dorset
Chubb Crater
Ungava Bay
Fort Chimo

Hudson Bay

Churchill
MANITOBA

C A N A D A

ONTARIO

Toronto

55°

# ARCTIC ODYSSEY

The Life of Rear Admiral Donald B. MacMillan

# ARCTIC ODYSSEY

The Life of Rear Admiral
Donald B. MacMillan

By *EVERETT S. ALLEN*

ILLUSTRATED WITH PHOTOGRAPHS

DODD, MEAD & COMPANY
*New York, 1962*

217267

Library of Congress Catalog Card Number: 62-14447

Printed in the United States of America
by Vail-Ballou Press, Inc., Binghamton, N. Y.

THIS BOOK IS DEDICATED to Miriam MacMillan, whose un-flagging interest greatly facilitated its conception and comple-tion. To borrow a phrase from Nasson College, which appro-priately saw fit to honor Miriam MacMillan, with a degree of Doctor of Humane Letters, for her nine trips to the Arctic with her skipper-husband, her published books and articles on the Arctic, her films of this little known area, her "record of always standing her watch in fair weather and foul . . . have won her a rightful place . . . as a working member of the team."

E.S.A.
Provincetown 1962

# ILLUSTRATIONS

vii

# ILLUSTRATIONS

The walrus, the most dangerous animal of the North
Eskimos ride sledges on ice
MacMillan's dogs rest on the icefoot
Aloft at *Bowdoin*'s crosstrees
S.S. *Roosevelt,* the Peary North Pole Expedition steamer

PHOTOGRAPHS FOLLOWING PAGE 214

Miriam MacMillan at the wheel of *Bowdoin*
MacMillan with a baby musk-ox
An Eskimo pup
*Bowdoin* takes refuge from dangerous drift ice
*Bowdoin,* stranded on a ledge in Refuge Harbor, North Greenland
Musk-oxen in customary battle defense formation
Baby eider ducks snug in their nest

PHOTOGRAPHS FOLLOWING PAGE 244

A strong snowhouse
The icefoot often is the only arctic "highway"
A polar bear protecting her young
*Bowdoin,* frozen in solidly for eleven months
An arctic puffin
Dovekies, known as little auks

# 1

<br>

CONSIDER THE IMPACT of an uncommon land upon a small boy, and vice versa.

The uncommon land was Provincetown, Massachusetts, which is to say, a sand finger poked obstinately into the tumbling swells of the North Atlantic at a latitude and longitude acceptable to the mackerel in summer and the hooded merganser in winter.

Uncommon, because of the people who lived there, who were, in turn, uncommon because of where they lived, a marination, if you will, of environment and heredity akin to the relationship of fish and plants in an aquarium, in which the two exchange oxygen and carbon dioxide and thus sustain each other.

Understand, then, that to live in Provincetown is to look out of the window and not at the calendar to find out what day it is. The seasons, the date, and even the hour are obvious to those who read what may be read from the caramel-backed dunes that are never the same shape from one wind to the next; from the clear pools in the flat sweep of beach

1

at half-tide; from wind-blasted pines and scrub oak butting their tortured shapes above the sandy sky line; from the gull's clean and lonely cry at daybreak; from the smell of weather to come, and from the predictability of the cheerful cranberry and the succulent, yet unassuming, sea clam.

At this time, which is to say specifically, 1874, the people who made Provincetown uncommon were more aware of all these things than are most of their thermostatically controlled children and grandchildren who, for better or worse, do not have to understand the anatomy and physiology of nature or die.

For Provincetown then, with its forty-odd docks at the tip of the "bare and bended arm of Cape Cod," was crowded with the cock-billed yards of the whaler, the broad and shallow hulls of the little coasters that bustled brick, coal, lumber, and fish with postmanlike fidelity, sleet and rain notwithstanding, and with the lofty and lean topmasts of the big schooners that went to the Grand Banks in summer and to the West Indies in winter, their lee rails under and sozzling all the way.

In those days the uncommon men could close their eyes and tell you what was going on. There is a sweet and clear music that comes from the stout heart of a calking mallet when it strikes home, a bustling optimism in the chuckle of a throat halyard block as its sheaves turn and a heavy foresail is boosted, a foot at a time, rasping and taut against the sky.

There are smells. Oakum and tar, copper paint and salt fish, a newborn chowder in the forecastle of the vessel to windward; wood smoke from the galley range, and sea smell, especially when the wind is east, blown halfway from the coast of Spain, and salty enough to taste.

Now of this small boy. Stand here at a particular point on what is called Commercial Street, that is, a street three miles long or the length of the town itself, narrow enough for two to pass if they are friendly, and where most of the houses are known, not for being plumb, but enduring, they being built close together not to encourage anybody to mind someone else's business, but rather to keep the wind out and because everybody wanted to have a door on the beach.

On one end of these houses is the street, on the other the sea, and whether, entering from the street, one comes into the kitchen or the living room depends on the temperament of the owner who did, after all, decide which way he wanted to face in his daily life.

On a particular door there is a bronze plaque which reads: "Birthplace of Commander Donald B. MacMillan, Arctic Explorer. This tablet placed by the Research Club, Provincetown, Mass., 1926." On November 10, 1874, Mac-Millan was born here.

From the beginning the world in which he found himself was fascinating to him. At the earliest, ice and snow held a compulsive interest for him—there was much more of it in Provincetown in those days. In the winter of his birth Cape Cod was locked in an ice field for all of the sixteen miles from Wood End to Manomet—and it is a titillating thought to wonder whether this interest of his arose from the subconscious if one is inclined to believe there is an inherent destiny that shapes our ends.

3

In the front yard of the house at 524 Commercial Street he saw his first snowhouse, built by an older brother. Eyes bright with wonder, he crawled through the oval door and sat there silent, feeling more than understanding the beauty of the glittering snow blocks, the truth of the clean coldness.

And there was the beach. No bribes of cookies, no motherly reprimands, could keep him from it, not even in winter, and it is something to remember that fear did not either, although it could have, had the boy been less uncommon.

On a certain day the harbor was completely filled with drift ice, scattered pans driven by a southerly wind from the shoal ground at the head of Massachusetts Bay to the harbor of Provincetown. It was one great, crystal mass in the December sun, from the shore to Long Point, a mile and a half away, broken here and there by dark blue lanes of water that an arctic man would call leads.

The boy hopped from chunk to chunk, finally took to sliding on his belly on the gently sloping beach, glazed by the falling tide into perfect coasting ground for one who had no sled. He ran, threw himself onto the slippery surface leading to the harbor ice, saw the black pool of water dead ahead, threw out his hands and arms to check his speed . . . and that was all.

Walter Crosby and Lew Morgan were beachcombing that morning, a pastime that is about as New England as possible, for it provides exercise, opportunity to appreciate the natural beauties, and, with luck, something worth taking home to eat, wear, or build with.

In that pool of water the boys saw a dark blob that looked like an old coat or a worn-out pair of pants. With a long stick Walter poked it toward Lew, who turned it over, revealing the white, cold face of Danny Baxter who lived across the street, so called because the Provincetown Scotch seldom used the last name in referring to anybody.

They carried him, with that tongue-tied timidity and helplessness that comes to boys when there is everything and nothing to be said, to his kitchen door. When the door opened, they handed the small and dripping boy to his mother, blurting, "He's dead." Then they ran.

Some things one was too small to remember, or perhaps it is that being subtle, these things were overshadowed by the more dramatic. Dan does not know why the mother did not call for help, but perhaps it was because she really believed he was dead. Yet women who live by the sea do not resign themselves even to death so easily, nor did Sarah Gardner MacMillan, shipbuilder's daughter and descendant of the Mayflower Compact signers.

She peeled the sodden clothing from him, pushed both his ice-cold feet into a bucket of hot mustard water, and placed a warm blanket over his head. For how long? Through an eternity, until a millennium . . . until he breathed deeply again and his eyes opened. She could not know it, nor he—although he remembered the strong smell of the mustard water eight decades later—but this was a charmed life's first of many brushes with death.

In the warmer days of the year, the winds blew gently from the southwest, the black-necked goose, flop-winged and lumbering, left for the north, and the bright notes of the ring-necked plover sounded on the flats. At such times the classroom of the village school, even for those eager

5

to learn, took second place to reality.

For on the docks and in the loafing room of Kibbie Cook's grocery were those who not only knew all that the geography books told of Maui and Lapland but such things as were never printed. Here were the crews of the staunch schooners and brigs that went a-whaling, east to the Azores, down to the South Atlantic and around the Horn into the Pacific. They all knew Hatteras in an easterly; many knew something of the girls in grass skirts smiling a welcome in a universal language, and one had seen a South Pacific native with a bloody blade in his teeth.

Here, too, were the sailormen of the hundred-vessel fishing fleet, the Scotch, Yankees, and Portuguese, from the Cape, Boston, Gloucester, Nova Scotia, and Cape Breton. Big-handed, red-cheeked, the men from the Provinces, McDonalds, McLeods, Mathersons, McFees, Kemps, Dowlings, and McKenzies. Flat-bellied and lean, boys from the island of Boularderie in the Bras d'Or Lakes who could pull a dory with two inches of freeboard to windward in half a gale for half a day and still have breath to laugh. Here were Portuguese from the Azores who knew each day what the codfish were thinking and thus could find them, even as they could find the pond lilies in summer and the beach plums on the dunes.

In September the fathers came home from the Grand Banks, colors flying at the masthead to denote a full fare, the vessels deep-laden with the big split cod that paid for underwear, bread, and shoes. These sailors were the full-bearded ones with hard, salt-reddened hands; strong, booming, and smelly, they were the heroes.

This small, uncommon boy listened to these men, and what they said consisted not of words, but of siren music. Now it was a whaleman talking, of a boat bitten to pieces, of the screams of the shipmate who disappeared into the chomping mouth. Whaling it must be then, when manhood came.

Again, it was a Banker with a tale of rough water and tumbling sea, of capsized dories, clinging to a dory-plug strap in ice-filled waters, of the hoarse bellow of a liner's horn in fog thick as cheese, of collision and the splintering crack of a wooden hull, of cries in the night and perhaps rescue . . . or perhaps not. So one decided then to become a fisherman, for that, indeed, was a man's way of life.

All of this is something that women may not understand, but boys do, and although death or near-death should logically be a deterrent, it does not work that way. At six this small boy stood on the sidewalk and watched a black horse pulling that type of wagon commonly known as a jigger. In the back, six bare feet protruded from beneath a canvas. Three lifesavers had drowned trying to rescue the crew of a sloop grounded and smashed on Peaked Hill Bar the night before.

Still, death was recognized as a part of life in a community whose "back beach" was a last resting place for the bones of many ships and men and whose natives understood that it was more important to know wind and weather than to know one's neighbor.

More important to those who listen and are compelled to listen, seduced from the beginning by the sea's call, is the fact that this life at the rim of death knows its own world

7

and lives in it, like a race apart.

These Bankers, carefully spelled with an upper-case "B" and no confusion, thank you, with the shore-based computers of assets and liabilities (for of the former, the sailor had too few to bother with, and of the latter, once the land was hull down over the horizon, too many for a practical man to waste time worrying about), these Bankers, then, spoke their own tongue, titled their own tools, named their own places.

The schooners went to the Banks, the Grand Banks, and this was an apt adjective to the mind of an uncommon boy. These sailormen talked of Quero and The Rocks and were as at home in the trackless roll and trough as is the lawyer reaching for the dining-table pepper shaker. And they could find things just as easily, too, though there was nothing out there for a lubber to see or smell—no fence, no wall, no sign saying: "Go this way, old boy, and keep dry!"

And in the fall they peaked their acres of baggy mainsails and coasted south down the parallels of latitude to Barbados, a name that rolled enchantingly un-New England-like on the tongue, to take aboard oranges, bananas, and coconuts, a cargo as romantic as Eastern gems, from a port as inspiring to the imagination as Camelot. These were, indeed, the dragon slayers come to life, the ever-questing brave. . . .

So with the whalemen, whose other home was vaguely off Hatteras, on Cornell, or at some mathematical way station of the world called Twenty-Forty, where they were, knowledgeably, in their own watery front yard, able to feed themselves three times a day, doctor most ills, repair anything that parted or carried away, and go about their business independent of the various continents.

These Provincetown fathers were no tinkers and tailors but captains, mates, bos'uns, and boat steerers. And it may have been even then, when Danny Baxter was at the age of six or less, that none of the stories they told were quite as fascinating as those of the halibut fleet that went to the blue water beyond the Arctic Circle.

Their sanctuary was Holsteinsborg in Greenland. It was the halibut catcher who talked of the pinnacles of ice, blue, white, and green, that at their best resemble crystal castles and cathedrals with Gothic spires and at their enveloping worst crush ships, turn them inside out, and shove the keel up through the deck.

Language of men of the sea is as individual as any foreign tongue, more distinctive than many, and requires an interpreter for those who do not speak it. It is not so much a thing of participles and pronouns, although they are there, but rather a collection of action idioms that meet every situation open-eyed and head-on, getting there fast enough to be of practical use, yet roundabout enough so that poetry is never quite excluded. It is important in understanding how this uncommon boy learned to talk.

Now take the wind, for example, which is close enough to a sailorman to be a half brother, for if it is gone, he sits and frets; if it is present, it takes him to work and back home again, and if it becomes unruly enough, it kills him.

As if it were a Pegasus, the wind backs. It also hauls, as it shifts. It breezes, it flattens, and when it breezes, it makes the going dusty, which is to say, wetter. The wind is called

9

for the place it comes from, not where it's going, for winds have predictable traits depending on their origins—as do people—and to give them a family name tells a lot about their breeding and behavior.

Anything nearer the wind is to windward; the other way, to leeward, which is pronounced loo'ard, because things do not, after all, have to be pronounced the way they are spelled. With the wind ahead the vessel lies close-hauled, full and by, and beats to windward in tacks that may be short, long, or split. With the wind astern, or abeam, the good ship runs or reaches, with sheets (which are, mind you, not sails, but lines) started. And mind the following sea, on which the luckless can trip or broach, capsize or swamp, and perhaps carry away everything aloft and the Charley Noble (which is the kitchen chimney) besides.

This is a world in which stairs are ladders, sheets are found topside, but seldom on the bunks, and it is eight bells at four o'clock. It is far, far removed from the universe of those who do not know what it is like to sleep in a bed that is never still.

This was the world of Danny Baxter MacMillan, age seven, in 1881. Necessarily, because he was a little boy still, he lived in it partly by proxy, but that would not be for long. His mother, knowing, as all women must whose men sail in ships, that courage is essential to life, never stopped him from doing anything that required it. As a first-grader, and ever after, he would climb to the masthead of a ship at the dock, lean his cheek against the tarred shrouds, look at the sea's curving blue as it bent to the horizon, feel kinship with the sweeping, curious gull, and dream, oblivious of the deck or the earth beneath him.

His mother saw him thus many times, but whatever fears she had, whatever impulses she stifled, she confided only to God, which is the way with such women. It was understandable then, although no less uncommon, that she had created a son who was, and is, a virtual stranger to fear.

She also knew, because it is the way with such women, that this boy who wrote so precisely in his copybook, who read, listened, and remembered so eagerly, who ran and climbed, pushing daily at the frontiers of his childhood existence, would soon enough be climbing mastheads that she would not see from her kitchen window, and it is far worse to wonder than to see.

So while she had him, Sarah MacMillan, slender and dark-eyed, gave her younger son love and tenderness and each night sang and played gentle tunes on her accordion at his bedside until he slept, knowing that a ship at the dock would not be enough for Danny Baxter, not for very long.

At eight he begged his father to take him north on the next trip to the Grand Banks.

He was big enough to cut out cod tongues. Other boys did it. Why couldn't he?

Captain Neil MacMillan, black-haired and dark-eyed, bearded and mustached in the fashion of the time, was built like his temperament. He was not big but solid, and of amazing strength and energy. He spoke softly, but with power. In a society of fearless and capable men, he was less fearful and more capable than most, and he had no need to remind his contemporaries of this, for they knew it well.

Understand, then, what this means when the last blue line of land drops into the sea astern and there is no sound but bubbles under the forefoot and no frame of reference but a bowl of sky and a plateau of water, either of which may be friendly or otherwise, with or without reasonable warning.

The master of the vessel thus becomes omnipotent, that is, to blame for everything, not excluding the weather. He is judge, jury, diplomat, father and mother; he is arbiter, calculator, seer and administrator, and occasional searcher of souls, including his own.

Will the current be fair six hours from now wherever one will be six hours from now? Does the peak halyard chafe? Is the cook falling down on the job or is that sea-lawyer talk from a troublemaker in the fo'c'sle? Is it time to shorten sail or can one wait a little and log a few more knots? What will tomorrow bring that must be prepared for today?

And all this is to say nothing of finding where the fish are, cutting out a cod hook buried barb-deep in an agonized palm, ghosting through the fog, blowing and listening all the night through, looking for the dory that did not come back when it shut in thick.

These things may not create an extraordinary man, but they do weed out the ordinary. Those who remain, held by luck or love, are likely to be the sort who take to things more quickly than to people. They do not hesitate to do what has not been done before if there is need for doing it, and do not talk about it afterward. Self-sufficiency of this sort brings a deep and lonely satisfaction. It also ages one prematurely.

This may have been why Dan's father said no. Perhaps he wanted childhood to continue a little longer, knowing that it is only a fragment at best. He said maybe next year. But this he would do: he would take the boy out of school early in May and let him sail northward with the schooner as far as the Bras d'Or Lakes, where Neil was born and where his father and mother still lived. Dan could spend the summer there; Neil would pick him up in the fall, on the way back home from the Banks.

The prospect was almost too miraculous for an eight-year-old to live with. He was going to sea; he was going to a farm on the shores of a lake on the island of Cape Breton, and there would be cows and horses, sheep, hens, pigs . . .

"Any real live Indians?" the boys at school wanted to know.

"My father says they're all over the place," said Dan.

There came the day when the sails were bent, halyards reeved, the sixteen dories stowed amidships, anchor cables carefully coiled, stores put in the lockers and under the forecastle floor, and the high-liner *Nellie Swift*, a deep-legged schooner with a Cape Breton Scotchman for a skipper, was cast off and away. The uncommon boy was on his first ocean voyage.

With started sheets and wind on the beam, the schooner slipped along the shore to Race Point and then squared away for Cape Sable, with a fair breeze.

As many men begin great adventure inauspiciously, this boy who would eventually become a rear admiral was seasick and remained so for two whole days. This in itself was an experience, for illness, then and always, was something about which he knew little and which he made a practice of refusing to recognize when it did come.

On the third day he awoke in the early morning in his bunk on the starboard side of the after cabin. His father was still sound asleep. The vessel was quiet, and he wondered why. No roll, no pitch, no complaining squeaks, and no footsteps on the deck overhead. He rolled out of his bunk, put on shirt and trousers, sneaked up the companionway ladder, and . . . faced the unforgettable.

Cape Cod has a beauty of its own. Thoreau knew; MacMillan knew, too, and being a boy, assumed that all places looked much the same, with buff-colored dunes, trailing arbutus, wild cherry and dogwood, and the warm red of cranberry bogs.

But here, fast to the stone quay at St. Peter's on the south shore of Cape Breton, all of these things were missing. Instead the smell of young spruce trees filled the spring morning. On the hillside sheep grazed, and, never having seen a sheep, he thought they were dogs, eating grass. They were either all white or all black but never black and white. "Why not?" he wondered.

Now the workmen arrived from the village and began cranking open the two ponderous doors leading to the canal lock ahead. Once the schooner was inside, the doors closed astern, others opened up ahead, and the *Swift* emerged into a narrow gorge leading to the lake. Engineless, as were all her nineteenth-century counterparts, and unable to use her sails in the narrow quarters, the schooner was towed through the cut by twelve of her own crew rowing six of the dories, and they did it with ease for she was designed

14

to move "with no more than a teacup full of wind, and a prayer in passing . . ."

Once in the lake, the vessel was anchored, in what appeared to a boy from salt water, to be "out in the country." No blustery winds, tumbling seas, or fog. Only hay and oat fields, and gentle lowing of cattle in the hillside pastures. "Why anchor?" he asked. Because no vessel could sail through the lakes with a head wind, particularly not in the narrow southern passage that wound among the islands. There was shoal ground close on either hand, and the "channel buoys," uncolored sticks in the mud, were frustratingly uninformative to a boy who knew that all such markers should be either red or black for safe navigation.

With a fair wind next day away they went, sailing through the woods, north through a mirror of fresh water forty by twelve miles big. Dan, who had never seen a lake, and all of whose ponds were of the lily-pad, knee-deep variety, was delighted but still only half convinced that anything so large wasn't the sea itself.

Within a few hours they arrived at the Narrows, in the middle of Big Bras d'Or, spanned by a drawbridge that opened with awkward slowness as they approached, revealing an exceptionally narrow passage for a big vessel.

It is worth wondering whether the opinion held by American youth of its fathers might be affected if every boy were able to watch his parent poke an ocean-going schooner under sail through such a needle's eye. Out of such things stem respect and desire to emulate. Sharing and understanding such experiences may be, who knows, superior to the usually uncomfortable "man-to-man" talks that have become an American institution.

Dan's father never hesitated a fraction; there was neither time nor room to do so, and a vessel under way makes no allowances for the indecisive. He luffed the *Swift;* her crew sweated in the long main boom until it hung amidships, then down with the wheel and she shot through the channel, under foresail and headsails, bound downlake for Red Head and the Plaster, and for Big Harbor, now called Port Bevis.

When the sun dropped red beyond the western hills, the breeze dropped with it, leaving barely enough to fan them in the darkness toward a black little hole among the shore's steep reaches.

Finally the anchor was down, the sails furled and stopped, and the quietness of the night, ruffled only by the sounds of lapping water and birds of the darkness, settled over them. On the far hillside shone a spot of light.

"That," said Neil to his son, "is where I was born."

Soon after daybreak, with breakfast over, they went ashore in a dory, Neil, Dan, and a barrel of flour for the grandparents. The grandfather was at the water's edge to greet his youngest son and the grandson whom he had never seen. His three older boys, Donald, a Manitoba farmer, John, a master mariner sailing out of New York, and Colin, a Massachusetts carriage maker, had not been home for many years, and this was more often the rule than the exception in that time and place.

Within a few yards of the landing a country school was in session, and Dan ran impulsively to the open window. Strictly disciplined though the pupils were, he disrupted them in large measure, and the Scotch domine who taught them as well, just by showing his face and speaking. He could hardly know they had never seen a boy from "the States," they had never seen a boy wearing "store clothes," and since they all spoke Gaelic, his manner of talking was a revelation to them.

This was merely the introduction to a new world of strange and wonderful things. Here Dan MacMillan, at an age when one remembers with miraculous efficiency, came to understand something of truth and beauty and to renew his perpetual thirst for the natural.

The small farmhouse hung on a side of high land, a toilsome climb, but chosen as a home site by his immigrant grandfather because from it one could see the yellow wheat fields of Boularderie, sailing vessels as far away as the Narrows, and the rising of the sun, and these things the old man deemed of more importance than aching legs and inconvenience.

Without words, and in spite of the difficulties of bridging Gaelic and English, the boy, when his father had sailed away for the summer, came to understand much of this philosophy. It began with his grandmother's hug, a priceless commencement which required nothing said, and somehow he carried with him thereafter this love, and love of life, crawling beneath the barn to gather eggs, riding the farm horse bareback over the green hills, rounding up the sheep, and playing games in the oat fields, with the tall stalks whispering above his head.

He chased squirrels along the rail fences and heard their chattering high in the trees; he caught fat trout deep in the shadows of the worn plank bridge. It was a wonderful time

17

of first things. He found his first bird's nest, with speckled eggs; saw his first kingfisher dart out of a hole in the bank; discovered his first hawk, cutting vigilant parentheses high in the blue.

Here he saw his first sleek-headed mink swimming along the shore, a rippling V-wake at its smooth throat; he gathered his first raspberries, hanging in clusters in the shade of the lime rocks. He went into his first cave, far back in the dark, and, intrigued, on into another one that adjoined, moist and silent. He saw his first brook, crystal clear and on its way to the sea over a golden bed of pebbles.

It was a breath-taking encyclopedia of experience, and even more.

This boy had gone back in time to the manner of living of the colonial eighteenth century, an adventure that few of his contemporaries ever shared. These people with whom he now lived did not depend on the outside world for food, clothing, or shelter; they did without what most of America even then considered essential for existence.

They lived on the results of their own efforts, the products of their own land. There was plenty of milk, cream, cheese, butter, meat, eggs, vegetables, cereals, fish from the lake, fruit from the orchard, and berries from the hills. They made their garments from the wool of their own sheep, their boots and shoes from the hides of their own cattle, by processes already forgotten in Provincetown and elsewhere.

The islanders went to bed and rose with the sun. They had no lamps and no stove; the big open fireplace furnished both light and heat for cooking. There were no ice boxes, no electric lights, no phones, victrolas, bathtubs, toilets, newspapers, magazines, or libraries. There was no doctor, either, but then, many of the islanders still managed to reach the age of ninety, as did Dan's grandparents, and one did not have to ask them if they were well and happy, for it was obvious.

There was something else in the nature of experience incident to pioneer life. MacMillan's daily companions frequently were Indian boys, Micmacs, who came early in the spring, paddling alongshore in their birchbark canoes, and living in the woods at the head of the harbor until late in the fall.

With them he stripped naked and dove for oysters at the base of the limestone cliffs. All summer long they were the instructors of his eyes and ears, showing him where the biggest blackberries were, where the latest flowers were in bloom, and where the spruce grouse built her nest. They knew where the fish hawks hunted and even when the young hawks first soared off alone.

September came too soon, and one crisp morning there lay the *Nellie Swift,* deep-laden and smelling of fish, swinging at anchor in the harbor below, waiting to take him home. Dan was glad to see his father, but all the way down the steep hill and even in the dory he thought of the Scotch boys ashore in their homespuns, of the Micmacs snug on the point among the firs, of the cold, bubbling water in the hillside spring, and the smell of the haymow in the heat of noontime. He knew, for the first time, what it was like to have to leave something, and not want to.

During the first night of the trip home he was snuggled in his bunk and heard the mate call down the companionway to his father, "Cap'n, it's comin' in hard from the no'th-east."

A gale from the northeast in the North Atlantic was the dread of every skipper under sail; it was a mean and nasty prospect; at the best, a cold and wet punishment that tried the endurance of man and vessel—at the worst, a litter of wreckage on some sea-pounded beach to mark one's passing.

His father hauled on his boots and oilskins, strapped on the sou'wester, and went on deck. Then there were the heavy thumps of boots on top of the cabin. The crew was either taking in the mainsail or putting a double reef in it to cut down the sail area to a maneuverable minimum. The pitch and roll of the schooner increased greatly; heavy seas tumbled against the planking and swished across her deck overhead. Wood cracked loudly, and there was the sound of running feet.

With back against the bunk board and feet against the sheathing, Dan braced himself in the heavy rolling, chewing on salt cod and sucking a lemon—his father's orders—to ward off seasickness.

Sometime in the pitch dark he could hear water running across the cabin floor and wondered where it came from. Then there was a heavy crash, the sound of breaking glass as the cabin skylight was smashed to pieces, and down poured cold salt water in torrents. There were hoarse shouts, sounds of running and hammers pounding; the men were nailing boards over the broken glass lights. They were also nailing up the companionways to keep the sea from breaking into them and flooding the vessel, including the one that led from Dan's cabin to the deck.

Even then he would have preferred to be on deck, lashed to something solid, so that he could see what the storm looked like in its foaming fury.

But within an hour he had company below. His father, jaw clenched in pain, was lowered down the ladder. A gurry butt filled with cod livers and weighing as much as a couple of men had broken loose from its lashings and pinned him against the rail. Possibly his leg was broken; they didn't know and there was no time to find out at the moment. Saving the vessel came first.

When daylight came, Dan went on deck. The wind had flattened out completely, leaving the schooner rolling heavily in a long, greasy swell, making no headway, and with her sails, blocks, booms, sheets, and a clutter of other tackle slatting and banging from side to side.

The deck had been scoured as white as a Dutchman's kitchen under the pounding of the sea. Every dory was gone, all sixteen smashed to kindling and the wreckage sluiced over the rail. Two mammoth coils of cable, normally forward of the foremast, used for anchoring on the Banks, had been washed overboard and now trailed far astern—not lost—because their bitter ends had been made fast to the vessel. Now they were being hauled back aboard, foot by foot, as a half-dozen of the crew pumped bent-backed at the clanking windlass.

It was Dan's first gale. He could not have known that in three quarters of a century of seafaring he would never experience a worse one. He could not have known either, as the white sands between Race Point and Wood End marked the end of his "back to school" passage, that even a good skipper like Neil MacMillan does not always fare so well when it gets that bad.

# 2

IT TAKES a good man to sail a big schooner away from a dock with every stitch of canvas on her; one mistake and the vessel, the dock, or one or more men may pay a swift and severe penalty. It takes coolheadedness, judgment, and a lot of experience.

That was the way Neil MacMillan left Provincetown in his new command, the *Abbie Brown,* the year that Dan was nine. The *Brown,* with new sails, new cordage, cabin trunks painted as white as snow, and her hull coal black and glistening, heeled to the stiff southwesterly and rapidly opened the gap of water between her stern and the dock.

It was November, and the *Brown* was especially selected by an eastern company, because she had a good skipper, to bring back a load of frozen herring for cod bait from the Bay of Islands on the west coast of Newfoundland. Neil's wife had not wanted him to go; she was afraid of what the Newfoundland ice had done to other schooners.

It is hard to say when time becomes too much time, because there are, after all, many variables in seafaring. Still, one senses eventually that too much time has gone by, even allowing for everything within and without reason, and in all places where men live by the sea the feeling becomes communal and is eventually whispered, then suggested more openly, and finally, as with pregnancy, there is a crystallization of the anticipated and suspected into undeniable reality.

Weeks had gone by since the *Brown* sailed, and in the bleakness of a Cape winter, with gray skies and grayer seas, even a day of waiting can be a long time. Dan came home from school one day and the house was empty. He found his mother on Miller's Hill, a frail figure against the weather, a shawl over her head and shoulders, eyes damp from straining into the northwest wind. He did not have to ask what she was doing there. She was looking for a sail. From then on she was there every day, for a long time, but each time she came down from the hill the brutal truth became more indelible and the woman more silent.

At school, during recess one day, two boys stopped talking when Dan walked up to them, but they didn't stop soon enough. He heard one of them say, "He's lost . . . lost with all hands, my father said so . . ."

Around the docks, where Dan played after school, the other skippers were talking about it. One remark he never forgot; they didn't know he heard. "I think," said one, "Neil probably drove her under. He was a devil for carryin' sail and he scared me time and agin . . ."

"Neil," said the little boy softly to himself. There were only two Neils in town, and Neil Ross had taken his schooner to the West Indies.

24

"Fordy," the Negro boy who walked home from Eastern School with him, did the best he could for Dan. He said, "Well, don't mind what they say. Your father'll come back. You wait and see."

Neil did not come back, although the mother and son watched from the hills, scanned the dune tops for weeks more, looking for the first sight of familiar topsails working along the back beach toward Race Point.

Finally, when December's snow flurries and bitter northerlies slammed the door on the last hope, his mother accepted the blow: the father of her five children had gone down in the North Atlantic, vessel, crew, and all, with no one to mark his passing or ever say how it came about or where. There would be no questions ever answered, although it would have helped to know even a little.

Was it day or night? Did they have long to wait, knowing what was to happen, or was it all ended in a thunderous green-gray sea that smashed aboard, foaming and chest-deep? Is the bottom where they lie clean, white sand or black rocks, with long, rubbery streamers of weed writhing in the shadows?

It was the end of 1883 and close to the end of many other things. In the cemetery northwest of the village a stone for Neil MacMillan, marked "Lost in the Gale," stood over an empty grave.

The MacMillans were poor. This woman, ill-prepared physically and financially for the burden that had been thrust upon her, could not even pay the rent of ten dollars a month for half of the little house at the end of John Kiley's Lane, where they had lived. Changes, pitiful and painful, had to be made.

With anguish that no one fully shared she permitted a Mr. and Mrs. John T. Oxnard of Freeport, Maine, to adopt her oldest daughter. Oxnard had heard about the Mac-Millan family through mutual friends; ruddy-faced and kindly, he was a well-to-do farmer-realtor and "one of *the* men" of Freeport.

The oldest MacMillan boy happened to be with his grandparents at Big Harbor that winter; he remained in Cape Breton for ten years before returning to the States. The three smaller children, Dan and his two younger sisters, the mother kept with her, and they moved to an ancient and neglected house at the foot of Lovett's Court.

If there are those, in New England or elsewhere, who yearn sincerely for the "good old days," at least let them remember all, and not merely the pleasanter part, of what such days were like. Since America's social revolution, which has produced United Funds, Community Chests, health and welfare agencies, and Social Security, was still unborn and even unhoped for, this woman MacMillan could do just one thing to obtain food for three children— a nineteenth-century errand of drudgery called "taking in washing."

She did it. Lean and sick, tired and underfed, she scrubbed the linen of the more fortunate, rinsed it in ice-cold water, and wrung it out with hands that were red, cracked, and veined and looked no longer like anything that a sailor with dark and laughing eyes might once have kissed. She hung the white sheets, the spotless shirts, even in the winter wind, although more wearily.

Of course all of this effort, noble and pathetic, was not enough. Not even though the neighbors brought in food, when their circumstances would allow, not even though they brought to the MacMillans the magnificent leftovers from the church suppers, still recollected fondly at a distance of nearly eighty years.

Dan was nine and a little more, because the struggle went on for about three years. He did what he could. He peddled cranberries in a wheelbarrow at a cent a quart; he sold lemonade and skinned codfish on a piecework basis, with the man on either side of him at the skinning bench helping him, because they understood what it was like for a boy to have to be a breadwinner.

In summer he dove for pennies tossed by excursionists at the end of Railroad Wharf when the Boston boat arrived. Rugged, and never ill, although he could undoubtedly have eaten more always, he did well in getting his share of pennies, because no other boy there was diving for food. But his biggest income was from the sale of a pamphlet entitled *Provincetown, or Odds and Ends from the Tip End.*

This text was principally a "sworn statement" by one George Washington Ready, who lived at the "head of Pearl Street," and who was not "unduly excited by liquor or otherwise," but who observed (he said) a sea serpent in Herring Cove with a head as large as a two-hundred-gallon cask, et cetera, et cetera.

The sunburned tourists found MacMillan's dockside pitch about the sea serpent irresistible, even though it cost them a quarter apiece to turn to page 172 and read all about it.

27

It was the spring of 1886. "I thought," said Dan, "that if only warm weather would come, Mother might live."

She died in March, unable to wait for that welcome softening of weather that comes when the raw easterlies that have thumped the beach with surf through the winter give way to the warm winds from the southwest.

It was cold, with ragged, wet chunks of fog dripping across the water front, when they stood beside the open grave. The woman whom they buried was not given to taking credit and certainly died in despair and exhaustion, believing she had failed in the only thing that mattered— raising her family. As with many such persons, she had built better than she knew.

At eighty-five, Dan was asked, "Why are you a moral man?"

Silent for a moment, he replied, "That's odd, I never asked myself that question. It was my mother, of course."

In the reply was recollection of all those childhood Sundays associated with the Centenary Methodist Church, his mother's church, transformed these days by curious alchemy into an art museum. But then it was where he pumped the organ for twenty-five cents a Sunday and won a prize for never missing Sunday School in a whole year. Those were the Sundays when one did not use a horse or boat or go swimming, when the band did not play or the Boston boat land. It was customary to spend part of each Sunday looking at Bible pictures; if one went outdoors, it was to stroll slowly, and with an attitude of reverence, the length of the long, four-plank sidewalk that bordered the water front. In the evening there was the prayer meeting, by lamplight, and the little church thundered as its congregation of women left alone shared the hymnbooks with their children and sang, "Pull for the Shore, Sailor, Pull for the Shore."

Those were the days when religion was an influence, not an institution.

Standing at a grave, even one's mother's, has to end. This is the moment of putting away, the painful regirding which has to be done because it is, after all, someone else who has died. Abruptly old at eleven, Dan did not want to go back to the house. It had become in a matter of hours a shell of brick and shingle with which he felt no kinship. He could not laugh there, he would not weep there, for its meaning had gone with the one who gave it meaning.

A mother of one of the boys with whom he played, Mrs. John McLeod, who lived a few yards easterly, looked at Dan's face, knew his inner thoughts, took him by the hand without a word, and led him from the cemetery to her home.

Dan wrote much later: "With the companionship of her two boys, one of whom was my own age, no home in Provincetown could have done more to make me forget that I was without father and mother. But being a mother to three rambunctious boys was perhaps too much for one woman. Within two months I was sent—I suppose you'd say, given away—to another home on the water front."

It is the home that is now his own, on Commercial Street; his boyhood bedroom is now his arctic library, and from the window one can see where the *Abbie Brown* sailed away for Newfoundland.

It was then the home of Captain Murdick McDonald, "Red" Murdick, skipper of the schooner *Gracie Parker*. He and his wife were born within sight of Dan's father's home in the Bras d'Or Lakes. The McDonalds had two little girls, one about Dan's age, now Mrs. Russell Doubleday of Glen Cove, Long Island, and her younger sister Lorena. It was a home so much like his own had been when Neil Mac-Millan was alive that Dan had virtually no transition to make. He joined the family in their weathered house over an abandoned store, shared their food and laughter, slept with the sea sounds in his ears, and did not feel alone any more.

Murdick, who followed the Provincetown pattern of going to the Banks in summer and the West Indies in winter, was an endless source of the same stories of the sea and ships of which Dan never tired. In this home the idiom and yardstick were the same as they always had been with him, framed in terms of quintals of fish, fair bottom or foul, shorten down when the glass drops, and hope for a fast trip home to market.

In perspective, the outstanding event of his two years with the McDonalds was a voyage as cabin boy aboard the *Parker* to Augusta, a place located, said Red Murdick, "to the nor'ard, up a river, state of Maine."

The voyage itself was like many another, except that it introduced Dan to his first river, and this was prophetic, for it was in another uncommon land that was destined to shape much of the rest of his life.

They "fetched" the mouth of the Kennebec at ebb tide, and to a boy who had never seen any such thing bigger than a Cape Breton brook, it was a clock stopper. Volumes of water boiled out of a hole in the land, met the stiff southwesterly head-on and ripped into white water, straight up and down, a tumultuous caldron of short, steep seas between the schooner and the pine-topped coast.

The impression was one of many entrances to the river, and there was no pilot to be had. Red Murdick stomped the quarter-deck, port to starboard and back, squinted into the spume, stood on the after cabin to get a better look, grumbled out loud, swung the vessel off and on while he thought about it, finally figured it out, sheeted her home, and boiled through it all into the quiet water of the river.

It was like going into a house, so suddenly quiet. The smell of pines was everywhere, and green fields sloped to the water's edge. Along the banks were huge rafts of logs and weathered sawmills, half buried in drifts of yellow wood dust, whining away through slab, clear grain and knot, with their slim, rusty stacks shooting purple plumes straight up in the still air. One had the sense of America, impatient to be built. It was a time of things going ahead, of solving the equation: one forest equals x number of rafters, keels, and wagon tongues.

Dan thought a lot about it on the way home. There was emerging the realization that, as with poems, the world should not only mean but be.

Destiny was not long in shaping. To one who never had received a letter, even though a freshman in high school, it was disquieting to hold the envelope, postmarked "Freeport, Maine," to see one's name, "Donald Baxter MacMillan," in bold hand, like a cry in the night that will not be ignored, a pointed finger indicating something at which one dares not look.

31

It was from his sister, Letitia—Lettie—now married and become Mrs. Winthrop C. Fogg. She wanted him to come and live with her, "to keep a fragment of kin and family together."

He put the letter in his pocket and went for a walk. Leave this? Leave the black-eyed Portuguese and the tow-headed Scotchman; the white-breasted gull scrooched with one leg up on the top of a spile? Leave the white-winged coot, bobbing in the swash of a no'theaster, and the suds of surf that pull sand out from under the toes as they suck their way back into the sea? No more gales that shook the house, sea that thundered in the night? It was impossible. He wanted to remain where he was born, where such ends-of-yarn memories as he had been able to retain of his father and mother were inextricably bound.

But this was a world without sociologists and psychologists. The decision was not his, only the tears, quiet and brief, in some corner where no one could see the spirit so naked. He received his orders in a manner customarily, although somewhat arbitrarily, described as "gentle, but firm," usually indicating that someone is doing what he is convinced is best, and the recipient wishes heartily that the Judgment Day or anything equally effective would intervene.

"Pack your small bag. (He didn't own enough to put in a trunk.) Go up to Railroad Wharf and buy a ticket for Boston. On arrival in Boston, turn to the right at Atlantic Avenue and walk until you see a large white steamer with paddle wheels at a dock. That boat goes to Portland, Maine, every night at seven o'clock. Buy a ticket, go aboard, and sit down in a chair. Go to sleep. In the morning you will be in Portland, Maine. A man by name of John T. Oxnard will be waiting for you at the gangway when you leave the boat."

"Yes, sir. Very good, sir. And are there any orders for the heart? Does it go or stay, or is it ripped raggedly down the middle, half for the little scrub oak on the dune, and the rest for the body that must, after all, walk and talk, and eat, whether it is at home or in an alien land, as all properly constituted bodies in society must do?"

Some of the boys from school walked down to the boat at Provincetown with him, enthusiastically equating what he was to become with the hero of the Harry Castleman thrillers, *Ned on the River* and *Ned in the Woods*.

"What luck!" they said. "Going down to live with the Indians, with men who catch skunks and foxes and big brown bears! They even have men there who walk on snow-shoes and live in log cabins! What luck!"

Luck? Going into the woods and away from the sea?

If you want to know about this MacMillan, this salt-water Scotchman, understand, then, that he found the "large, white steamer" without difficulty and that, once aboard, he not only sat down in a chair, as ordered, but he went to sleep too. Not because his grief was less, but because his forbearance and his resiliency, then as now, were greater.

There is a patience in some men, not to be confused with either fatalism or surrender, that can outwait the turning of the world's leisurely axles. MacMillan could not know how uncommon it was in him, how essential it was to what

33

he was to become.

In the morning, as predicted, there was Oxnard, prompt, and more important, gentle. Heavy-set, slightly stooped, he lived next door to Lettie, whom he had raised; so impressed was he by the MacMillan clan that he was going to take one of Dan's younger sisters, Jessie, and eventually a Mr. and Mrs. Ansell Davis would take the other, Eva, brought to Freeport by Lettie.

Dan fell in step beside Mr. Oxnard. As yet no woods, no Indians. They walked along the Portland water front, a teeming place of barges, drays, deep-water craft, boxes and barrels, until they came to a wharf where a small steamer lay. *Phantom* read the gold letters across the top of her wheelhouse.

MacMillan looked at his guide dubiously. To Freeport by water?

This was the first delightful surprise in the new world, steaming up Casco Bay, a stretch of water studded with more islands than he had known there were in the world, rock-faced little islands, he thought, which were determined to resist forever the sea's wearing. By coincidence, on Casco Bay, which struck him as a thing of hope and beauty from the first moment, he was to discover the forces that eventually reshaped his life.

The *Phantom* brought them to the mouth of the Harriseeket River, to the village of South Freeport, a couple of miles from their destination. They went the remainder of the distance by horse and buggy, arriving in the afternoon at Freeport, population three thousand. Here the chief functions of those who labored were to furnish supplies to the adjacent farming communities, to manufacture shoes, to operate the gristmill and granite quarry.

There was no sea. There were no seamen. One had to learn to live in a new way.

The first thing he had to lose was a year of life, academically speaking.

Until then the idea of going to college had been far less remote than going to the Far East. He could not remember the name of a single schoolmate at home (no, he corrected himself, not "at home" any more—"in Provincetown") who went to college.

But all except one of the five boys in his class at Freeport High wanted to go to college and two of them to Bowdoin. Why Bowdoin? Because this college of eminents, alma mater of Nathaniel Hawthorne, Henry Wadsworth Longfellow, Chief Justice Fuller, Elijah Kellogg, Senator Frye, and John S. C. Abbott, was only nine miles away.

Wilmot B. Mitchell, a Freeport native and Bowdoin alumnus, was MacMillan's high school principal. Mitchell said to him, "You must go to college." MacMillan replied, "I haven't any money." Mitchell, who remains the admiral's idol after seventy years, said firmly, "You can. You must."

It posed problems, and not all financial either. Dan had had a year of high school, intending to take the non-college course, and had taken no classical languages. Bowdoin entrance requirements called for four years of Latin and three of Greek. "You can. You must," Mitchell had said. Back MacMillan went to take his freshman year over again, this time with Greek and Latin.

As for the money aspects, he had seven dollars in the

Seamen's Savings Bank at Provincetown. He was too proud to request a loan, even if anybody would have given him one without security, which they probably wouldn't have. "Get out and earn it," he said to himself.

So he became janitor at the high school, he pumped the organ at the Baptist Church for twenty-five cents a Sunday, and sold a book from house to house entitled *The Religions of the World,* which was a rather odd way to make money when you stop to think of it, because no one in nineteenth-century New England was expected to be interested in or even to recognize any religion other than his own.

He cut linings in a shoe factory, often working until midnight. He drove a milk "team" in the early morning, long before school opened, delivering and selling the product for a nickel a quart.

None of these jobs was as interesting to him, however, as the private gymnasium he established. During his first two years of high school he had developed exceptional facility in gymnastics. In part this probably was because he did not drink or smoke, not for disapproval's sake, but for lack of interest. There was more to it, however, for his instructors had recognized from the beginning that he possessed, in a relatively small, lithe body (about 148 pounds), exceptional co-ordination and a vitality that resisted ordinary fatigue and ailments. This birthright has made possible the life he has led.

# 3

THE LITTLE black horse that drew the rattletrap wagon danced along the hard-crowned road and his mane shook like laughter in the bright fall. In the back, one desk, one chair, one bureau; overhead, a scolding crow and a fat-tailed squirrel, noisy among the yellowing leaves. Thus Mac-Millan went to college.

There was no money, but with all of life bursting its shocks and pods, full blown in the afternoon sun shafts, neither death nor defeat seemed more than myths.

Bowdoin is not a collection of buildings but an intellectual atmosphere, a place of pines, weathered brick, and clean snow, in which it is quiet enough to think about what is happening. MacMillan was assigned to 32 North Winthrop, a room not far from that which Longfellow once occupied.

In that year of 1893, being poor, MacMillan found it more economical to live at home in Freeport much of the time, rather than buying meals at the college. The round-trip train fare was twenty-two cents; occasionally he would "save three cents" by staying at the college, purchasing enough frankfurters for supper and breakfast for nineteen cents, and cooking them on an oil stove in his closet. He could not afford to buy textbooks but established his schedule so that he could study when others were not and therefore borrow their books.

Whenever he decided to remain at the college overnight, usually for an examination or an important football game, he would go to the gymnasium for mat work. He spent hours tumbling through a succession of handsprings, front and back somersaults, and workouts on the horizontal bar, parallel bars, and flying rings.

He attracted the favorable attention of **Dr. Whittier**, the college physical director, who appointed him an assistant instructor in the gym for the winter months; the salary he received allowed him to buy an occasional meal at the Theta Delta Chi house. He also was captain of the freshman football team, a member of the gymnastic team and Indian club squad, and ripped off a hundred yards in ten and a fifth seconds in varsity track.

Because so many college students have done similar things in so many colleges, it is less important that he climbed 120 feet by walking up the side of the chapel, holding onto a copper cable (although this remains an unparalleled feat), than that when he got there, in the middle of the night, awed by the magnificence of the stars and the dark of an approaching storm, he sang "Nearer, My God, to Thee" before coming down from the steeple with the freshman flag.

The incident made something of a name for him state-wide, but it didn't help the fact that his money was gone and three frankfurters weren't enough to stave off hunger. He obtained permission to leave for the "mid-term," make up his work in the spring, and went looking for a job. He found it, teaching reading, writing, arithmetic, and geography to six pupils in Freeport's Pratt District schoolhouse. For walking the eight miles each day through snowdrifts and Maine cold, teaching five days a week for ten weeks, he received $60.

MacMillan wrote not long ago: "The regular routine in schools today, a succession of bells and marching which jangles the nerves of many of our talented teachers, can be varied to provide relief, I should think. I visited the Pratt District recently. It was quiet at the four corners. The small schoolhouse was gone. The clearing was heavy with tangled briars and raspberry bushes. But the soughing of the northwest winds through the tall white pines was as musical as it was sixty-odd years ago.

"I could see the drifts still, smell the burning chunks of wood in our iron stove, feel the comfortable warmth of the poorly furnished room. In our quiet corner, we were happy, learning something that might be of use in a busy outside world."

From then on college became a challenging pattern, yet a defeatable problem. Summers he spent working in the White Mountain hotels; in midwinter, if broke, he would go back to public-school teaching, and academically he completed three years. At that point typhoid acquainted him with the fact that he was not indestructible. Being bedridden for weeks was particularly shattering because it was his first illness; in addition, he was penniless after paying his medical bills, and it was too late to begin his senior year anyway.

Lean but not discouraged, he went to Boston, job hunting. Soule, Dillingham Company wanted a paymaster and timekeeper (both Soule and Dillingham were Freeport men) and they hired him, to work on the building of the new "electric road" between the Massachusetts cities of Taunton and Brockton. It was a restorative through the spring and summer of 1897. He was hungry for the sunshine, eager for the feeling of strength to come back, and with those sweating, big-handed Irish and Italian tile tampers, track layers, and rail drillers, those sun-baked, good-natured chewers of thick, smelly sandwiches on black bread, he walked gingerly back into the fraternity of life and laughter. One day he found himself breathing deeply again, for the joy of it, and knew he was ready to pick up where he had left off.

So he returned to Bowdoin and was graduated with the class of 1898, a year late, but with all bills paid and without having called on relatives or friends for money. On the afternoon of graduation he went to work in a hayfield at four dollars a day and never has seen his diploma from that day to this.

Levi Hall High School in North Gorham, Maine, wanted a principal, for which it was willing to pay $500 a year, and he took the job. It wasn't much, and moreover, North Gorham is one of those little communities so common to northern New England where the trees tend to outnumber the people about sixty to one and the most exciting thing all year is the unconquerable stubbornness with which the inhabitants, red-nosed and icy-footed, stick out another winter.

But its residents, as in most such towns, were congenial country people. About as subtle as a granite block, but about as durable too.

MacMillan "lived in" with Mr. and Mrs. Marshall Moses. For his "quarters" he paid six dollars a week, this covering both room and board. When this was paid, he obviously did not have much monetary profit to show for his efforts at the end of a forty-week school year.

A typical room purchased under such circumstances, usually second floor with sloping ceiling, was unheated and lit by a glass kerosene lamp carried with caution up the narrow, steep stairs. It was Spartan neat, with a washstand, a white iron bed, a lithograph of a trotting horse, and a sampler with fancy capital letters that cautioned: "Love Thy God."

The food, although these were towns where folding money was pretty rare, was beyond compare. Nobody said "homemade" because there wasn't any other kind. The gravy was better than most soups now, and the chunks of juicy meat—beef, venison, pork, and partridge, and who knows what all—hardly left any room on the flowered plate for the fluffed-up potato with its rivers of yellow butter and Kentucky Wonder beans off the poles out back. The pies, with crusts all short, hubbly and brown, were crisped up by the wood stove that could drive anybody out of the kitchen even in January and maybe filled with huckleberries brought up from the cellar preserves and poured into a pie plate that was two inches thick or better. This was the original country, the real birthplace of the tall cake, the deep pudding, the thick stew so rich it won't pour, and yet most of the people are lean-waisted as the birches that sway on the rock-faced mountains.

Dan spent two years here. He wrote: "With the boys, I walked through the fields and over the hills studying glacial scratches and discovering erratics which, locked in the embrace of the great ice field 40,000 years ago, had been carried down from the White Mountains. These country boys could hardly believe that every inch of where we were standing, every square foot of the state of Maine, was buried beneath a solid sheet of ice five thousand feet in thickness, and not once, but at least four times.

"In the spring I strolled through the woods with my class in botany. We found the two varieties of lady-slipper, pink, and yellow, and the three kinds of dandelion, the lion's tooth.

"We dug into the dry beds of brooks, to be thrilled with the discovery of hexagonal quartz crystals. And how excited we were to find the twin crystals of staurolite, the two crystals crossing each other at right angles!"

At the end of his second year he was invited by a Mr. Tomlinson, founder and head of the Swarthmore Preparatory School in Pennsylvania, to teach Latin and physical education; MacMillan had been recommended, wrote Mr. Tomlinson, by President Hyde of Bowdoin.

From North Gorham, at $500 a year, to a flourishing Pennsylvania prep school at $1,200, was a big step forward. He accepted at once and in September embarked at Philadelphia's old Broad Street Station and rattled his way over the rails to the Quaker school twelve miles south. Here he might have stayed for a long time, for he liked it, and as for Mr. Tomlinson, he liked MacMillan well enough to offer to build a gymnasium for him; but the sea intervened in two instances and that is not so strange, for one who has heard the surf on Provincetown's back beach does not get over it easily.

But it was Casco Bay MacMillan was thinking of; he had fallen in love with it when he first saw it, in the summer of 1889. There were hundreds of spruce and fir-clad islands, their gray edges breaking with surf; blue-water channels sparkling in the sun; gulls, ducks, and geese, feeding or aloft on gentle wings, and in the cold, blue depths, the firm-meated cod and lobster for the taking.

At the end of his first year at Swarthmore he started a summer camp called Wychmere, at Bustin's Island in Casco Bay, with the help of a fellow teacher, Sam Palmer. It was very likely the first of its kind in this country, a place where boys could learn to sail a boat and study seamanship and navigation.

Wychmere also skyrocketed to sudden fame when Dan rescued nine persons in a single week, these being victims of a couple of boating mishaps. The resultant publicity produced a most unexpected letter:

Dear Mr. MacMillan:

Having read of your "nautical camp" on Bustin's Island, and being favorably impressed with your apparent aim to teach boys to be self-reliant, I write to ask whether you would consider undertaking the pri-

43

vate tutorship of my son, Robert, in certain matters of this nature.

Robert Edwin Peary
United States Navy.

Peary was a resident of nearby Eagle Island. He wanted his son to know how to sail a boat, paddle a canoe, swim, and shoot a rifle. MacMillan's first encounter with the elder Peary, already famous for his arctic exploits, was on a Casco Bay dock where they waited for boats to take them to their respective islands.

Peary asked Dan if he had ever considered "going North."

"I told him," Mac recalled, "in how many ways my boyhood had had ties with the North. That my father brought back to me a pair of Eskimo kamiks, sealskin boots, that he had sailed to Iceland, Greenland, and even to Holsteinsborg, beyond the Arctic Circle, that he had told me what the ice and the arctic seas look like, and that, finally, he had sailed north and not returned."

Peary was impressed and evidently surprised. He studied MacMillan openly for a few minutes without saying anything, then he said it had been a pleasure, turned, and walked down the dock toward the boat about to leave for South Harpswell.

In 1902, while Dan was still teaching at Swarthmore, the sea made another effort to influence his destinies. According to a newspaper story, a full-rigged ship named the *Young America* was to cruise around the world as a "preparatory school afloat."

John R. Kent, a Harvard graduate, was headmaster of

the floating school and was touring the country interviewing prospective teachers. MacMillan sought him out in Philadelphia and was hired. They were to sail from New York in June 1903.

It sounded great, until he received news the next spring that the "beautiful, all-steel, full-rigged ship" could not be completed in time and the voyage must be postponed for a year. This was awkward. He had resigned from Swarthmore and now had no job.

By midsummer, however, he had been hired by Dr. Abercrombie of Worcester (Massachusetts) Academy, as physical instructor, and he spent an enjoyable winter there, nevertheless watching each day's mail like a tern seesawing over a school of shiners, eager for news of the *Young America*.

Eventually the letter came. The school ship was to sail, but it was not a "full-rigged ship." Instead, Lieutenant Commander Harlow, U. S. Navy, who, as ensign under Commander W. S. Schley had aided in bringing back the six survivors of the ill-fated Greely arctic expedition from Cape Sabine in 1884, had chartered the "beautiful ocean liner *Pennsylvania*." MacMillan was to report on board in the Hudson River on the first of June.

He did. In a double-breasted, dark-blue suit, and wearing a yachting cap with a gold insignia, he walked the deck of the big white liner as she lay at anchor in the river, awaiting visitors. Launches were purring back and forth, bringing to the ship parents who thought that a school at sea was just the kind of a school where their boy should be.

Once they had looked over the layout from stem to stern,

45

some were not so sure. They were impressed by the idea; they thought it would be fascinating to study French in France, Latin in Rome, and Greek in Athens. But still, there were storms and collisions and disease in foreign ports.

After two weeks in New York, during which they entertained hundreds of visitors aboard, the *Pennsylvania* and her crew sailed, of all places, to Providence. No one knew why; it seemed to be an official secret. It was encouraging that some of the boys began dribbling aboard in ones and twos, although the rate seemed slow since the *Pennsylvania* was supposed to get under way in two days. Even on the scheduled day of departure they had enrolled only 120 students instead of the 300 needed to pay expenses.

MacMillan recalled, "We steamed slowly down the harbor, too slowly, I thought, to be headed for Europe. We anchored in Bristol, Rhode Island, that night. In the evening I was on the upper deck. As I strolled past the pilot house, I happened to glance in. What I saw there confirmed my suspicions . . . something was decidedly wrong with the whole affair.

"Lieutenant Commander Harlow was in trouble. He sat there with his head in his hands, looking completely crushed. I pitied him with all my heart. He was a wonderful fellow and straight as a string in all his dealings.

"A small boat approached and tied up to our side ladder. I went to the rail. It was the law . . . a 'sheriff ship' with all equipment, come to thrust upon us the harsh realities of assets and liabilities, to end what was supposed to have been a 12,000-mile voyage when it had covered only twelve of those miles."

It was hardest of all on the teachers aboard. They, who had been selected from some of the best preparatory schools and colleges in the country, sat quietly in the wardroom, wondering where and how to pick up the thread of professional life again.

The collapse of the *Young America* project was discussed in some detail in the newspapers and this was not without advantage, at least to Dan. A few days later he received a telegram: COME BACK TO WORCESTER ACADEMY. WE NEED YOU. DR. ABERCROMBIE.

Dan packed his single bag and late that evening reported at Dr. Abercrombie's home on the campus. Yes, admitted the good doctor, it was true the school already had employed a physical director for the coming term because they had not known MacMillan would be available.

"Well, if you already have one . . ." Dan began.

Yes, replied Dr. Abercrombie, but the school was growing, responsibilities were increasing, and the board had decided it would like to have two physical directors.

The two men looked at each other in wordless understanding.

"I knew very well," said Dan in retrospect, "that the school did not need two physical directors. Dr. Abercrombie and Worcester Academy just wanted to help Donald MacMillan. I felt a great fullness within, looking at him."

There came a morning in the early spring of 1905. Mac was walking across the campus to his classroom at Worcester Academy's Davis Hall when a boy riding a bicycle came up to him.

47

"Is your name MacMillan?"

"That's right," Dan answered. "A telegram for me?"

There was. He tore open the envelope, glanced at the message, and stood there, stunned. Slowly he read it again, to be sure.

HAVE PLACE FOR YOU ON NORTH POLE TRIP. WHEN CAN YOU MEET ME IN PORTLAND? R. E. PEARY.

He felt the quick rush of tears of frustration blur his vision as he signed the yellow pad. The boy looked at him. "Do you want to send an answer?"

"No," said Dan slowly. "Not today. I'll take it down . . . later, myself."

With Peary's telegram there had crystallized all of those forces, building since childhood, that urged him to go to the Arctic. Every experience, every book he had read impelled him to wire Peary immediately: "Yes. Yes, of course! I will come and go to the Arctic with you for a year, for several years if you will have me."

But it was not so simple. Only days before he had renewed his contract to teach for another year at Worcester Academy. If he went with Peary, he would have to break the contract, because certainly Dr. Abercrombie would not, and could not practically, consent to his going.

For the remainder of the day he was oblivious to school, dormitory, class, and gymnasium, performing his functions mechanically for perhaps the first, and last, time in his life. He kept telling himself that there must be some honorable and practical way in which he could do what he wanted to . . . but he knew there wasn't, and it became increasingly obvious with the passage of each hour.

At the end of the day he made his way to the quarter-mile cinder track and walked around it slowly, again and again. He remembered how he had felt after the *Young America* voyage had collapsed when Dr. Abercrombie said the school needed two physical directors. He felt a sudden flood of shame that it had taken him so long to decide whether to abide by an agreement with a friend, and he made his quiet way down the hill to Union Station and the telegraph office.

SORRY. UNABLE TO ACCOMPANY YOU THIS YEAR. MAC-MILLAN.

"This year!" he thought to himself. It would be forever. Nobody turned down an opportunity to go to the Arctic with Peary. Peary would assume MacMillan wasn't interested, and that would be the last offer; unquestionably there were dozens of equally qualified people available. But the irony of it, the fact that he, of all persons, wanted so much to go, and with Peary . . . and Peary would never know it now.

In June, when the Bucksport-built, stubby-nosed steamer *Roosevelt* that was going to take Peary north sailed from Portland, Maine, on her trial trip, MacMillan was in the crowd on the dock, a sad-eyed young man purposefully anonymous. Neither Peary nor Bob Bartlett, the skipper, knew that MacMillan cast off the steamer's lines and sat there on the cap-log long after everyone else had gone, watching the *Roosevelt* steam out past the breakwater and on beyond Portland Head to sea.

There, he told himself bitterly, goes the one and only opportunity to visit the land of which my father knew, the ground made historic by Lieutenant Edwin J. De Haven, the intrepid Dr. Elisha Kent Kane, by Dr. Isaac Israel Hayes, Charles Francis Hall, and Lieutenant Adolphus W. Greely. He was convinced the door to what he wanted most was slammed shut with the *Roosevelt*'s departure. Surely this time Peary, who had tried so long and so hard, would reach the Pole, and the great effort would be over.

Ironically disappointment itself provoked in him an avid desire to study the Arctic through the works of those who had been there. He roamed bookstalls and secondhand stores for the out-of-print and the obscure. Thus began, even without intention, the accumulation of an arctic library that now numbers more than three thousand volumes.

In the fall of 1906 came news of the Peary North Pole Expedition. The headlines said: "Peary Fails to Reach Pole. Breaks World's Record of Farthest North, 87 Degrees, 6 Minutes North Latitude. Party Lands Starving on North Shores of Greenland."

Details had to wait until the weakened *Roosevelt,* battered from conflict with the relentless growlers and pack ice of Kennedy Channel and the bergs of Melville Bay, finally tottered back to New York.

True, Peary had failed, but at least he knew why he had failed. A gale, which drove the polar pack eastward, had scattered irretrievably his carefully placed caches of food for dogs and men, established upon the trail northward by his supporting parties against his return with empty sledges. Every ounce of this food was lost, and the same violent winds that disrupted the pack destroyed the trail back to land and safety.

Still, feeding dogs to dogs, he had gone on to a new world's record, surpassing the farthest north of Nansen of Norway and of Captain Cagni of Italy. America again was out in front in the battle for the Pole, for the first time since Lockwood and Brainard had put the United States in this position in 1882.

It was a brave and wonderful world in which arctic explorers lived, populated by giants. The question was: how did one enter it . . . or did one?

ON DECEMBER 15, 1906, President Theodore Roosevelt presented to Peary the National Geographic Society's Hubbard Gold Medal.

Peary's reply was especially revealing to those who wondered whether he intended to make another try for the Pole. He said, "To me, the final and complete solution of the polar mystery, which has engaged the best thought and interest of some of the best men of the most vigorous and enlightened nations of the world for more than three centuries . . . is the thing which should be done for the honor and credit of this country, the thing which it is intended that I should do, and the thing that I must do."

In Worcester, MacMillan read it with avidity . . . "the thing that I must do." Peary was going North again. Now the question was, would he think twice about the man who had turned him down? It was not until spring of 1908 that the answer came.

IF YOU ARE STILL INTERESTED IN ARCTIC EXPLORATION,
COME TO SEE ME AT ONCE GRAND UNION HOTEL, NEW
YORK CITY. PEARY.

MacMillan reached New York too late that night to see
Peary, but there was a note for him at the hotel desk: "I'll
see you at breakfast. . . ."

In the morning there was Peary before him, a man of
lean body and powerful shoulders with the hands of an
artist. In his face, with steel-gray eyes, bushy brows, square
jaws, and deeply lined features, there was evidenced the
same contrast of disciplined strength and profound sensitivity.

"MacMillan," he said, "I am fifty-two years old. This is
probably the last attempt of my life. I want you to be in
command of one of my supporting parties. We may go beyond the limit and never come back. This nearly happened
on my last trip.

"Go back to school. Think it over. Let me know at the
end of two weeks."

MacMillan did not require two weeks to make a decision that had been crystallizing for twenty years. He
looked at the explorer. "May I sign the contract now?"

If Peary was surprised, he did not show it, although obviously he had not been prepared for this. Without a word
he reached into the breast pocket of his jacket, produced a
large brown envelope. He scribbled on it with a pencil, re-
read what he had written, and passed it to MacMillan.

It said that Donald B. MacMillan was to go on the next
North Pole Expedition as Peary's assistant. He was to com-

53

mand a supporting party, to be the ornithologist of the expedition, make a "complete collection" of northern birds, take tidal and meteorological observations, and make a "running survey" of the unknown fjords on the north coast of Grant Land.

He was never to write or lecture concerning the trip. All pictures taken by him were to become the property of Peary. He was to receive no salary.

MacMillan, with a "most exciting sense of things beginning," stabbed at the envelope with his signature, feeling that the brown piece of paper was as important to him as any since his birth certificate.

After breakfast they went to Peary's room, cluttered with samples of arctic gear provided by eager salesmen who wanted to supply his next expedition. For MacMillan it was a first look at the trappings of his new way of life, an introduction to his arctic apprenticeship.

There were alcohol and oil stoves, all designed to weigh little, fold up small, and burn thriftily. There were rope samples, intended for making woven and braided sled traces of such nature that no dog, however hungry, would select them for a meal. Here also were sticks of tough wood for sledge construction, durable, straight-grained stuff which would take the punishment of the Polar Sea's hard blue ice.

Stacks of boxes contained precision instruments, theodolites, pocket sextants, artificial horizons, and ethel chloride thermometers that record temperatures as low as ninety below. Among the tinned foods MacMillan spotted some big cans, some red, others blue.

"These?" he asked Peary.

It was pemmican, blue label for men, red for dogs, the staple of the dog-team explorer. Pemmican, dried meat and suet, is a word of the Cree Indian. In the drying the product loses three fourths of its weight, which makes it good for carrying, but retains all of its nutritive properties. White men have added to it vegetables, oatmeal, raisins, currants, sugar, wild cherries, and even honey. Each nation that produced northern explorers had its own version; Amundsen ate a pemmican made of dried fish and lard.

Peary was tired; he wanted to go to Casco Bay for a rest. He wanted MacMillan to continue the buying for the expedition and would provide him with a "shopping list."

"When can you report here to New York?"

"I'll go back to Worcester, finish my schoolwork, and be back here in two weeks."

It sounded simple, but there was more to it.

Dr. Abercrombie was in Europe, so it was necessary to take up the matter of leave of absence or resignation with the chairman of the board of trustees, a Mr. Gaskill. Mac was somewhat relieved that it was not Abercrombie whom he had to face; it is easier to take leave of a stranger.

Gaskill's office was near City Square. Dan knocked at the door; at the last minute he remembered that Gaskill had made a point of telling Abercrombie what good reports he had had of MacMillan's work at the school.

Once in, he began, "Mr. Gaskill, I would like to resign from the school."

A look of surprise and anxiety. "What's the trouble?"

"No trouble at all, sir. Five very happy years." Mac hesitated. "I'm going to the North Pole, sir."

55

A look of perplexity and disbelief. "No!"

"Yes."

"With whom?"

"With Peary, sir. He would like to have me go with him as one of his assistants."

"How long do you expect to be gone?"

"Fifteen months at least, perhaps two years," said Mac.

A long pause. Gaskill pressed his finger tips together and made a peak of his two hands.

"Well, I'm not going to accept your resignation. I'm not even going to call a meeting of the board. On my own responsibility I'm going to give you a leave of absence. When you are through with this crazy idea of yours of freezing to death at the North Pole, come on back here where you belong and stay with us for the rest of your life."

Judge Gaskill stood up and stuck out his hand.

Fifty-four years later Dan wrote: "I never saw Judge Gaskill again. I have never been through with that 'crazy idea.' I am still on leave of absence from Worcester Academy."

Back in New York, one of the first things he did was to go down to the dock and look at the *Roosevelt,* a powerful 184-foot, three-masted vessel with an eleven-foot propeller, built to steam her way into the Frozen North and, in the event of a fuel shortage, to come home with no power but the wind in her eleven sails.

Of staunch white oak construction, she was sheathed with a six-inch belt of ironwood. Her wedged-shaped bow and ample beam, carried well aft before it began to taper, were designed to shunt the ice away from her churning screw, the Achilles' heel of every arctic ship.

Mac boarded her and walked into the after cabin house. Wrinkled and benign-looking, a man with a white apron tied around his middle stood at the big black galley stove. This would be Charlie Percy, late of Brigus, Newfoundland, the expedition cook.

"Who be you, sir?" said Percy.

"I'm MacMillan. One of the commander's assistants. We're going to be shipmates."

"Well, now," said Percy, "you're bunkin' there"—and he jerked his head to port—"in the room next to mine."

For the next two weeks the steamer's crew principally wished to get away from the "Recreation Pier" at the foot of East 23rd Street. It was hot in New York—there were twelve deaths in the city from heat prostration in a single day—and the very thought of the Arctic was comforting.

Their impending departure necessarily attracted attention of several sorts. Many of those who visited the pier, even some of the apparently cultured, had only vague ideas of what the North Pole was. Their conversation suggested they thought it might be something sticking up in the air which, with luck, could be broken off at the base, hoisted aboard the steamer, and brought back to be exhibited in a museum. They hoped this might be achieved; they would pay the admission fee, whatever it was, to see this thing, and they said they thought the men of the *Roosevelt* were daring and brave; they pumped their hands up and down heartily and wished them well and Godspeed.

But suddenly all of this phase was over and they were ready to sail. On the dock the ladies waved kerchiefs and the men standing beside them felt a tug of adventure in their office-bound souls and almost wished they were going too. A drunk perched on a bollard yelled out, "Where you off to?"

MacMillan, in sheer ebullience, cried, "To the North Pole!" and the drunk retorted, "The hell you say!" and fell off the bollard, provoking nervous laughter among those who had come to say good-by.

Then down the big river they went, down to the sea.

In scanning the 1908 crew list of the *Roosevelt,* there are clues to be had as to what kind of man went North in those days.

Robert Abram Bartlett was the captain. He came from a long line of "ice-water sailors" and had served with Peary as mate or master since 1898. He was a Newfoundlander, as were most of the crew, a strong, able, vigorous, and good-natured breed that had been sailing to the ice fields since boyhood. Because there were no public schools in Newfoundland then, many of them could not read or write. These were men of Brigus, quiet spoken and shy with outsiders, but at home in a gale of wind.

Matthew Henson was the only Negro aboard. Born in Maryland in 1866, he had been North with Peary on six expeditions. Of outstanding vigor, a good handler of sledge dogs, he was highly respected by the Smith Sound Eskimos with whom the expedition would have to deal. It was he who had stood with Peary at the world's most northern record in 1906.

Ross Marvin was an instructor in civil engineering at Cornell University. He had been North with Peary in

1905–06 and had had no intention of making this trip. Marvin came down to the Twenty-third Street dock to bid the *Roosevelt* good-by; Peary found out that he really wanted to go along and told him to pack a bag and join them at Sydney, Cape Breton, Nova Scotia, which he did.

There were, then, sailors, scientists, and adventurers among them.

The expedition had no official support from the U. S. Government, contrary to popular belief, but was made possible by a private group, the Peary Arctic Club, headed by Thomas Hubbard, Zenas Crane, and Herbert L. Bridgman. Nevertheless, the *Roosevelt*'s first stop was at Oyster Bay for a rendezvous with the President of the United States, for whom the steamer had been named.

Shortly after three in the afternoon the launch *Gleam* steamed alongside with the President and his wife and guests; in a second boat came his sons, Kermit and Archie, and several of their friends. T. R. climbed the rail, walked the deck, visited Peary's quarters, insisted on going down into the engine room, returned topside with perspiration streaming from his face, insisted on shaking hands with every man aboard, and declared repeatedly, "What a fine ship! How I would like to go along!"

Bartlett apologized somewhat for the way the steamer looked and said he guessed she wouldn't come up to U. S. Navy standards.

The President said briskly, "Don't care what she looks like . . . it's what she does," and Bartlett said, "It's ninety or nothin' . . . the North Pole or bust this time, Mr. President!"

Roosevelt laughed and said, "Boys, I believe you'll get there this time."

On the eighth of July they arrived in Sydney, Nova Scotia, the "jumping-off place" where everything previously forgotten must be purchased, for this was the last of civilization. The final duty was to secure permission to clear the port; ordinarily, when going into the Arctic with destination uncertain, the master clears for "points at sea," a roving license. But when the Customs House officer said, "Where bound?" Bob Bartlett roared out, "To the North Pole!" and without a doubt the S. S. *Roosevelt* is the only ship in the world to have sailed away with the Pole as her destination.

Mac noted in his journal: "While standing on the bridge en route to North Sydney, I engaged in conversation with a well-known U. S. geographer who had come to see us off and first learned that a Dr. Frederick A. Cook was at Etah, North Greenland, and had been there for a year, that he had sailed away in 1907 on an expedition sponsored by John R. Bradley of Palm Beach, Florida, the main object of which was to hunt polar bears. Upon the return of the expedition, it was announced that Dr. Cook had decided to remain in the North and make an attempt to reach the Pole, having found the Eskimos well supplied with walrus meat and with an abundance of dogs."

Northward the *Roosevelt* steamed, heading across Cabot Strait for Cape Anguille on the southwestern coast of Newfoundland. The land had dropped back into a blue haze; there was no sound but the rhythmic chung-chung-chung of the thousand-horsepower engines, the splash and gurgle of the sea alongside, and, occasionally, the tinny cheer of the mechanical piano in the commander's cabin.

The night crossing of Cabot Strait was sloppy. With an ebbing tide against a strong easterly wind, everything not securely lashed down was moving. The eight-by-six-foot stateroom shared by MacMillan and George Borup, a Yale graduate who had never been to sea before, was cluttered with rifles, cartridges, summer and winter clothing, arctic books, candles, candy and chewing gum for the Eskimos, notebooks and pencils, heavy walking shoes, rubber boots, oil clothes, field glasses, pocket compasses, and pocket sextants.

The rough night scrambled the whole assortment, especially since nothing had yet been stowed in its right place.

One call at 5 A.M. was sufficient to rouse them out after a night of pitch and roll, and they had coffee and toast in the starboard messroom reserved for Peary and his staff. After breakfast they lined the rail for the first look at Newfoundland, probably the "Markland" of the Norsemen nine hundred years ago, visited by Cabot more than four hundred years past, taken possession of by Gilbert in 1583 in the name of Elizabeth, and visited repeatedly by French, Portuguese, Spanish, English, and American fishermen for the last five centuries.

Mac viewed with more personal interest its shores and hills, especially the entrance to Bay of Islands, for this had been Neil MacMillan's objective when he sailed away from Provincetown for the last time.

Commander Peary considered the Eskimo dog the most important item of his equipment. He knew from his three journeys out over the Polar Sea that no man could expect to go far without them; he knew also they had to be well fed to keep going. The pemmican aboard was to feed them when they actually were on the ice of the Polar Sea where he never had observed a living thing. But it would cost a fortune to feed them on pemmican before they got there; thus other food had to be found for them. So they headed next for the whaling station at Cape Charles where, as good fortune would have it, two finbacks had just been killed. Dogs will thrive on whalemeat, and it's cheap.

The station crew hauled the two carcasses out of the water by steam power, hacked them up into pieces convenient for handling, and in two hours had 17,000 pounds aboard the *Roosevelt;* her afterdeck was filled, level with the rail.

Nor was it enough. They headed for Hawke's Harbor, a few miles north, and the site of another whaling station. Here they were to meet their consort, the steamer *Erik,* which had been chartered to accompany them to Etah. The *Erik* had orders to take on another twenty-five tons of whale meat.

Finally both ships, *Erik* and *Roosevelt,* were away together in the evening, bound for Turnavik West, two hundred miles to the north, the summer fishing station of the Bartlett family for generations.

Within a few days well supplied with cod and pink-meated Atlantic salmon just out of the cold waters of the Labrador Current, they steamed out past Turnavik East into open sea. They were now butting against an arctic current flowing southward along the shores of Labrador at the rate of about nine miles per day, which carries on its surface 10,000 square miles of ice and thousands of beautiful bergs born on the west coast of Greenland, nearly all offshoots of some of the largest and fastest-moving glaciers in the world, including the Jakobshavn, Rink, and Upernavik.

These huge bergs, when "calved," do not go south, as suggested in many scientific reports, but rather north along the west coast of Greenland, far north into Melville Bay, thence west to the eastern shores of Baffin Island where, meeting the southward-flowing current from the Polar Sea, and from Kennedy and Robeson channels, they begin their long drift southward following the shores of Baffin Island and Labrador.

Their course is then eastward along the northern shores of Newfoundland to the warm waters of the Gulf Stream, in which death by daily diminution soon comes to them.

On July 27 the *Roosevelt* crossed the Arctic Circle, that imaginary line drawn 23 degrees, 28 minutes from the Pole, which equals approximately the declination of the sun at the time of the summer solstice. The increase in the amount of daylight from day to day as one goes north may be an enigma to some and thus warrant explanation.

As twilight is in the east before sunrise and in the west following a sunset, and will remain until the sun is 18 degrees below the horizon, there is a continuous twilight in much of the far north as the sun rolls along only a few degrees beneath the horizon because of the inclination of the earth on its axis.

With every degree of latitude that a ship proceeds northward, the sun is "raised" one degree nearer the northern horizon or, with every mile advanced thus, it is raised one minute of arc, until the day comes when it does not set but skims along the edge of the sea and rises into the morning of a new day.

The ships were now well among the icebergs. White dots on the blue of the sea stretched on indefinitely. Nothing in the North quite compares in beauty to these crystal palaces of nature. Two and three hundred were in sight at one time —stolid, solid, immovable, dignified, betraying to the eye not one inch of motion as huge waves dashed insignificantly against their glittering white sides.

The summits of many were covered with arctic terns (*Sterna paradisaea*), boyhood friends of MacMillan, for they visit Provincetown in May when on the way to their northern nesting grounds. They love to roost on icebergs, although why one does not know. Perhaps for the same reason that the herring gulls sit for hours, immovable, on the sunny side of a sand dune.

MacMillan noted, "As we approached the Greenland coast, the glaucous gulls, too, came out to welcome us to the Northland, a bird that I had seen as a boy only during the winter months. Questions such as where our winter birds go during the summer were being answered before my eyes.

"And here, in these northern waters, I discovered my old friend, the 'noddy!' This was the fisherman's name for him; henceforth I was to know him by his own, the murre (*Uria troile troile*), and also Brunnich's murre (*Uria lomvia lomvia*), which differs only slightly."

Now close ahead of the *Roosevelt* lay the apparently

peaceful waters of Melville Bay, for one hundred and twenty-six years the "battlefield" of the Dundee whaling fleet in its struggle with the relentless ice field.

"To the bay itself, I give the name of Melville's Bay," wrote Captain John Ross in 1818, "from respect to the present First Lord of the Admiralty. It is situated between latitude 75 degrees, 12 minutes, and 76 degrees, and abounds with whales, many of which were taken by the ships which were persevering enough to follow us."

In this bay the eighteenth-century Dundee whalers were "tracked" or guided through cracks in the ice pack to the accompaniment of fifes, bagpipes, and drums, the skirling of salvation, if you will, for those ships fortunate enough to find a way in and out. In 1830 twenty-one of the fleet, solidly built, deep-water ships, were smashed to pieces. Many vessels have been abandoned here, together with tons of provisions, clothing, and gear. Tragedy moves fast in Melville—it requires only a wind shift, the ice closing in inexorably, and then there is cruel rending of massive timbers, nipped by the pack. Some ships actually were turned inside out, the bottom being thrust up through the deck.

To those who knew what Melville Bay could be like the *Roosevelt*'s crossing was accomplished with magnificent lack of delay or incident. With Bob Bartlett conning the ship from the crow's-nest at the mainmast head, and with the husky engines pulsating as regularly as a heartbeat, the steamer chugged on merrily, around large flat pans, threading its way among huge bergs, never slowing or stopping for a second.

Within two days they were at Cape York, 840 miles from

the North Pole.

They had reached the threshold of their task and, incidentally, the very place where white men in 1818 first came in contact with the so-called "Polar Eskimos," who were living, on that day in 1908 virtually as man lived thousands of years ago. Without their help no man could have sledged to the Pole.

At 4:45 P.M., August 18, the *Roosevelt* moved out of the harbor at Etah, bound for Cape Sheridan at the edge of the Polar Sea, 251 miles north. From there, with Eskimos and dog teams, Peary hoped to reach the Pole, accomplishing what had lured men into the frozen unknown for 300 years and rewarded them principally with death and disaster.

The *Roosevelt* had become a floating madhouse. The sledge dogs, 246 of them, were crowded into the waist of the ship; each was on his toes ready for a fight, snapping and snarling. The last ton of soft coal had been jammed into the bursting bunkers, and the persistent smudgy dust of it was everywhere. The Eskimos had arrived by the boatload with their families, forty-nine men, seventeen women, and ten children. With them this unwashed community in animal skins brought seal-hide tents, soapstone pots and lamps, wooden harpoons, sixteen-foot kayaks, bags of grass for bedding, and tin cans in which to cook. The children, excited, bled from the nose, a customary procedure among their kind.

The *Roosevelt* blew its whistle. The last link with civilization was broken.

# 5

A JOURNEY from Etah northward to the edge of the Polar Sea is a succession of leaps and bounds, requiring all the power of the ship at one moment to push through the ice, and offering at the next blue, open water.

One day the 184-foot *Roosevelt* would lie inert, locked in the pack and drifting south, losing all the mileage so stubbornly gained the day before. On the next her steel-shod stem and eleven-foot propeller would be thrusting her northward through the frozen mass. If the moving ice —the "pack," proved too formidable, there was only one course, to dodge into a niche in the land and let it go by. Peary obviously knew where the niches were.

The truth dawned early upon MacMillan that no ship, however strong, can be built to cope with a shifting ice field, driven by wind and tide. The only hope for safety lies in a vessel's small size, enabling her to hug the beach so closely that, because of shoal water, heavy ice cannot reach her. The small ship also rises readily and easily under ice pressure; she can wind her way through narrow leads and find safety in the lee of protective ledges, however limited.

Bartlett worked the *Roosevelt* along toward Cape Union, keeping so close to the shore that the steamer nudged the bottom time and again. Finally, at the last turn in the channel, they could look into the Polar Sea, 1,500 miles in diameter and 1,500,000 square miles in area; it was white from horizon to horizon with bluish ice pans forty to fifty feet in thickness and many of them a quarter-mile square. The ship seemed minute by comparison as she scurried under the lee of the cape.

Here the steamer was moored just inside a long line of stranded bergs which would serve as protection against the growling pack ice. The *Roosevelt* was driven aground near the mouth of a dried-up river bed. When the snows melted in the spring, the torrents of water pouring down from the hills would help refloat her. Here she had wintered before; undoubtedly she could do it safely again.

The hills were white with snow now, desolate and barren, with not even a stunted spruce on the sky line. They were alone in a white world, the stillness broken only by a low-toned swishing sound from the Polar Sea, the movement of the heavy pans which, born off Siberia's northern shores, were elbowing their restless way over the top of the world to the blue waters of the Atlantic.

The expedition's attack upon the Arctic really began on September 16, when sixteen heavily loaded sledges started northwesterly along the ice foot, that frozen belt that forms along the arctic shore between high and low watermarks as a result of the rise and fall of tides. At times it is the only "highway" existent there, and in certain areas, the only one ever.

Peary, well aware that the drift ice of the Polar Sea moves from west to east, had decided to make his departure from the land at Cape Columbia, the most northern point of all North American soil. On each of his efforts to attain the Pole he had increased his distance westward to overcome the ice drift; Columbia was the most westerly of all his starting points.

Those of the expedition who had not been to the Arctic before watched with interest the increasing daily darkness, the "dreaded arctic night." Actually only one expedition had ever experienced real darkness for twenty-four hours during the winter season, and that occurred when the ice-locked Norwegian ship *Fram* drifted within 243 miles of the Pole. Even at the North Pole, there are not six months of darkness, as simple mathematics reveals.

Darkness occurs when the reflected light of the sun disappears from the sky. This is not possible until the sun is 18 degrees below the horizon. The *Roosevelt* was at 82 degrees, 28 minutes North Latitude, or 452 miles from 90 north, the latitude of the Pole. On December 22, the middle of the "long night," the sun was at its farthest south, 23 degrees, 27 minutes south of the equator, or 15 degrees, 48 minutes below the horizon. On the shortest day, therefore, there still was a glimmer of twilight in the south.

At the North Pole the sun goes beneath the horizon on September 21 and returns on March 21, a period of six months, but during this non-sun period there are actually fifty-three days of twilight in the fall and an equal period in the spring, leaving only two months of real darkness during the winter.

Aboard the *Roosevelt* the period of long night produced no "premature aging, faltering steps, or traces of insanity," all of which have been attributed to the effects of arctic darkness. MacMillan recalled "not a single cross word, heated argument, or any feeling of ill will among the ten men in the after cabin." It never was necessary for Peary to do as did one of his predecessors, Lieutenant Greely, who directed his expedition's attention to the 133rd Psalm: "Behold, how good and how pleasant it is for brethren to dwell together in unity."

The Peary expedition may have been unusual in this respect. Explorer Charles Francis Hall shot two of his men; Greely felt compelled to shoot one of his, and Dr. Elisha Kent Kane, another arctic pioneer, shot at one of his expedition but missed him. Mutinies over the years were so prevalent that the British Admiralty agreed all arctic expeditions should be under military discipline.

The men of the *Roosevelt* remained calm in the long winter night, but "piblokto" proved common among the Eskimo women. Little understood, it probably is a form of hysteria and seemingly can stem from such widely diversified emotions as fright, joy, sorrow, jealousy, craving for affection, or remorse or anger because of a husband's abuse.

This is how it happens: A low, crooning note is heard. Within a few moments this is accompanied by a swaying of the body, a beating of the hands, and suddenly, with an abandoned yell, the afflicted woman is off for the snow-covered hills or the rough ice of the Polar Sea, en route ripping off her clothes with teeth and hands, clasping ice and snow chunks against her bare breasts, and spitting, clawing, and biting if restrained in any way. Usually those afflicted are dragged back to sanctuary and are normal a few hours later.

Near the *Roosevelt* the Eskimos had built two rock-sod winter houses, the "igloo" of the Smith Sound people, rather than live jammed together aboard the ship. One evening, hearing singing from one of these, MacMillan jumped the ship's rail, walked across the ice foot, and crawled into the igloo's narrow passageway. When he came to the semi-darkened interior, the singing stopped, but he entered, took a seat on a bed platform, and waited patiently.

The occupants were an old woman and two teen-age girls, the half-light accentuating their tangled, black hair and Mongolian features. Perspiration covered the woman's face; the girls appeared highly excited.

In a moment, as if he had not entered, they began again. Slowly, faintly, the crooning started, a mystic chant, accompanied by swaying body and beating hands, the guttural note of age blending with the treble of youth, the old teaching the young what was undoubtedly some of the most ancient music on earth. MacMillan, feeling that he had suddenly become contemporary with the cave man, sat transfixed as the girls became frenzied under apparent hypnotic influence. They appeared without control of emotion or motion. All three women were bathed in perspiration, and eventually physical exhaustion quieted them, although they still seemed confused as he left them, shaken by this intimate image of mankind's long-hidden past.

Arctic nights, which can kill, can also be beautiful. On one of these, MacMillan walked northwest along the trail, now well marked by sledge runners and dog prints, leading from the *Roosevelt* to the hunting areas. In Provincetown, for example, the moon is a great silver disc, resplendent with reflected light. In the Arctic it is a crimson oval, distorted by refraction as it rises over the rim of the Polar Sea; the colder it is, the greater the distortion, a weird flattening of the true circle into a shortened ellipse.

When risen, the arctic moon assumes its true proportions and color and makes a wonderland of the white wastes. Then appear the long shadows of the floe bergs, the shorter ones of the crunched-up mass next to the ice foot, high lights on the far hills and deep blotches in the dark valleys. In the glistening whiteness, silence blends with silence, and all is immeasurable, motionless and empty; even time and distance are no more.

As he approached the ship once more, the spell was broken by, of all things, the laughter of children at play on the ice foot. There they were, at the top of the world, unbelievable yet real, the Eskimo children of nature frolicking on the pans, unmindful of the long night and a six-below-zero temperature.

The expedition was busy, hunting food for present and future, making studies and surveys, and forging white men, Eskimos, and dogs into a smoothly operating team. On the fourteenth of October fourteen sledges and 140 dogs were lined out along the ice foot, ready to leave for work. It was, as always, an animated scene. The dogs were yelping (they

(*Left to right, top to bottom*) Rear Admiral Robert E. Peary, discoverer of the North Pole. Matthew Henson, his chief assistant. Captain Bob Bartlett, skipper of Peary's steamer *Roosevelt*. Donald MacMillan, assistant to Peary. The four Eskimos who, with Peary and Henson, reached the North Pole on April 6, 1909.

MacMillan's arctic schooner *Bowdoin*, close-hauled and northward bound in Baffin Bay on a sparkling summer day.

The midnight sun, North Greenland, photographed at 20-minute intervals, 11 P.M. to 1:20 A.M., July 25.

Homeward bound, the MacMillans hold two full-blooded Eskimo pups, given them

by Aage Knudsen, former Danish District Manager of Jakobshavn, Greenland.

This wanderer of the North, its dramatic architecture a product of sun and sea, drifts south to extinction in the warm waters of the Atlantic.

ABOVE: Donald MacMillan, Dr. Gilbert Grosvenor, former president of the National Geographic Society, and Dr. Wilfred T. Grenfell, English missionary of Newfoundland and Labrador, aboard *Bowdoin* at Battle Harbor, Labrador. BELOW: MacMillan's Eskimo assistants on the North Greenland expedition of 1923–24. Etukasuk, Kakotcheeah, Nookapingwah were loyal hunters and dog drivers.

did not bark), jumping, standing on their hind legs, and tugging at their traces, eager to go. Eskimos, black-haired and fur-clad, shouted gutturally as they finished loading the sledges, being frequently interrupted by the unruly dogs, which they whacked and kicked into temporary submission.

MacMillan had been assigned two sledges and two Eskimos to make a survey of Clements Markham Inlet; the other twelve sledges were to continue to Cape Columbia, each with full loads of five hundred pounds of food and equipment.

That first moment of being under way was unforgettable. MacMillan sat close behind the broad, caribou-skin-covered back of his Eskimo companion on the heavily laden sled. Out ahead the fast-stepping dogs, as precise as a chorus line, leaned into their taut harnesses with big shoulders rippling. Sledge after sledge strung out behind, following the ice foot's twists and turns. Abruptly conscious of the magnitude and daring of this polar undertaking, of the years which Peary had dedicated to it, of the men whose lives it had already cost, Dan was silent, even in enthusiasm.

That night they slept at Porter Bay, a run of thirty miles. Here years before, George Porter of the British expedition of 1875–76 died and was buried in the sea ice.

Since good building snow was lacking, they were compelled to use a canvas tent to protect them from a twelve-below-zero wind.

A deep red sky in the morning portended wind, the enemy of every arctic traveler, for it blinds with its stinging drift, freezes both face and hands, stops both dogs and men dead in their tracks, and at times actually blows them bodily off the trail.

They were away at nine-fifteen, however, for the crossing of the Fielden Peninsula, anticipating trouble because a land crossing in the North generally means a wind-swept area of grit and gravel which ruins the traction surface of the carefully polished sledge runners.

Within minutes it began to blow, dead ahead; in another quarter hour they knew they were through for the day. Whirling snow blinded the dogs, whitened the cheeks of the leading men trying to find the trail. White men and Eskimos grabbed the upstanders of their sledges for support, buried their faces in their fur-covered arms, and trusted to the dogs to follow the team ahead. Faces numb with pain, they arrived at the shore of James Ross Bay and huddled in the lee of a provision cache. Here tents were pitched, miserable shelters against such weather, and here they spent a restless night, with the canvas slatting and banging.

In the morning it was bright and calm, and MacMillan parted company with the other sledges, gaining the Markham Inlet late that day. Here he established a carefully measured base line at the mouth of the fjord and by triangulation, or "fix," recorded salient points on both sides. At Peary's suggestion he had measured his own pace on snowshoes (thirty inches) and paced off his distances, thus saving much time and acquiring in the next fourteen days the practice of counting as he walked, a habit that persisted for weeks and acquainted him with the fact that he took 2,400 steps to the mile.

It was a job that required persistence; one, two, three,

count, and another round of angles with the transit, while the Eskimos, Egingwa and Ooblooya, drove at a snail's pace up the inlet, half asleep on their sledges. Being practical minded, they could not understand why anybody wanted to measure the inlet and put it on paper anyway; as for them, they could remember every indentation, point, and knoll.

When the job was done, they were, all three, like boys out of school on a Friday night. The two Eskimo drivers, characteristically of sharp and roving eye, spotted a cone-shaped pile of rocks a quarter mile ahead as they sledged back along the trail. It was a cairn, such as explorers build, and the drivers were jabbering about it; they figured it was a food cache with *nanook* (bear) *nerke* (meat), and they were right.

Field rations had been beans, tomatoes, and biscuit, and all hands unhitched the dogs and pitched the tent in a hurry at the prospect of a change in diet. MacMillan's "boys" found a frozen brook, chipped fresh-water ice, and filled a pot over the fire. Then they boiled the big red bear steaks . . . or rather this is what happened:

Egingwa took off the pot cover, jabbed his long hunting knife through the cloud of steam to test the meat's tenderness. *"Tima naga* [Not done]," he said. They all sat back, ravenous and licking their lips, yet endeavoring to appear unconcerned. Finally patience gave way to hunger pangs. Whetting knives, they dragged the tin pot off the stove, placed it among them on the floor, and peered through the steam cloud. There was nothing in it; they had in their eagerness forgotten to put in the meat!

75

To MacMillan the most memorable aspect of this incident was that the two Eskimos fell back on the ice and roared with laughter at the joke on themselves. It was his first insight into the nature of primitive polar humor and did much to convince him of the Eskimo's good-naturedness and emotional stability.

Of the polar-bear meat itself, since it was his first, it may be said that it varies greatly, depending on the age and sex of the animal. Some is delicious; some is tough, stringy, and uneatable. Young bear is almost always good; MacMillan, at least, finds bear meat much better raw than when cooked, but only when it is frozen. Freezing removes its peculiar rancid taste.

The Peary expedition had received special orders from President Theodore Roosevelt to attempt certain scientific work, including tidal and meterological observations at the two most northern points of land in the world, Cape Columbia and Cape Morris Jesup. When MacMillan returned to the *Roosevelt,* he received the following: "SS *Roosevelt,* November 6, 1908—Sir: Proceed to Cape Columbia with your party, comprising the sailor, Jack Barnes, and the two Eskimos, Egingwa and Inugeeto, and their wives, for the purpose of obtaining a month's series of hourly tidal observations. R. E. Peary, Commanding."

Columbia was a long, low spit reaching seaward from the black bluff of Cape Aldrich; it was the site of a large provision cache placed there by Bartlett's and Borup's divisions a few weeks before. MacMillan's survey party arrived there in thirty-eight-below-zero temperature, groping through a smother of swirling snow. They began probing the sea ice by lantern light, and after two fruitless borings revealed gravel, not sea, four to five feet down, they gave up for the night, discouraged by cold, wind, and dirt. Mac concluded they were on a mass of ice attached to the land —not a glacier or ice foot which is formed by the rise and fall of tide, but a "glacial fringe," unlike anything found in any other part of the world.

Drift and wind continued. It was quite necessary to do something or be buried. The men crawled out, drove their snowshoes into a snowbank as anchors, and pulled the tent back into shape. Just how far out on the Polar Sea it might be necessary to go to find water MacMillan didn't know. Time was valuable, and the lunar month was passing.

Studying a rough map of the coast, he noted that to the east of the cape there was an indentation in the land, bordered by high hills. Invariably these characteristics denoted a considerable depth of water, so he decided the best chance of finding water was in that section and there, luckily, they found it, nine feet deep, with perfect shelter nearby for the snowhouse they must build.

The plan was to sink to the bottom a butterbox weighted with rocks, which would support an upright staff graduated to the tenth of an inch. Necessarily this rod should be of sufficient length to project well above the level of the highest tide and thus record the rise and fall.

While Barnes and MacMillan were engaged in excavating roughly three tons of ice to bring this about, the two Eskimos were hard at work constructing living quarters, the largest snowhouse Dan had ever seen, eleven feet, seven inches by twelve feet, with a height of eight feet, two inches, and incidentally the first in which he had ever lived.

One foot and a half above the level of the floor and occupying one half of the interior was the bed platform, upon which were placed, as a protection against dampness and cold, boxboards, snowshoes, and sheepskins. The snowhouse completed, the women lighted the soapstone oil-lamps and closed all openings. Within an hour the thermometer registered forty-two degrees above zero, causing the inside of each snow block to drip. Then they extinguished the lamps, cut a small round hole in the top of the house, and removed the covering from the exit leading to the outer passage. This sudden lowering of the temperature stopped all melting; the result was a hard glazed surface which strengthened the whole structure against violent winds and drift. As they were to inhabit this snowhouse for at least a month, they lined it with the canvas tent, thereby creating an air space between the walls of the tent and the snow blocks, a non-conducting unit of the best kind, rendering the living quarters very comfortable.

A woman's touch in this home of snow blocks and canvas was highly appreciated. Returning from a six-hour "watch" on the frozen sea where the thermometer registered thirty to forty degrees below zero, having lain on one's belly for an hour, peering at figures on an ice-covered staff every five minutes, the shelter was palatial.

The "girls" each day smoothed out the tumbled beds, rearranged the boards and snowshoes beneath the skins, trimmed the wicks of the small oilstoves, replenished the oil, constructed drying racks for socks, padded dry grass into the sealskin boots, prepared meals of hash, corn, and beans, and even tried, in vain, to polish the tiny mica windows.

Barnes and MacMillan continued their work religiously, lying flat on the frozen sea for hours, chipping away with a huge snow knife, the ice constantly gathering on the tidal gauge. MacMillan wrote: "We sincerely hoped that what we were doing under such severe conditions proved or disproved something. What that something was we did not know, and could not guess."

It was on one of these six-hour watches that MacMillan froze both heels, a development that was to have major consequences.

It dawned upon Dan one night as he recorded the events of Wednesday, November 25, that the next day was Thanksgiving at home. Family reunions, crackling-brown turkeys, and homemade mince pies were out of the question for the two most northern white men in the world, living in a house of snow blocks, and for their four primitive companions, but he determined to mark the day.

He recorded faithfully: "I started the day by having a good wash; some of us washed once a week and some not at all. I then told the four Eskimos, as well as my limited vocabulary would permit, what the day meant to us in the land far to the south, and that always on that day we gathered around a big table heaped high with food—the very best that our mothers could prepare. We certainly should have something extra to commemorate the day. Since canned corn was apparently our favorite dish, I decided to increase the half ration can to a whole can. And instead of eight small crackers, we were to have ten. And instead of one cup of tea, we were to enjoy two."

MacMillan also recorded each day the Eskimos' guttural sounds for everything that happened, and he looked forward to the time when he could converse freely, for he sensed in them a high degree of intelligence and civilization despite the lack of a written language or opportunity for formal education.

Night after night he studied stars and planets and tried to tell them of what men knew of the moon. He permitted them to peer through his telescope. Yes, these were names which the men from the south had given to certain objects in the sky seen through the brass tube.

He called their attention to the constellation known as the "Big Dipper," the Ursa Major of the astronomers. Yes, they knew. The seven stars were seven reindeer feeding on the hills up in the sky. The Pleiades, the so-called "Seven Sisters," is a team of dogs in pursuit of a bear. The three bright stars in Orion's Belt are three steps cut in the face of a glacier, steps to aid the traveler.

They had no watches, these Eskimo people, to tell them when to get up, when to go to bed, when to eat, when to do everything; watches weren't necessary. The bright star, known to us as Arcturus, tells them all. It revolves in the sky and tells them how long they have been traveling, how long they have slept. And when the stars have gone to their rest, the sun, revolving in the sky, tells them all they need to know.

Moreover, there is a land beyond when we are through with this one. That is why we must take with us the things that we really need. A man must have his hunting equipment, for no man can live without food. Thus one always finds such equipment near a grave from which the spirit, of course, has been released.

Similarly a woman must have her soapstone cooking pots and lamp to light her igloo. They are both placed at her feet in her grave. And you will also find there a needle, a thimble, and thread, as well as her *ooloo,* a knife that she cannot do without.

These people believe in a hereafter but not in an all-forgiving, all-loving God. Night after night, and especially on nights when progress to and from the tidal hole was nearly impossible, their omnipotent one Old Tornarsuk, the mightiest of all, was intently watching every move. They heard his voice repeatedly. He was in the moaning of the winds, in the swish of drifting snow, in the loud cracking of the bay ice, and in the rumble of the distant pack.

He stood at the *toksut,* the entrance to the snowhouse, for hours, listening, listening to every word said. At times his voice was so loud, discordant, and threatening that their only recourse was to frighten him away. This was frequently done by having Egingwa or Inugeeto load the heavy 40-82 Winchester, drop quietly through the round hole in the floor, creep stealthily through the narrow snow passage, and upon gaining the outside, turn quickly and fire repeatedly at the face of the frowning black cliff at the rear.

This done, they could hear the Eskimo scrambling for his life to get back into the house. Then they all would jump quickly into bed, snuggle down under the coverlets, and remain perfectly quiet.

Evil spirits (*tornarssuit*) ever threaten to destroy; a mul-

titude contend against the one protective guardian spirit
which is always on watch to protect when danger is near.
The evil spirit lurks among the crags above the ice foot; it
hurls boulders down upon dog teams and their drivers; the
evil spirit of cracking ice threatens to engulf all; the spirit
of blasting winds sweeps down from the great *sermiksuah*
(icecap), stops all travel, destroys the *tupiks* (tents). Such
spirits must be appeased and pacified continuously and in
many ways if one would have happiness.

Man has a spirit or soul, of his own, not within the body,
but apart from it, always attending it until it goes to its rest
beneath a rude pile of rocks, and even to that enclosure the
spirit often returns. Upon the death of the body this *inua*
(its real self) goes on to the great world above or down into
the sea. Eskimos fear neither one nor the other prospect,
decidedly different from the "hell and brimstone" theories
of MacMillan's early church days in Provincetown. For
*inua* may have many abodes and wanderings. It may live
in the body of a walrus, to seek retribution for some offense
committed by a certain hunter in the community, and of
that particular walrus the hunter must beware. The soul of
one who has passed on may return to life in the body of a
newborn infant; therefore great importance is attached to
its name. Panikpah's father was a man called Etukasuk.
Panikpah named his first boy after his father, knowing that
his father had returned. In view of the fact that the soul of
his father was in the body of his son, he always addressed
his boy as "father" and the young Etukasuk addressed his
father as "son."

At length the cold and tedious project of tidal observations was completed. The day came when the last statistic had been recorded, the lights in the snowhouse were extinguished. They rolled up the skins on the snow couch, gathered up their few belongings, and crawled through the passageway leading to open air and sledged to the *Roosevelt,* frozen in at Cape Sheridan, ninety miles distant.

For MacMillan it had meant attainment of new perspective, his first real insight into the nature of the Eskimo.

# 6

ALTHOUGH THE SUN, according to the *Nautical Almanac*, would not appear above the horizon until March 1, the attack upon the Pole was to begin on February 15, 1909, the coldest time of year, when temperatures between sixty and seventy below zero could be expected.

On that date Bartlett and his three Eskimos received instructions to leave the ship and go to Cape Columbia. There was no fanfare to mark the occasion. In the afternoon Mac-Millan was looking for Bartlett and someone remarked casually, "He left this morning."

Dr. J. W. Goodsell's division left the next day for the same destination, with orders to return for additional loads. Henson and MacMillan got away on the eighteenth, the former several hours in the lead.

The dogs in this expedition were driven by experts, not the least of whom was Henson, who, with a turn of the wrist, undoubtedly avoided obstacles that would have put a novice out of business for hours. The technique of the long whip in dog driving, much like casting a fishing fly, is an art; it is not the suffering inflicted by a skillful arm that speeds the team on but rather the dogs' knowledge that pain can be inflicted. Once it dawns on the dogs that a novice is in the driver's seat, then eight bushy tails begin to wag and the skylarking begins.

Accordingly, day after day, MacMillan had sat on a box in lieu of a sledge and flicked his whip at the backs of eight dead dogs, frozen into various attitudes. He sprinkled the back of each with snow and, upon hitting the mark with his whip, a puff of flakes would indicate his accuracy.

Many an expedition has failed to attain its goal because of mistakes made before it ever left home in the selection of food and clothing. On this trip subsistence per day was to consist of sixteen ounces of pemmican, sixteen ounces of biscuit, four ounces of condensed milk, and a half ounce of compressed Chinese tea per man. Whether or not this was a balanced diet no one, including Peary, could be sure, for this was more than a half century ago, and little attention was paid by explorers to proteins and carbohydrates.

The dogs were to receive sixteen, rather than thirty-two, ounces of food daily, for they weighed roughly half as much.

For clothing, Peary provided each man with the following: a blanket shirt with hood; a sheepskin coat for sledge work; a caribou-skin coat, to be exchanged for the sheepskin at the end of the day's march, and for sleeping at night; one pair each of polar bearskin pants, bearskin boots, caribou-skin boots, and sealskin boots, and three pairs of sheepskin or hare-skin stockings.

Underneath all was worn a light woolen "union suit" to

absorb body moisture; from this all buttons were removed and the garment was sewed on. Thus there were no sleeping bags or sleeping covers provided because each man really was walking in his sleeping bag; this was Peary's own theory of arctic dress; he was the only arctic explorer before or since who ever resorted to such extreme measures. Peary reasoned that if the Eskimos managed to sleep in their clothing when on the trail, his men could.

Also of great importance was the type and construction of sledge. If the polar sea ice were smooth, as it is in Labrador, or as level as the icecap of Greenland, a toboggan could be used successfully. But such a contraption would not last an hour when drawn by eight dogs through, on, and over the rough sea ice between Cape Columbia and the Pole.

The 1908 model of the Peary sledge was twelve feet long, two feet wide, and seven inches high, with a strong, blunt nose to resist shock and a "knockabout" bow for rough work, that is, for surmounting massive blocks of ice forced up into "pressure ridges." Bound with rawhide instead of nails or screws, to give it elasticity and flexibility, the whole structure thus was rendered relatively immune to shock and breakage.

Peary's plan for reaching the Pole was based on supporting parties. The distance from Cape Columbia to the North Pole is 413 geographical miles, or a total distance to be traveled of 826 miles. Ice conditions do not permit a direct course, and at least a hundred miles should be added to this figure for deviations.

The weight to be carried by each sledge does not depend

upon the strength of each dog or the total number of dogs but upon the strength of the driver, who is called upon to push, pull, lift, and struggle with his load throughout the day. The frozen Polar Sea is not a pond but a slowly moving mass of ice sections, "leads" of varying length and width, and of pressure ridges ten, twenty, and even thirty feet in height, over which the driver must repeatedly lift at least one half of his total load.

Considering the total amount of food to be consumed by a man and his eight dogs, it is clearly impossible for one man and one sledge and eight dogs to journey to the North Pole and back from any known point of land. It is an utterly impossible feat for two or even one hundred sledges, in consequence of the simple fact that when the total amount of food on one sledge is consumed, it has been consumed on all, days and weeks prior to the attainment of one's objective.

Thus is created the essential need for supporting parties, the number depending on the distance to be traveled, each supporting party to carry food for the total number of men and dogs in the main party for a certain number of days, and when this has been consumed, to return to the land.

The five supporting parties, as planned by Peary, were to place him within striking distance of the Pole, with sufficient food remaining on his five sledges to enable him to return to the land. With lightened sledges on a beaten and well-defined trail, all marches were to be doubled on the return, and dogs were to be eaten if necessary.

In order to control the Eskimos in their daily work and in the distribution of food and oil, each division was to be under the command of a white man and was to be outfitted as a complete, self-supporting and independent unit. Each, therefore, carried its .44 Winchester rifle, cooking outfit, snowshoes, snow knives for building igloos, and its *ahwataq,* or sealskin float, to be inflated and placed beneath the sledges in the event that open water cut off the retreat later in the season.

With orders to meet Peary on the last day of February, the Eskimo Koolatinah and MacMillan pushed on to overtake Henson at Porter Bay. Dan's dogs were now pulling together and were so much improved in their relations toward one another that he was encouraged to take on the maximum load of five hundred pounds, which is about the limit for one man on the rough Polar Sea.

On February 22 five of the supporting parties were encamped at Cape Columbia. Marvin and Peary were somewhere back on the trail between the cape and the ship. The camp was a busy place, with all hands drying and mending clothes, feeding dogs, repairing sledges and harnesses. Borup and MacMillan received orders to transport all gear left on the ninety-mile trail to Columbia to the base camp at the cape; they doubled up their teams and got away early on the twenty-fifth.

This Borup was a good man with whom to travel the arctic emptiness, for what he was did not suffer from the closer scrutiny that is inevitable when life is reduced to its lowest common denominators.

He was a completely sociable being who chose to like everyone and to whom laughter was a way of life. The newspapers called him "the boy athlete," but he confided to Mac

that he never had made a team in his life. Boyishness there
certainly was about him, an irrepressible love of living and
doing that encouraged him to tackle anything, alone if necessary, with a zestful courage so ebullient that it had no time
to consider failure.

Principally, he was without meanness; he was not devi-
ous; he thought everybody was a good fellow, and so they
all thought he was too.

For an hour the two of them and their sixteen dogs were
apparently the only living things on a great white desert,
but then they met Marvin and his men, then Dr. Goodsell's
party, and within another few minutes Peary himself. Mac-
Millan wrote: "The great, desolate-looking white hills must
have wondered at the congested traffic; they had looked
down upon twenty-six men and one hundred and fifty
dogs, passing and repassing . . ."

Commander Peary, in a red skullcap, with his hair
clipped short and his mustache shaved off, looked absolutely fit. In a matter-of-fact way he turned to MacMillan
and, removing a bearskin mitten, applied the palm of his
warm hand to Dan's face; he said, "MacMillan, your nose
is frozen." It was still there but hard as a piece of wood at
the tip end.

Application of the warm hand is the Eskimo treatment
for frostbite. Civilized man rubs the afflicted part with
snow, but snow, at the temperature of air (it was fifty-
seven below that morning), would freeze the nose harder,
if possible. If an Eskimo has cold feet, he puts them on his
wife's stomach, not in a snowbank.

The next day, February 26, the thermometer stood at

fifty-eight below. The day after that they never knew how cold it was, for Peary had disappeared into the haze to the west, taking the thermometer with him.

MacMillan spent the night of the 26th camped in a snow-house at Goode Point with two Eskimos who said it was the coldest night they had ever experienced. Whisky and gin were frozen solid. Kerosene froze into a white mush. Condensed milk was as brittle as rock candy, and even the sledge traces were stiff as sticks.

The new men of the expedition, including MacMillan, were beginning to realize that many accepted "truths" pertaining to the Arctic were not truths at all. It is written, for example: "It is fatal for a man in such low temperatures to breathe through his mouth; one must inhale carefully through the nostrils."

Throughout the cold days of February and March, Mac-Millan took careful note of the fact that every man, native and white, breathed through his mouth when working in low temperatures. Personally he found this practice to be "absolutely necessary for two reasons: First, a more rapid and needed supply of air is drawn through the open mouth than through the small, narrow passages of the nose, and second, air at sixty and seventy below zero drawn through the nose quickly freezes the tender tissues, resulting in excruciating pain."

Outside the Arctic it also was a generally accepted belief that to eat snow was injurious to health, possibly fatal. Actually snow proved refreshing when sucked, although exasperatingly lacking in thirst-quenching qualities. When working and perspiring beneath a warm suit of furs, members of the Peary party often ate snow all day long, first warming it in the hollow of the hand, inside a fur mitten.

February 27 found them all at what Peary designated as Camp Crane, in honor of Zenas Crane of Dalton, Massachusetts, vice-president of the Peary Arctic Club. From this point they were to leave for what the newspapers persisted in calling the "dash" to the Pole, although it would involve all plodding and no dashing, a persistent struggle across the bending ice of a lead, over the summits of angular pressure ridges, to find a pin point on an ice pan at the end of the earth's axis.

Every man was tense with expectancy. Sledges were bottom up, their steel runners being filed and burnished; gear was scattered out in heaps, awaiting final loading; harnesses were being renewed and traces mended; broken crossbars were replaced and new whipstocks made, and dogs were exchanged to make up the best possible teams. Work done for the day, they finally gathered in Peary's igloo for the last instructions, looking at each other silently and realizing they would not be all together again until it was over . . . and perhaps not even then.

The commander said they were to profit by his mistakes. He knew very well why he had failed three years before. That mistake was behind him and would not be repeated. He had depended on food left in caches on the ice by his expedition teams. Due to motion of the ice pack, driven eastward by strong winds, he had lost every ounce. On this trip, therefore, he would supply his dogs, his men, and himself from the food carried on the sledges by the supporting parties.

He had purposely taken to the edge of the Polar Sea twice as many dogs as he actually needed. Now, even after a winter's work of hunting and advancing food supplies to the departure point at Cape Columbia, he still had 140 of the original 246. This would enable him to place in the field twenty teams of seven dogs each. That was the substance of the last briefing; his assistants, Henson, Bartlett, Marvin, Borup, Goodsell, and MacMillan, came away in thoughtful silence—the power of Peary's determination, more formal than fiery, had dominated the gathering, and the strength of it lingered with them.

The sun had not yet returned. The expedition must do its immediate work in the dawn of the long arctic day, difficult for many reasons, the chief of which was a lack of shadows, often resulting in failure to detect depression in the ice surface—even deep holes—into which men and dogs fell repeatedly in a tangled, struggling mass.

The departure was quiet. No bantering, no handshakes, no good-bys or good lucks. Each fur-clad figure gathered up the traces of his dogs, fastened them to the *peeto* attached to the sledge, and with a "Huk" was away, swallowed up almost immediately by the drifting snow, and even the commands to the dogs were quickly muffled by the wind's force. So began the final chapter of Peary's eighth expedition, twenty-two men and nineteen sledges on the glacial fringe, with more than four hundred bitter miles to go to reach their destination under the North Star.

Civilization they left behind, even its trappings, its "indispensable necessities." They had no soap, washcloths, towels, razors, toothbrushes, tooth paste, combs or brushes, ties, socks, wrist watches, fountain pens, or hair clippers. They carried nothing except what was required to keep them breathing and working.

Once behind the ice foot and the ever-present pressure ridge adjoining the tidal crack, the going was much better, although two Eskimo sledges were smashed beyond repair in the first few hours. Ten miles from land, following the trail of Bartlett and Borup, they arrived at their first camp, a place of soiled snow, two igloos, and some empty pemmican tins. With two divisions in advance, selecting by compass the shortest northward course, the main party could always be sure of two snow shelters awaiting it at the end of the day's march.

March 2 was typical of a day on the Polar Sea. Mac-Millan's heavily loaded sledge preferred, more often than not, to travel bottom up or to lie quietly in a deep hole in a crushed mess of ice. During such an occurrence the activity of the dogs is the cause of more exasperation than the predicament itself. Invariably they take delight in sitting on the edge of the pitfall, greatly interested in the situation, cocking heads, wagging bushy tails vigorously, rolling in the snow and, above all, congratulating themselves that work is over, at least for the time being.

About the middle of the afternoon the advance sledges were sighted, assembled near a large pressure ridge. There would be only one reason for the delay—a lead, a crack in the ice field with open water preventing further progress. From an ice pinnacle Peary studied the lead; one can only wait until it closes, either by freezing or ice movement or both, when it can be crossed safely.

Waiting at this "Big Lead," tied down to inactivity by the necessity of halting until the open water ahead of them froze enough to permit crossing, was the worst thing in the world for the Eskimos. They fretted and chafed and frankly wanted to turn back. It was MacMillan who communicated to Peary that there was "mutiny in the air," that something must be done to preserve the Eskimos' will to continue. It was at this point, as MacMillan's colleagues later indicated, that he "proved his full worth and in a way made possible the discovery of the Pole." Dan had what Peary called a "natural talent" for handling the Eskimos, and during the bleak days at the "Big Lead" he kept them busy and happy through a continuous succession of games and tests of strength, an effort to which they brought the delightful enthusiasm of children.

According to dead reckoning, based on the judgment of the four men best qualified—Peary, Bartlett, Marvin, and Henson—their last march had placed them beyond the British record of 83 degrees, 20 minutes made by Commander Albert H. Markham, north of Cape Joseph Henry, on May 12, 1876. Since the sun still was absent, there was no opportunity for meridian altitudes for latitude of either sextant or theodolite, both of which they carried.

In the morning MacMillan was awakened by the pounding of a hatchet on the floor of the igloo, the call of Peary to his men in the other snowhouses to light their alcohol stoves, eat their eight ounces of pemmican, pack their sledges, and be off.

A quick survey of conditions through the peephole of the entrance to the snowhouse was not encouraging. It was clear, but the wind, the curse of the Arctic, blew with steady violence. Beyond, what had been a lead was now a mass of rafting, crushing, tilting slabs of young ice.

Question: Was the broken end of the lead to the right or left? In other words, which course to take across in order to get on sound ice again? There was one thing to do. Send Kaiota west over a bending surface of newly formed ice, and Ootah east. In a short time Kaiota was seen on top of a pressure ridge waving his arms vigorously; he had found a way across.

Fresh-water ice breaks without warning and there you are in water up to your neck, but not so with salt-water ice. The ice they crossed that morning on the run had the properties of a sheet of rubber. It seemed incredible that it could bear the weight even of the eighty-pound dogs, but it did, and the entire party crossed, found Bartlett's trail, and headed northward once more.

The first day out of camp they covered at least twelve miles over a fairly good surface. Holes and rough stretches gave some trouble, however, leaving their union suits wringing wet even in the bitterly cold weather. MacMillan wrote: "Secret for cold weather travel, and for restful, sound sleep at night—do not permit yourself to become overheated to the extent that you perspire. I wanted to 'get under' something. It was wholly unlike retiring for the night to drink a quart of tea, munch frozen pemmican and hard biscuit, and then tip back on a snow bed."

The "Peary system" of dressing for arctic travel has its advantages, but there is no denying that all suffered, every man. There were black patches on every face, both white

95

and Eskimo. The rims of their ears often were frozen when, in desperation, they had shoved back the hoods of caribou-skin coats to cool their sweating heads and necks. The tips of their fingers were horny, cracked and bleeding. The working coats of sheepskin, in which they did their sledging, were a mass of ice about the face, from condensation of the breath, and about the bottoms, where warm, moisture-laden air escaped from the body.

Driving dogs through a shattered ice field presents difficulties to the point of hardship, but there was something else as bad. That was the ordeal at the end of the day of getting out of a sodden, half-frozen garment and standing for a moment exposed to the wind at fifty degrees below zero, while putting on a dry caribou-skin *kooletah* for sleeping. Even that task was heavenly compared to the one that awaited them each morning—removing the warm, dry coat over the head and exchanging it for a mass of ice, snow, and wool, which at times refused to open up and conform to the shape of the day before.

To prevent the escape of warm air from about the body, a good Eskimo seamstress fashions the neck of the *kooletah* to equal the diameter of the wearer's head. Consequently, when the neck of the garment is frozen, the head will not pass through. There is nothing one can do but pull and struggle with freezing fingers and then remain patient for a few minutes until the heat of the head thaws and softens the neck-hole sufficiently.

It is true that the veterans did not suffer as did the novices. Peary, Henson, and the Eskimos knew how to wear fur clothes and never became overheated. But even so, the

march out over the drift ice was cruel. As strong a man as
Bob Bartlett, his underclothing soaked with perspiration,
the face opening of his coat heavy with ice, his cheeks black
with frost, his legs chafed to sores by endless walking, broke
down and called for his mother as he shivered in a snow
bed, miles from land on the polar pack.

On the twenty-third day away from the ship Peary requested MacMillan to pack up and go ahead with the advance party to break trail; it was not so cold, only forty-
seven below, but this was a brief respite. The next day it
dropped twelve degrees, and they struck an area of deep
cracks and pressure ridges which required great effort and
constant vigilance.

For MacMillan, Sunday, March 14, was both a day of
rest and a day of sorrow.

His feet, which he had frozen lying on his belly making
the Cape Columbia survey, were in bad shape. Both heels
were seriously maturated and getting worse each day. When
occupying the same igloo with Peary, which he frequently
did, Dan made a conscious effort to conceal this condition,
yet it was constantly on his mind.

Prior to leaving the *Roosevelt,* Peary had come to Mac-
Millan's stateroom, something that had never happened
before, a gesture perhaps motivated by the fact that they
both were Bowdoin College graduates, a tie deeply mean-
ingful to each. Sitting on the edge of MacMillan's bunk,
the commander reminisced.

He had made his first trip to the Greenland Icecap in
1886 with a Dane named Maigaard, his only companion.
Impressed by the sight of this great white highway, he rea-

soned that he had discovered the route to the Pole itself. Yet he had failed to reach the Pole by way of the icecap in 1892 and again in 1895, or by way of Smith Sound and Kennedy Channel in five other attempts. Now he was trying again.

This time, said Peary, Goodsell was to return from the Polar Sea first, since he was unable to drive a dog team. Borup, young and inexperienced, and with no knowledge of navigation, was to be the second to turn back. Ross Marvin was to be third.

Turning to MacMillan, Peary said, "After these men have left, I shall depend upon you and Bartlett to feed us and our dogs, up to within two degrees of the Pole. Henson will go all the way, I hope. He has been with me on every important northern trip. His influence over the Eskimos is invaluable."

This decision to keep MacMillan with him for most of the trip to the Pole was honor indeed for a young man on his first trip North. MacMillan was thrilled, eager to be found worthy of all tasks, and it was this very conscientiousness that bothered him now. Peary was depending on him for support during the most critical part of the expedition, and what if injured feet should cause him to fail at a time when not one man, dog, or sledge could be spared?

MacMillan knew that with Borup, Marvin, and more Eskimos in camp than really were required, now was the proper time for him to allow Peary to decide whether changes in plans should be made. "To be the person responsible for failure," MacMillan wrote, "would be more than I could bear."

Dan went to see Matt Henson, finding him alone in his igloo. Henson had had years of experience with this sort of thing. Removing one of his *kamiks* (boots) lined with a sheepskin stocking, MacMillan said, "I want you to look at my foot, Matt. Tell me what I should do."

"My God, man! How long has it been like that?"

"Since I went to Cape Columbia. The other one is the same. But I can still do my work."

Henson was silent.

"You think I should show my feet to the commander and let him decide?"

"Absolutely."

They went to the commander's igloo. Peary examined both feet carefully, straightened, and said, "You are going back in the morning and have them attended to."

For MacMillan the bottom had dropped out of the Polar Sea.

The next day he said good-by to them all, with a final farewell for Marvin, with whom he had shared so many hours, and a moment with his dogs, whom he knew he should never see again. Peary walked back on the trail with him for some distance. He wanted Dan to establish food caches west of Cape Columbia and along the northern shore of Greenland if there were dogs enough available and his feet would permit. MacMillan promised, mindful that this short walk might be their last.

Peary grasped his hand. He said simply, "MacMillan, if I am not back by the first of June, and Bartlett is lost, tell

Mr. Gushue to get the ship ready and go home."

Why wait further for him to return? He would not be alive.

On short rations and with inferior dogs, MacMillan nevertheless covered the one hundred miles back to the *Roosevelt* in three days, arriving there on March 25. In spite of the condition of his feet he sledged west along the northern shores of Grant Land and left a record and food for Peary on Ward Hunt Island. This record, left in 1909, was found in 1954 by Geoffrey Hattersley-Smith, a member of the Ellesmere Ice Shelf Expedition. It read: "Sunday, March 21, 1909. To whom it may concern: At the request of Commander R. E. Peary, who is now out on the Polar Sea at Lat. 85, I am leaving this cache as a possible aid to some one landing near here by a westerly drift. D. B. Mac-Millan, Assistant."

There remained now only the task of caching food along the North Greenland shore, as far up as Cape Morris Jesup. If Peary came back by this route with no food left, the caches could mean the difference between life and death.

On April 17 MacMillan was waiting at the ship for Marvin to come back from the main party, since Peary had requested that the two of them establish the Greenland caches.

Far in the distance there appeared two dark objects and a dog team coming out of the west; these were the latest to have left Peary on the Polar Sea. MacMillan jumped over the *Roosevelt*'s rail to greet the young Eskimo drivers Kudlukto and Inugeeto. They stood with heads down, visibly agitated.

"What is wrong?" he asked them.

Kudlukto stared at the ice. "Marvin gone. Young ice. I told him look out."

Thus death became a member of the expedition. Each of them reminded himself privately that this was a dangerous undertaking, that death always had been among the calculated risks, and that this matter of a life snuffed out was an additional burden to be carried on the daily march without, as it were, breaking step.

But it was a shock, because there were not many of them in this icy vastness, and even though they had never felt near to Marvin, who was quiet and serious and did not play their games, an empty seat at a small mess table is impossible to ignore. Professionally they would miss him also, for he was a precisionist, a highly competent navigator, and a good dog driver.

Someone remembered that Marvin never had laughed, and, as is the way with men in the face of death, they now thought of this as a prelude to his tragic end, a clue dropped by destiny, which all of them had missed.

The monument they erected to Marvin near the winter quarters at Cape Sheridan read: "Drowned April 10th, returning from 86 degrees, 38 minutes, North Latitude," for at this place and time in history the greatest homage they could pay to this man, who never had intended to make the trip, was to describe the mathematical position in the world of a piece of ice on which he had stood for a moment.

# 7

MACMILLAN'S NORTH GREENLAND "expedition" consisted of five Eskimos, his assistant, Borup, six sledges, and forty-eight dogs. They left the *Roosevelt* on April 19, in twenty-five-below-zero weather.

The route lay across Robeson Channel, a narrow opening leading south from the Polar Sea and choked with ice blocks. The going at times was so bad that all seven were required to handle one sledge, which even then occasionally somersaulted into the bottom of an ice hole. Finally they lowered the sledges with ropes to the more level ice foot, which gave them a "highway" to Black Cape and on to Lincoln Bay.

There they ascended the highest pinnacle to survey the channel; it looked favorable and so it proved to be, for on the twenty-first they reeled off twenty-five miles, going into camp on the Greenland shore at Repulse Harbor, so named twenty-eight years before by Charles Francis Hall, "in commemoration of my defeats." Here they picked up Marvin's trail of four months before, for the impression made by the steel runners of a heavily loaded sledge in snow persists for a long time. Due to the absence of heavy rains in summer, moreover, deep tracks may remain for years in the Arctic. Near the *Roosevelt*'s winter berth were wheel tracks of a pushcart made thirty-four years before by men of the British exploration ship *Alert.*

At length they were beyond the British record of "farthest north" of 1876, and MacMillan recognized Rief Island and Dragon Point. It was weary plodding and they welcomed the littlest changes—discovery of a lost cake of chocolate, a biscuit extracted with difficulty through a crack in a box, a dogfight, or a dropped sealskin mitten. So their spirits surged at the ringing cry of *"Oomingmuksuit!"* from one of the Eskimo drivers atop an ice pinnacle.

What was it? As old Kaiota scanned the hills a mile away with field glasses, MacMillan ventured, "Rocks," for with the naked eye one could discern black spots outlined against the white of the snow. Kaiota grinned. "The rocks move." Sure enough, they did. *"Tedlimat oomingmuksuit!"* he said. "Five musk oxen."

This animal, whose contemporaries now are extinct, has been living in the Far North for 500,000 years. It does not inhabit those places where snows lie deep but clings to the wind-swept areas, feeding on moss and lichens and on the grass that grew during the summer months. With the hills and plains dotted with black boulders, it takes an experienced eye to spot the musk oxen. Add to this that he bears a grayish-white patch on the center of the back; the result is that, when lying down, he looks exactly like a large rock with its top sprinkled with snow.

Tired Eskimos are no longer tired when they sight game. Loads were dumped helter-skelter, and away they drove toward the hills, each man holding a knife in his hand to sever the traces of the dogs if necessary. Eight dogs, bound to a sledge and heading at full tilt into a herd of musk oxen, can be wiped out in a few minutes if the oxen fight and the dogs get their stumpy legs entangled in the traces.

Minutes later the deep bark of the Winchesters rocketed across the ice. The Eskimos killed them all, five bulls and a cow, and returned in triumph. Enough travel for the day. Pitch the tent, put the pot on to boil, for this day one eats fresh meat and that is cause for good cheer.

That night MacMillan and Borup decided their supporting party had supported them long enough. They felt confident that they could cover the remaining distance with the food on their sledges, together with help from an occasional hare or ptarmigan. It was a bold decision, but they missed the men and their dogs the next day and were compelled to "double back," a tedious and discouraging procedure.

When sledge loads are too heavy, half the load is dumped and left on the trail. At the end of five or ten miles the sledge, relieved of its load, returns for the other half, thus traveling the same distance three times instead of once.

John Murray Island looked innocent enough on the map, but it proved to be heartbreaking. Throughout the day deep snows, treacherous tidal cracks, black and deep, huge blocks of ice tormented and delayed them. Reluctantly they finally gave up the struggle and camped, thoroughly worn out. Then and there they decided to lighten the sledges by establishing the first cache for Peary. It is of interest that the cache remained untouched for eight years, at which time the Danish explorer, Rasmussen, recorded, "We are back again in the tent at eleven o'clock, gourmandizing to our heart's content on Peary's pemmican; no marzipan cake could have tasted better."

Constantly they scanned the expanse of the Polar Sea as they sledged along its edge day after day, hoping to see some sign of Peary coming southward along the ice foot. They went over the imagined scene many times, MacMillan and Borup, telling each other how the tired dogs and men would look and what a thrill it would be to have food for them, so far from the ship.

Then they struck a spell of howling wind and *piltsuk-suah*" (drift) which forced them to halt for a couple of days and tried their patience sorely. Searching for something to break the monotony, MacMillan remembered that Charlie Percy, the *Roosevelt*'s cook, had given them a "surprise" box when they left the ship. It wasn't supposed to be opened until they had reached their farthest northern point, the tip of Greenland, but that shouldn't be later than the next day, he and Borup reasoned, and surely Charlie wouldn't mind twenty-four hours one way or the other.

To make the game longer and more delightful, they guessed at what was in the box, suggesting everything from cookies to reindeer steak. But when the thick cover was ripped off, none had been correct—it contained two loaves of Charlie's best bread, a big lump of butter, and a tin of cocoa. Savoring the meal, a welcome change from tea and biscuit, they were buoyant enough to predict the next day would bring better weather, and it did.

Two days of rest makes a big difference to sledge dogs. With curled tails, tightened traces, and sturdy legs working like pistons, they covered sixty miles in the next fourteen hours of march, bringing the party up to the face of a glacier. Rather than sledge out around it, MacMillan decided to cross over the top of it and proceeded to do so. He recorded that "to our alarm, great sections of the glacier dropped with a muffled report from beneath our feet, causing us to catch our breath and await the end.

"When two of my dogs disappeared completely, I tiptoed to the edge of the crevasse. I could hear them whining and calling to me for help. Shading my eyes from the glare of the sun, I could see them far below me, huddling on a projecting ledge. A lasso improvised from my sledge lashing brought them both up, choking for breath and limp as dish rags. However, they were soon wagging their tails and rubbing their great heads against my bearskin pants in gratitude. We edged out of there very gingerly, and without further mishap . . ."

The day came when they reached Cape Morris Jesup, the most northern point of land in the world. Only Peary and Henson had preceded them to this spot, nine years before, and they found Peary's cairn of 1900 on a little hill east of their camp.

This was a desolate land of rolling terrain, dotted with patches of willow, arctic poppies, purple saxifrage, a few hardy species of grass, and lichen-covered boulders. Even in this lonely place there were occasional tracks of the musk oxen.

Within their tent, preparing a meal at the top of the

world, they heard an unthinkable sound . . . the crack of dog whips. Four sledges were dashing in from the south, two of their support parties and two Eskimos from the *Roosevelt*. What on earth had happened that would bring them two hundred miles from the ship?

One of the Eskimo boys handed MacMillan a letter:

> S.S. Roosevelt, April 28, '09
>
> My dear MacMillan:
>
> Arrived on board yesterday. Northern trip entirely satisfactory.
>
> Concentrate all your energies on tidal observations and line of soundings north of Cape Jesup to 85th parallel and use intended depot supplies for this purpose.
>
> Push and get back to Jesup before the full moon of June the third, which will open things up again.
>
> Marvin's death is a great shock to me and a great loss to the expedition, to the future, and to me personally. If your inclinations are that way, you must figure on filling his place in the coming Antarctic work . . .
>
> R. E. PEARY.

Borup and MacMillan yelled aloud. "Entirely satisfactory" could mean only that the commander had attained the Pole. That mission completed, his next expedition would attempt the South Pole and they had been asked to come along, for Borup also had received an invitation.

Though heady with exhilaration, wondering what the world would say, eager for details of what the polar conquest had been like, they buckled down to work in short

107

order, because the calendar would not wait. It was May 8, and no time could be wasted if MacMillan was to reach the eighty-fifth parallel so late in the year. Already a survey of the Polar Sea from the hillsides revealed thin, black lines —lanes of water extending like threads of a great spider web until their ends were lost in the maze of rough ice.

The next day he was away with Kudlukto. From May 11 to 14 the trip out on the ice and back to land offered the hardest arctic traveling he had ever experienced. He wrote, "There is hardly a spot flat enough to pitch a tent in this jammed-up ice. I have stumbled and fallen forward and backward, wrenching arms and legs and bruising my body in numberless places, at times wading through snow up to my waist and falling in holes over my head."

At length, however, he recorded, "Meridian sight gave me 84 degrees, 17 minutes, 5 seconds as the site of our last camp. . . ."

This was as far as he was going and it is important, in terms of arctic history, to understand why and what it meant. Since Cape Morris Jesup was the northermost point of land in the world, it might be asked why Peary in May 1900 had not made his North Pole try from here. In working northward, he had got only to 84 degrees, 15 minutes north, a mark that Mac now had surpassed.

What eventually stopped both of them was a succession of rough ice, pressure ridges, and widening leads of open water that later was described by Borup as making any such arctic obstacles he had ever seen before look like "ice cream sundaes in comparison."

Regretful that he had failed, Mac logged:

"Started back at once, stopping here at the last of the young ice for another sounding. Got 56 fathoms here, which I judge to be twelve miles out. Will sleep for a few hours, then push on for land."

MacMillan finally reached the land. Borup was not "at home," but a note told of his tribulations and initial failure to find water. A second note, however, was briefer: "Tidal observations station located about one and a half miles east." He had finally been successful.

With the bad weather it was difficult finding him, but Mac eventually did. There he was, on half rations of biscuit, oil, and canned milk, with plenty of musk-oxen meat, but very, very lonesome. He was breaking the ice in the five-gallon oil tin cut in half that served as a teapot and was about ready to abandon everything and go south to Cape Washington. The tide statistics bored him anyway, and since the rise of the tide here was only five tenths of a foot in six hours, and he was expected to note carefully the rise in inches every five minutes, it was far from an exciting assignment.

MacMillan reminded him the results were of value to physicists and oceanographers and were to be sent to Washington. He encouraged Borup to record everything accurately and neatly and, above all things, to keep the tidal book clean. Mac also volunteered to stand the next watch at the tidal gauge.

After recording "accurately and neatly" the results of the six-hour duty, he handed the book to Borup and returned to the tent for lunch and a few hours of reading. At 6 P.M. he returned to the tidal hole on the sea ice to relieve his companion, suggesting that he go in to the land, eat his supper, and sleep until midnight. Borup left.

Opening the record book to enter his first observation, Mac noted with consternation that Borup, under the page headed "Remarks," had written with an indelible pencil: "I do not know whether the God-damn tide is going up or down."

MacMillan was not amused. He strode back to the tent with militant indignation and told Borup what he thought of it. He received little satisfaction. Borup replied, "Mac, that was the page for remarks and that's where I put them."

They finished the job, in any event, completing the observations and establishing a bench mark. True, Mac had failed to reach 85 degrees North Latitude, but he was somewhat consoled by the fact that Peary himself had been halted nine years before, almost to the day, by the same conditions, "extremely rough ice intersected by water cracks."

Bound for the *Roosevelt*, Borup and MacMillan surpassed even Peary's record for fast traveling on this route; they averaged thirty-four miles per march for eight marches, a journey that had taken them eighteen marches on the way out. Peary, who had worried over their safe return, fearing they might be prevented from coming back by open water, was delighted to see them. They were fully as glad to see him, congratulating him upon attainment of the Pole, the conquest of which had been virtually an obsession with him for twenty-three years. Henson and four Eskimos—Ootah, Egingwah, Ooqueah and Seeglo—were with him.

Back aboard the steamer, one night was enough for both

MacMillan and Borup. The stateroom was too small, the air too stuffy, and there was not enough doing. Both of them were pleased when Peary gave them new assignments. Borup was to sledge back to Cape Columbia, build a substantial cairn, and place within it a document attesting that Peary had reached the North Pole. This document, which was found by a Canadian expedition in 1957, read:

"This monument marks the point of departure and return of the sledge expedition of the Peary Arctic Club, which in the spring of 1909 attained the North Pole. The members of the expedition taking part in the sledge work were Peary, Bartlett, Goodsell, Marvin, MacMillan, Borup, and Henson."

MacMillan was to go to Fort Conger, which had been headquarters of the Lady Franklin Bay Expedition of 1881–84, roughly sixty miles to the south. His task was to take tidal observations for a lunar month to supplement those taken on the same spot twenty-eight years before. No assignment could have pleased him more than to live in the house that had been occupied by Lieutenant A. W. Greely and his men for two years before they finally left for Cape Sabine and death by starvation for most of them. Jack Barnes was to go to Conger with him.

Thoroughly familiar with Greely's *Three Years of Arctic Service,* a heroic, pathetic, and even horrible story in part, MacMillan felt, as he snowshoed around the end of Distant Cape, that every landmark near Conger was an old friend. There was Bellot Island, as he had pictured it, and there was Proteus Point, named for the ship that brought Greely here. In the distance there was Archer Fjord to the southwest, named for Lieutenant Robert H. Archer of H.M.S. *Discovery*. And there, standing by the house itself . . . was a man!

After the first moment of disbelief he realized it was Goodsell, who had been sent into the interior of Grant Land to collect rock specimens, particularly so that American geologists might seek to determine the age of the land mass. Goodsell, tanned and healthy, was greatly pleased to see him but also somewhat concerned. He urged MacMillan to speak to the two Eskimos assigned to the geology expedition because whenever Goodsell turned his back they lightened their sledge loads by throwing away his precious rocks.

Mac spoke to them. They were blunt and to the point. First, they said it was foolish to cover many miles to pick up stones. There were plenty of stones near the ship. Second, no man can be sane who carries rocks in his pockets. The interview was finished, ending about where it started.

Dr. Goodsell added something welcome to the menu, large, red-meated trout, a species of charr (*Salmo arcturus*), which he had taken from the waters of Lake Hazen. Here these fish inhabit waters beneath ice eight and ten feet in thickness, their only change of scene being a short annual visit to the sea.

Looking about the house for something to go with the trout, they discovered tin after tin marked "Potatoes," which had been provided for Greely's men twenty-eight years before. Delighted at the prospect, they whacked open a half-dozen cans with a hatchet, but there were no potatoes therein. Instead, all the cans contained rhubarb, which proved to be delicious in spite of its age and the temperature extremes to which it had been subjected.

It was of great interest, yet with inevitable tragic overtones, to examine what had been a home for the twenty-three Army men and two Eskimos of the Greely expedition, a party dispatched into the North by the U. S. Government for scientific observation. Since, upon abandoning these headquarters, each man was allowed to take with him only nine pounds of possessions, the house and grounds were littered with boxes of geological specimens, stuffed birds, sections of petrified trees, fossils, photographic plates, and countless yards of blue Army cloth. Kudlukto donned a long-tailed coat with epaulettes and visored blue cap of the vintage of 1861 and walked the grounds daily with martial air, a shining officer's sword at his belt.

The house, now greatly dilapidated, was originally sixty by seventeen feet with double walls, two coverings of half-inch boards separated by an air space of about a foot. A section of the floor was intact and a part of one room was standing, which MacMillan judged to have been the kitchen since it contained a large coal-burning cookstove. He opened the oven door. It was filled completely with human skulls, all arranged so that they stared vacantly into space.

Knowing that no one had died at Conger, Dan concluded they must all be Eskimo, particularly since old igloos had been discovered in the locality and even along the shores of Lake Hazen, far in the interior of Grant Land. The shape of the eye socket was another clue to identity, as was the skull shape, all being hypsicephalic, a characteristic of the Mongol. Why the Eskimos chose the oven for a last resting place for the souls of their departed is anybody's

113

guess; in his record Dan suggested, half seriously, "Perhaps following the extreme cold of winter, they wanted their relatives to enjoy through all eternity the warmth of a white man's stove . . ."

On the floor of what he judged to have been the main living room lay a small white card, miraculously intact and undisturbed. It read, "Lieutenant A. W. Greely, 816 21st Street, Northwest, Washington, D.C." Scattered about were coats, pants, caps, shoulder insignia, boots, swords in scabbards, and even Indian clubs and ice skates.

A book lay upon a small table, thick with dust. On the fly leaf, written in a boyish hand, it read: "To my dear father. From his affectionate son, Harry Kislingbury. May God be with you and return you safely to us."

Lieutenant Kislingbury, the "dear father," was second in command of the expedition. Singing the "Doxology," he died of starvation at Cape Sabine, in the arms of his commanding officer. MacMillan wrapped the book in oil cloth and long after, following months of searching, returned it to the son, then a resident of Arizona.

Life at Fort Conger for MacMillan and his party was very pleasant after the cold winter and months of sledging. Sunlight, never more appreciated than in the Far North, drew forth many varieties of flora and fauna that offered delightful contrast to a desolate winter vista of rocks and snow. Seals sunned themselves on the harbor ice and occasionally even popped up in the tidal hole to see what on earth (or rather, on ice) was going on. Barnes, true to the tastes of his native Newfoundland, thoroughly enjoyed its

114

"national dish" of seal flippers. For delicacy, both Kudlukto and MacMillan preferred heart and liver of the arctic hare.

Lemmings, best known for their periodic and unexplained migration in which they swarm over hills, through valleys, across rivers, and into the sea, where they swim on until they die, proved among the party's friendliest neighbors. This particular species (*Myodes torquatus*), the tracks of which they often observed throughout Grant Land even during the coldest days of February and March, was about five inches in length. It had a pepper-and-salt appearance, the rusty-brown hairs being tipped with white. Later in the year it was darker in color, but whether or not it turned white during the winter for protective coloration, they never did discover.

They were amusing little creatures, possessing a comic way of standing on their hind legs, clicking their teeth, and pawing the air with their front feet. Disposed at first to struggle and fight, within a few minutes they would be content to snuggle in one's hands or pockets, their beady little eyes shining with interest and evident pleasure.

By now the birds, too, were increasing rapidly and there seemed to be new arrivals every day. Dan wrote in his journal: "The cries of the 'old squaws,' the so-called long-tailed ducks, were heard from every pool in the harbor, one of the most musical sounds in all nature. It is not so wild and maniacal as the cry of the Great Northern diver (*Gavia immer*), or so musical as that of the Canada goose (*Branta canadensis canadensis*), but thrilling.

"I was glad to see an old boyhood friend, one which

115

came to our harbor at home every spring, played about on the sandy beach for two or three days, and then disappeared. Where? Our mothers didn't know.

"And when other water birds returned in the fall, bringing their young, we watched for this swallowlike bird with the black cap and coral-red feet, but never saw it. But in the spring, on or about May 22, there it was, diving directly down with a splash into the clear waters of the harbor, emerging with a small fish in its bill. As boys, we always called it the "mackerel gull," but it is *Sterna paradisaea,* a tern, and not a gull at all, and there are three species that come to Provincetown, the common and least terns, and the arctic tern . . ."

Search high, search low, they could not find the bench mark of the Lady Franklin Bay Expedition, and it remains something of a mystery to this day. According to the scientific report, they should have discovered a "brick pier set in cement" with the "X X on its south side," but they did not.

On June 24 they built another so that the next observer, whoever he may be (and whenever), will have a basis for scientific comparison. The real value of such a mark is to aid in determining the oscillation of the earth's crust in the particular area and the rate of the evaporation of the 6,000,000 square miles of ice resting upon the earth's surface, all of which eventually will go back into the oceans of the world from which it was taken thousands of years ago.

In the cairn, built over and around the bench mark, the record reads:

> Lady Franklin Bay, Fort
> Conger
> June 25, 1909

To whom it may concern:

This iron stake has served as our bench mark for tidal observations through a period of fifteen days. Its top was 25 feet, 9¼ inches above the zero of tide gauge, or 22 feet, 7.3 inches above the mean range of tide.

Arrived here June 10th. Shall leave today for Str. *Roosevelt* at Cape Sheridan.

> Donald B. Macmillan
> Jack Barnes
> Kudlukto

They left the place reluctantly. The flowers were in bloom, birds were in the air, trout in the lakes, musk oxen back in the hills, and a quantity of good coal within a short distance of the house. One could live here indefinitely without supporting parties or relief ships.

# 8

ABOARD THE *Roosevelt* all was bustle. They were going home! It was July first, the sun was warm and high, and the smells of tar and paint were in the air, a delight to any sailor in spring, for these signify "fitting out."

Once under way—a gradual process in working out of the winter berth—they had drifted, more than steamed, to a point between Cape Tyson and Bellot Island by July 31. There they tied up to an ice floe that was, by actual measurement, three and a quarter miles long.

MacMillan decided that a plunge into the ice water off the port side might "close the pores of the skin," and he decided to try it. The temperature of the water was 29.2 Fahrenheit; he figured on swimming across the open "pool," which was approximately twenty yards in length, pulling himself out on the ice and running back to the ship. Borup discovered he was going to do it and yelled, "Wait for me!"

Seeing Dan perched on the rail naked, waiting for Borup to undress, the Eskimos streamed from their quarters, located forward, and stood about him with a jabber of

118

tongues. He had, they decided, gone *piblokto,* and when Borup appeared, they concluded both had succumbed to hysteria, for obviously no person in his right mind would strip off his clothes and jump into ice-filled water. The Eskimos lined the rail during the swim-and-sprint (which went off without incident or ill effect) principally because they had never seen a man swim and often wondered, they said afterward, whether he could.

As customary, the Eskimos aboard were to be landed at the locations of their choice and assisted in gathering a sufficient food supply for the coming winter. These Smith Sound natives are nomadic and seldom asked to be dropped off twice at the same place. Ordinarily, from the time when the seals begin to appear on the ice in late April, they are accustomed to hunting them, caching away the flesh for food in the cold-weather months. Although occasionally a bear is shot by moonlight, an arctic hare or a white or blue fox snared or trapped, the main supply of food consists of seals, walrus, and dovekies, also known as little auks, the latter being swept out of the air with nets during June, July, and August.

Now, with the hunting season well gone, the Eskimos aboard the *Roosevelt* faced a long, cold winter without food unless they were given help.

Thus there followed nine days of hunting in which the white men joined, a period of excitement that proved exhausting. Each day the huge pile of meat grew on the *Roosevelt*'s deck, now red with blood.

At the end of August 10 they were tired. On that day alone Mac, Borup, and the others had killed thirty walrus.

One "hooded" seal (*Cystophora cristata*) taken measured eight feet, eleven inches and weighed 624 pounds! Following the evening meal, they rolled into their bunks and within a few minutes MacMillan and Borup were sound asleep.

It had seemed only a few minutes when the breakfast bell rang. Sleepily Mac dropped from the top bunk to the floor and, with eyes half open, felt for his clothes. He looked out of the opened porthole. It was raining and blowing and they were anchored, he noticed, up under the lee of one of the Whale Sound islands. This was an indication the commander had decided the weather was too rough in which to hunt. Good; back to bed, then.

The brief response to the breakfast bell probably saved his life. He had been sleeping with his back against the partition which divided their room from that of the mate, Mr. Gushue. Upon getting back into bed, he faced the wall, placed his left hand on his right shoulder, and with his cheek resting in the hollow of his forearm, dropped off to sleep.

Following breakfast in the messroom on the starboard side, Commander Peary had handed a loaded Winchester 40-82 rifle to Chief Engineer Wardwell—a weapon that the hunters had returned late the day before—asking him to remove the cartridges, for safety. Ordinarily this is done by turning the rifle upside down and, with a movement of the lever back and forth, pumping the shells out onto a table or something similar. This the chief proceeded to do, and in the process a finger must have touched the trigger, for the rifle discharged with a loud bang, and the bullet was on its way.

This mushrooming lead slug crashed through a pine partition in the mate's room, passed approximately a foot over his head as he lay sleeping, and tore through another wooden bulkhead virtually into MacMillan's face. It clipped his right eyebrow, passed between the ulna and radius of the left forearm, emerged near the artery in the left wrist, entered the right shoulder an eighth of an inch above the collarbone, missed the subclavian artery, passed through the right shoulder, clipped the third finger of the left hand, crossed the room, dented a third partition, and fell to the floor, much squashed out of shape.

MacMillan climbed out of his bunk, saying, almost with disbelief, "He got me." Borup, who saw only the blood, and there was considerable of it, sprang up and out the door, to get Dr. Goodsell. They returned almost immediately. Goodsell said to Dan, "Get back in bed!"

Examination revealed that the bullet had put four holes in MacMillan without breaking a bone or severing a single major vein or artery. When Peary heard of it, he came to Mac's room and, with tears in his eyes, said he would much rather it had happened to him.

Wardwell, tracking the course of the bullet from room to room, boomed in calm, matter-of-fact tones as he came to MacMillan's cabin, "Well, well, who've I killed now?" When he found out what had happened, he sat down quietly, shocked at the narrow margin by which tragedy actually had been averted.

As for Borup, he wrote later: "When the doctor came in, he found Mac . . . spread very loose on the strand, but soon had him glued together."

Leaving Etah on August 21, they proceeded down the coast, dropping the Eskimos as they went. Two days later, with considerable surprise, they met the small auxiliary schooner *Jeanie,* skippered by Samuel Bartlett of Brigus, an uncle of Bob Bartlett. She had been sent north by Herbert L. Bridgman, secretary-treasurer of the Peary Arctic Club, with coal to replenish the *Roosevelt*'s dwindling supply.

From the *Jeanie* they learned the latest news. Howard Taft had been elected President. Henry Huttleston Rogers, the noted oil magnate, was dead. Harvard had defeated Yale in both football and rowing—a terrible shock to Borup of Eli. Shackleton had succeeded in getting to within 97 miles of the South Pole. The Danish expedition had lost three men by starvation in attempting to map the northeastern coast of Greenland. This latter item was bitterly ironic, for Borup and MacMillan might have saved them easily when they were at Cape Morris Jesup had they known the Danes were in the area and in need of food.

On August 25 they arrived at Cape York, where they found two families who reported that a whaleship had called there in the spring, leaving a box of mail for the *Roosevelt* up among the rocks. With the aid of the Eskimo children they located it within a few moments. Comfortably seated on the green hillside, with their backs against a boulder, MacMillan and Peary opened their letters. Dan was startled out of his reverie over news from home when the commander said abruptly, "Read that!"

It was a note addressed to Peary from Captain Adams of the Dundee whaler *Morning,* stating that he had met a Dr.

Cook in South Greenland during the latter part of June when on his way to Denmark, and Cook had told him that he had reached the North Pole.

Mac turned to Peary, saying, "Do you think for a moment he will carry that story home?"

"Absolutely."

"Who is this man?"

"Eighteen years ago he was my expedition physician when I first came north. He also was a member of the party that accompanied me on the Greenland Icecap. I did not take him with me on my next trip two years later, although in many ways his work was quite satisfactory."

On August 26 the *Roosevelt* headed for home, her immediate objective being Turnavik on the Labrador coast, where coal for the hungry boilers awaited them.

On the morning of September fifth they left Turnavik for the run to Smokey Tickle, the farthest north Marconi wireless station on the Labrador coast, which they reached just before dark.

As they were bound in, Peary knocked on their cabin door, and when Mac and Borup sang out, "Come in," the commander entered and sat down on top of a box, their only seat. He was passing the word to all hands: "We are now in sight of the first wireless station. After I have cleared the official messages, you may tell your friends that we reached the Pole. Say whatever you wish, but remember, there is to be no mention of Dr. Cook's name."

The first dispatch was sent to Mrs. Robert E. Peary, South Harpswell, Maine. It read: HAVE MADE GOOD AT LAST. I HAVE THE POLE. AM WELL. LOVE. WILL WIRE AGAIN

FROM CHATEAU. BERT.

MacMillan informed his sister in Freeport: ARRIVED HERE TODAY WITH POLE ON BOARD. HAVE HAD THE BEST YEAR OF MY LIFE. LOVE TO ALL. He also sent one to Worcester Academy: TOP OF THE EARTH FOUND AT LAST. GREETINGS TO FACULTY AND BOYS.

Within a half hour after their arrival the Canadian revenue cutter *Fiona* steamed in. From her officers, those aboard the *Roosevelt* learned that on September 1, four days before, a message had been received by a Dr. Frederick A. Cook who claimed to have reached the North Pole on April 21, 1908, a year before the Peary expedition. The message had been sent from the Shetland Islands, and Cook was apparently en route to Copenhagen.

It was an unthinkable circumstance; there was the greatest excitement—and already the roots of bitter controversy, even among lay persons—as America and all the literate world realized what had occurred. Geographers, experts in arctic travel, famous explorers such as Nansen, Amundsen, Sverdrup, and Greely had suggested repeatedly that attainment of the North Pole over that "hell of shattered ice" was impossible.

Now, within a five-day period, two men claimed to have accomplished this feat.

On September 8 the *Roosevelt* dropped anchor in Battle Harbor, where the wireless station, perched high among the rocks back of the village, was destined to play a dramatic part in an argument that rocked national capitals then and the spark of which never has died. They were not surprised to find the little shack flooded with radiograms, both from the United States and abroad. MacMillan was appointed to receive and deliver all messages.

Several were urgent, from geographic societies in Europe, eager to honor Cook before he sailed for home, if they could only ascertain the truth. Others were from news agencies; Reuter's of London made a specific request— that Peary give the world his opinion of Dr. Cook's claim. This, to Peary, posed a major problem.

In his personal papers MacMillan wrote: "Peary is before me now, even after fifty-one years, walking, walking, walking until long after midnight, walking the quarter deck from rail to rail, a lonely figure in the dark, wrestling with the question as to whether or not to expose an opponent, to belittle a rival, to tell the deluded public that they were being fooled, that through their ignorance of the demands of exploration, and of equipment required to combat the drifting, tumbled-up mass of ice of the Polar Sea, they were being cruelly deceived.

"Was it his duty to comply with the request of Reuter's or permit the lie to go down in history as the truth? Here, pacing the deck, was the one man who knew. He could have relinquished the burden to Bartlett, Borup, or to me, but Reuter's knew that he knew, and wanted the honest opinion of the most expert man . . ."

Peary sent for MacMillan to come to his room. He was sitting in a wicker chair, tapping a pencil on the top of the table.

"MacMillan, what is a synonym for a 'gold brick'?"

"I don't know," Dan said. "As far as I know there is no word like it in the English language."

"It's an ugly word," Peary replied thoughtfully. "I don't like to use it. Let's think it over for a while."

They did but failed to come up with an acceptable substitute, so Peary wrote the radiogram that hurt him more than it hurt Cook: "Do not trouble about Cook's story or attempt to explain any discrepancies in his statements. The affair will settle itself.

"He has not been at the Pole on April 21st, 1908, or at any other time. He has simply handed the people a gold brick. These statements are made advisedly and I have proof of them.

"When he makes a full statement of his journey over his signature to some geographical society or other reputable body, if that statement contains the claim that he has reached the Pole, I shall be in a position to furnish material that may prove distinctly interesting reading for the public. Robert E. Peary."

Out of the rain and mist of September 13 emerged the tug *Douglas H. Thomas,* and three days later the *Tyrian,* both vessels bringing representatives of many of the most influential newspapers of the United States. Commander Peary, facing them, made a characteristic gesture, jerking his neck upward out of the collar of his blue flannel shirt. He cleared his throat and announced incisively, "Gentlemen, I will see you this afternoon at two o'clock in Mr. Croucher's loft—that building there," pointing with his forefinger.

The afternoon scene on the second floor of this whitewashed building, clapboarded and ancient, near the rickety wooden dock at Battle Harbor, September 16, 1909, was unique. Out of doors, for setting, were the barren gray hills, the narrow "tickle" (Newfoundlandic for a "ticklish" place in which to navigate), its eastern entrance white with breaking seas. Worn wooden steps led to the loft, which was stained with age, smoke, and dirt. There were two windows, one at the very end of the littered room, one piercing the sloping roof. High-lighted against the former was the coarse, reddish hair of Peary. In front of him and about him in a half-circle, seated on the floor, on barrels and boxes and on piles of nets, were the eager inquisitors, come to learn the truth for a waiting world.

These men knew how to ask questions, and one followed another like gunfire.

And then came the question that probably had been most discussed in the "outside world": "Why did you send all of your white men back to land and take a Negro to the Pole?"

Peary's critics had suggested he chose to keep Henson with him because the latter did not understand navigation. Why, they wanted to know, had not Peary chosen Bartlett, Marvin, or MacMillan, all of whom were well versed in handling a sextant or theodolite?

In his journal MacMillan, who was present at the press conference, answered this question at length in what was essentially a tribute to Henson.

Dan wrote, "Why did he take a Negro? Why did he take Henson?"

"When Peary rounded the most northern point of land in the world in 1900, the first ever to reach it, Matt was with him. When Peary stood at the world's record of 'Farthest North' in 1906, Matt was by his side. When Peary crossed the 'Big Lead' over the cracking, bending thin ice on the return—the most exciting and the most dangerous undertaking of his career—Matt followed him.

"I could have told these reporters that Peary had given his life to this one obsession—the attainment of the Pole; that in his final attempt, he owed it to the members of the Peary Arctic Club who had backed him financially, and who believed in him although he had failed time and time again, to his wife, to his family, to his friends, to cut off every dead limb on the tree which impeded his progress toward the goal of his ambition.

"We, Bartlett, Borup, Goodsell, Marvin, and myself were the dead limbs after we had accomplished that which we were selected to do, namely, feed him, his expert dog drivers, and their dogs for the final dash.

"Matthew Henson, following his long years of service, was an expert dog driver, without a doubt one of the best in the world.

"Matthew Henson, the colored man, stood beside his commander because he was more experienced and, therefore, more valuable to Peary than any one of us."

The *Roosevelt* was away again on September 18, its crew now well aware that they were not only sailing home but into a hotbed of trouble as well. An old cannon on the crest of the harbor hill boomed farewell and a passing tramp steamer gave them their first nautical salute, a long and mournful whistle blast in passing.

They learned at St. Paul's Island that reporters were waiting for them in North Sydney, Nova Scotia, and that a tug was awaiting them off Cape North, evidently to escort the *Roosevelt* into the harbor.

Leaving St. Paul's on the morning of the twenty-first, they proceeded at half speed in order not to be too early at Low Point. At about 6 A.M. they sighted a large steam yacht flying an American flag at the fore-topmast and a British flag at the main. By 7:30 they could read her name, the *Sheelah,* and discern on her bridge Mrs. Peary, with Marie and Robert, the commander's daughter and son. The reunion was joyful, as they proceeded toward Sydney.

Now other boats were seen rushing down the harbor— power launches, excursion steamers, and sailing yachts— all with the intention of escorting the *Roosevelt* up the harbor, the shores of which were black with people who cheered and waved flags. As Peary landed at the dock, a delegation of school girls dressed in white met him at the gangplank. The daughter of Mayor Richardson stepped forward, made a salutary address, and presented the commander with a bouquet of flowers. Standing in an open carriage before the principal hotel, Peary addressed a large audience, referring to his many departures for the North from their city, and regretting that this was his last, now that the mission had been accomplished. Following a banquet in his honor, he left with his family for Eagle Island in Casco Bay, by night train, with orders for Bob Bartlett to sail in the morning for the island, en route to New York. Peary did not know it, but he had received greater homage in Sydney than he was to receive in his own country.

Deeply moved for the remainder of his life by the events that followed, MacMillan wrote in retrospect: "That the glory of such an achievement should be tarnished by bitter controversy is regrettable. The majority of the people of the United States believed that Dr. Cook reached the Pole a year before the commander did and therefore should be recognized as the true discoverer.

"Geographers and scientists, however, could not believe that, although Dr. Cook had discovered a new route to the top of the world, one through a game country, he could possibly have covered more miles on the Polar Sea with two sledges than Peary did with 24 men, 19 sledges, and 33 dogs.

"These men recognized the basic fact that in order to live, a man must eat,—something to which Dr. Cook's supporters appeared to have given little consideration—and that two fully loaded sledges, such as Cook had, could not possibly carry sufficient food for the purpose. If Commander Peary, following some twenty years of experience, and with four trips to his credit on the Polar Sea, and with a world's record of Farthest North in 1906, used this large number of sledges, each loaded with food for dogs and men, there must have been a very good reason for it.

"The world believed in Dr. Cook for five days. The world doesn't like to be disillusioned; it dislikes to believe that it has been fooled. There are people today who still believe, but not the officers and members of geographical societies, not one of which has ever bestowed honors upon Dr. Cook. All have recognized Peary as the discoverer of the Pole."

# 9

---

THE S. S. *Invermore,* the mail and passenger steamer en route from Bay of Islands, Newfoundland, to Battle Harbor, Labrador, in the summer of 1910 carried four American passengers. More by impulse than design, since he had been headed for the Grenfell Mission to correct navigational charts of the area, MacMillan had thrown in his lot instead with William B. Cabot of Boston and two medical students, George Howe of Peabody and Schofield Clark of Salem, whom he met on the steamer.

These three planned to spend the next two or three months exploring the interior of Labrador with the aim of reaching the home grounds of the primitive Nascapi Indian on the banks of the George River; they succeeded in persuading MacMillan to change his plans and come along. Dan, planning graduate work in anthropology at Harvard in the fall, had the summer free and actually required little coaxing.

Not only was the project interesting, but so were his traveling companions. Cabot, a Boston Brahmin with plenty of time and money, was a complex mixture of impatience, intelligence, and sensitivity. Possessed of great physical strength, he had devoted much of his life to acquiring the art of living in the woods. He had learned a smattering of the language of the Nascapis; through studying their manner of life he had come to love them, and it was his hope that he would some day gain enough of their confidence and friendship so that they would adopt him into the tribe.

Clark and Howe were excellent traveling companions, each possessing a stable cheerfulness that did not wear thin or out and a healthy intellectual curiosity about things and people. Howe, whose sight was greatly impaired, smashed his glasses at the beginning of the trip and had to stumble about half-blind, but he was still undaunted.

At Turnavik, from which the *Roosevelt* had departed for Greenland two years before, Dan renewed acquaintance with Captain William Bartlett, Bob's father. Mac explained they were bound north, the immediate destination being the Hudson's Bay Trading Post at Davis Inlet, eighty miles distant. There they would "fit out," purchasing smoked hams, bacon, flour, corn meal, molasses, tea, coffee, canned milk, and sugar, as well as picking up a second canvas canoe, left there by Cabot the year before. Would Captain William sell them a trap boat in which to get to Davis Inlet?

He would. For fifty dollars. And he helped launch her, a craft big, clumsy, none too sound, and so sun-dried from disuse that the water bubbled up through her seams. No matter, she would tighten up, Mac decided, and tighten she did. The other three decided he should be the "captain" because of his experience afloat; this meant that he was to handle the steering oar while they rowed.

Alternately sleeping in the boat and rowing northward, they arrived at Davis Inlet, purchased the equipment, and were off after a night of fighting mosquitoes, the "curse of the Labrador," bound for the mouth of the Asawaban River. Here they anchored the trap boat, packed their gear into the two canoes, and started upriver.

This was a land of thick spruce, high cliffs, rapids, and waterfalls. Here were boiling rapids, studded with boulders, pools with two-pound trout waiting for the frying pan. Deep-laden, they paddled where they could, waded through shallow water where they could not, and portaged when they had to. It was stiff work, sometimes heavy going, but the sights, sounds, and smells of the quiet and unspoiled country were both incentive and reward.

At the "high portage," forty miles inland, they struggled eleven hundred feet virtually straight up the mountainside, following the centuries-old trail of the Nascapis, carrying gear and one canoe with them. After that, lake after lake, into the interior of Labrador, the land that Jacques Cartier declared God gave to Cain. There was not much but water and stunted spruce, wind-swept and much of it fire-swept, the barkless, whitened stumps standing lifeless in the summer sun. And now they were on the Mistinipi, the waters of which were so placid that they all crowded into a single canoe, making a total weight, with equipment, of at least nine hundred pounds. The other canoe they cached, awaiting their return.

For days it had bothered them that time was running out

and they had seen no Indians. Now they did—twenty in all, on a slope leading to the water's edge, bound for the Davis Inlet trading post from a lake known as Tshinutivish.

Their reception was colder than the frigid North itself. Cabot, most familiar with their language, gathered from their long-sounding words that they wanted whisky and tobacco, the two things that none of the four had or even used. Cabot told them so. The Indians said sullenly that white men never were without those two things, and they packed their belongings in poorly built canvas canoes, grasped their short, spruce paddles, and were away toward the east. Only two remained, an old man with one eye called Longshan, and a small boy.

Cabot asked where they were going. The man pointed toward the west. How long would it take them to reach their tent? He waved his arm through an arc of the sky— that long. Could the white men go with him? He smiled for the first time and waved them on.

What a journey! Trying to match pace with those fast-stepping Indians was a struggle. They seemed to glide like snakes, through bushes and across marshes—it hardly seemed a trail—with scarcely a fast breath, at length arriving at a small stream. Here they pulled out from the bushes a misshapen canvas boat; all six piled in, and away they went downstream, with gunwales nearly level with the water and the equilibrium extremely delicate.

Shortly they heard dogs barking; this village, at the Tshinutivish estuary, was the destination. At the sight of the canoe there was a crowding to the beach, for no more than two white men in history had landed at this settlement, and they were the first whites that the children ever had seen. Once ashore, they were surrounded by grave, hungry-looking men uttering grunts of welcome, by women giggling and laughing, and by staring children, tugging at the bedraggled skirts of their mothers.

It was getting dark and raining. Standing outlined against the sky at the door of his caribou-skin tepee, alone and dignified, was a male figure in tight-fitting red pants. Obviously the chief, he had not joined the throng surrounding the "strangers from the sea."

"Cabot," said Dan, "go tell Red Legs that we can't go back to our tepee tonight. I don't even think we can find it. We have to stay here, welcome or not, until daylight." Somewhat uncertain, Cabot went, but he need not have been anxious.

With a low bow the chief pulled aside the skin flap of the tent and ushered them in. Fawn skins for distinguished guests were spread on the ground to the right of the brightly burning fire, and over the blaze hung an iron pot filled with pink-meated trout.

What a welcome on a drizzly night! Bronzed Indian girls, with long braids down their backs, removed the travelers' wet socks, hung them by the fire, and served the lake-trout stew. One by one, with permission of the guard at the entrance, other tribesmen entered to look at them, puzzled not so much by their appearance as by their being there. Did they come to trap, to trade, or to hunt? No, said Cabot, the white men just came to see the red men. That the Indians could not understand or accept; they smiled in gentle puzzlement.

In the morning when they left, Chief Red Legs himself accompanied them back to their camping place and embraced Cabot with such obvious affection that the latter gave him a pair of eye glasses which had been much admired throughout the visit.

Two days later, canoeing eastward, they spotted smoke on the horizon and, coming up to it, found two unfriendly Nascapis, one of them the son of Red Legs, cooking a meal. Mac and his "crew" gave the Indians candy, chewing gum, tea, and coffee and other food, and they camped together that night, but the Nascapis remained hostile. In the morning, after partaking generously of the white men's breakfast, they trotted off on foot, loads on their backs and tumplines on their foreheads, without raising an arm skyward in the gesture of friendship or so much as an *"au 'voir."* The white men were to learn that this was the beginning, not the end, of hostility.

The Cabot expedition pushed eastward. Paddling the canoe around a point in the lake, suddenly they could smell it—the stunted spruce trees were on fire! And that was the location of their second and last cache!

They dug their paddles into the water and, once in the shallows, scrambled ashore. White reindeer moss was blackened; stumps of trees were still smoking. The cache was completely destroyed—coats, sweaters, underclothes, towels, notebooks, a shotgun, rifle, and all the ammunition. The latter could be a serious loss; in case of food shortage they had planned to subsist upon the abundant country.

One thing remained in that blackened area. High up on the top of a pole planted firmly in the ground was the sun-

World's most northern children, Polar Eskimos, probably unchanged in appearance from their ancestors of 20,000 years ago.

Battling the Polar Sea's rough ice at MacMillan's point of farthest north on the Crocker Land Expedition.

This is a treacherous passage for man and dog, for the icefoot "highway" has fallen away from the cliff face.

An Eskimo summer encampment near Pond Inlet, Baffin Island.
The tupik (tent) is made of sealskin, the drying rack nearby of
driftwood and oars, for wood is scarce.

Nanook, mighty "King of the North," takes his stand on an
iceberg and defies the approaching Eskimo hunters.

Thirty miles south of the Arctic Circle, this Greenland glacier feeds iceberg

the sea. Frozen rivers such as this one flow constantly from the vast ice sheet.

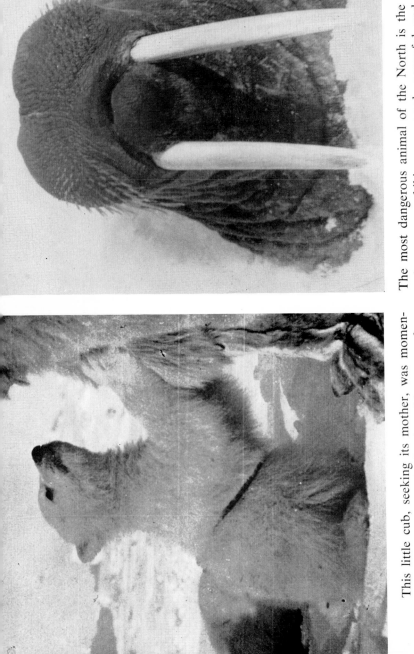

This little cub, seeking its mother, was momentarily misled by the polar bearskin pants of an Eskimo boy.

The most dangerous animal of the North is the walrus, an amphibious mammal, powerful and well-armed; this one weighed 1,800 pounds.

ABOVE: When the ice of bays and fjords is as smooth as this, Eskimos ride, rather than push, their sledges and the dogs, tails characteristically curled in contentment, can make good time. BELOW: After hard sledging, MacMillan's dogs rest on the ice-foot leading north along the Greenland coast beyond Renssalaer Harbor.

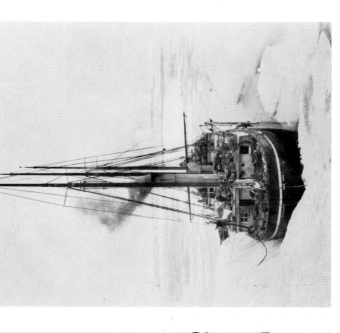

S.S. *Roosevelt*, the Peary North Pole Expedition steamer, refills her water tanks from the pools and streams of Cape York Glacier, North Greenland.

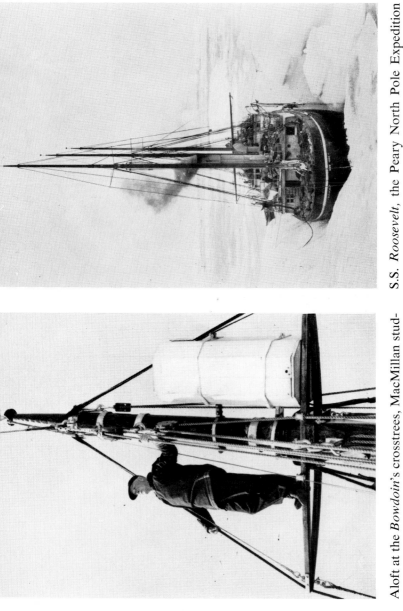

Aloft at the *Bowdoin's* crosstrees, MacMillan studies the best course through the pack ice of Melville Bay. Beside him is the crow's nest or "ice barrel."

whitened skull of a bear.

"What does that mean, Cabot?" MacMillan asked.

Cabot was grim. "We made a serious error. We camped on sacred ground."

"If we made the same mistake at the first cache where we left the canoe," Mac said thoughtfully, "we're going to have trouble getting out of this country."

Arrived at the base of the "high portage," they reached in under the bushes and dragged out the other canoe. It had been ripped from one end to the other with a sharp knife.

To Cabot, who for years had developed interest in and affection for the Nascapi, it was more than a mechanical difficulty; it was a rebuff from a friend. He paced for a moment, head down and close to tears. "There is no doubt what they mean by this. They want us to get out . . ."

For the next several hours they slapped adhesive tape, roll after roll, over every cut and crack of the damaged canoe, producing what Howe called a "damned old basket" of mottled red and white. MacMillan and Howe, neither as experienced as the other two, nursed this conveyance the forty miles downriver; it leaked like a sieve, especially in rapid water, but they made it without serious mishap to Voisey's Bay, where the trap boat waited.

This trip inspired MacMillan, the following summer, to purchase a sixteen-foot canvas canoe with the idea of "exploring the Labrador." He went as far as possible by train and steamer, eventually debarking at Davis Inlet, and his first objective was the Moravian-Eskimo village of Nain, where he planned to stay awhile if "I could find the route,

137

through the confusing network of islands ahead."

Developing an increasing interest in ornithology, he found this area delightful for bird watching. In his journal he wrote: "What an idyllic existence. A close companionship with the herring and glaucous gulls, hovering with outstretched wings above me, wondering whither I was bound and why."

At night he made a bed of reindeer moss on the shore, put the coffeepot on, ate his bacon, beans, and "Newfoundland No. 1" biscuit, wrapped his head and shoulders in mosquito netting, and turned in under the canoe. He never really knew just where he was at any given time, except that the sun told him he was headed slightly west of north, the general direction of the Labrador coast. Since Davis Inlet he had not seen a house or a living person.

One morning it was not the note of the white-throated sparrow (*Zonotrichia albicollis*), one of the many species he noted, that awakened him, but the rumble of a steamer's machinery and the clang of shovels on a metal boiler-room floor. He scrambled out from under the canoe. A bark-rigged black hull . . . what was she doing here? And then he remembered—the S. S. *Harmony* of London, bound for Nain, the Moravian Mission Station, his own destination. If he could follow her, he would find the station.

He dragged the canoe to the water's edge, crammed odds and ends into the duffel bag, and ran for the beach. The steamer was still in sight. He fitted the oars into the rowlocks and pulled with all his energies, pausing in a moment to look over his shoulder to see where she was. She had disappeared, and he did not know whether straight ahead or to left or right. On he rowed for about a mile, more slowly now, scanning the shore for a sign.

Well over on the starboard hand there appeared a white conical object which proved to be a tent, with a little girl standing before it. In a few moments she was joined by her father and mother, the first Eskimos MacMillan ever had seen on the Labrador coast. He knew a smattering of the Innuit, acquired during his year with the Polar Eskimos, and he was delighted to hear its words again: *nuna* (land), *pannek* (daughter), *seeko* (sea ice), and *nanook* (polar bear), exactly as he had heard them in North Greenland. The Eskimo language from the shores of Bering Strait to the east coast of Greenland is the same, except for local idioms.

They were a friendly family and the little girl showed him her books, including *"Kristib Nipliajorutinga Nutaung-itok"* (*Christy's Old Organ*), a volume printed by the Moravian Church, and *"Takkorngartaub Arvertarninga"* (John Bunyan's *Pilgrim's Progress*).

In the evening the father handed MacMillan an Eskimo Bible, opened to the fourth chapter of St. Mark, and read to him, pointing out the words with his finger: *"Tessersublo kiglingane ama ajokertuiler; inugasaksuillo kattilerpok; inugasaksuillo kattilermatta tapsomunga, umiakortomut tessersoarmetomut ikkijariakalerpokingidlunelo; inugasaksuillo illunatik tessersub kiglinganeput,"* which is to say, "And He began to teach by the seaside, and there was gathered unto Him a great multitude, so that He entered into a ship, and sat on the sea, and the whole multitude was by the sea on the land."

Then the mother sat down at the little organ and their three voices blended in Eskimo, singing, "God be with you till we meet again." All this in a small cotton tent, by the descendants of a once-savage horde of which both English and French fishermen had been mortally afraid. But since the day when the Moravian missionaries held out their hands to the natives of Labrador, saying, "We are your friends," life had been safe there.

In the morning, with directions from his hosts, he was off again and in due course found Nain and the mission station at Okak as well, and much else in the way of rich experience.

On a certain day he could see what he judged to be Cape Mugford, named for the master of the Jersey packet that brought the Moravians to Labrador in the eighteenth century. Its eastern end rises sheer out of the sea to a height of two thousand feet. Here, to these rocky shores, come the codfish in early July, schooling in from the Grand Banks to remain until October, and to this place come the Newfoundlanders to fish in summer, fortified principally by flour, a bag of biscuit, and a tin of tea. On these vessels water for tea bubbles perpetually on the cheery wood stove "for'ard."

MacMillan found the fleet anchored in Mugford Tickle. He selected what appeared to be the best-looking schooner of the six and climbed over the rail. Most of the ten-man crew were below in their bunks, waiting for the "fish" (which to them is a synonym for cod and no other) to arrive. Hearing footsteps on deck, they emerged from the cabin aft and the forecastle forward and stared. Kayaks they had seen, but not red canoes.

One who proved to be the captain asked, "Where be you from, zur?"

"From Boston." It was close enough, and he tried to pick a city with which they would be familiar. Many Newfoundlanders could then be found on Boston's fish piers.

"Hey, boys, come up! Here's a man from the States! Stay with us tonight, zur. We is glad to have ya. We has nah'n to do; fish hain't come yit."

Dan pulled his canoe over the rail of the *Carrie C.* and settled down with them.

"When you are not at sea, what do you do during the winter?"

"We's go wooding, zur. And some's of us works to the mines."

"Mines?" Mac inquired, surprised.

"Yes, zur. Mines at Belle Isle, for iron. They takes it to Sydney, they does, by the million tons of it."

Then it was their turn to ask questions. What was he doing in Mugford Tickle in such a "wee boat?" He tried to explain that he was interested in geology, in the formation of the big hills along the coast, how they were molded, cut down and leveled off by a big sheet of ice that once covered all of Labrador, all of Canada, all of their own Newfoundland, and much of his country, the United States.

They looked doubtful. They wondered why he did not come in the biweekly passenger and mail boat with a good room, good food, and companionship instead of this canvas-covered cockle, sleeping under it, and on short rations too.

But they were interested, and he persisted. He called their attention to the size of spruce and larch trees and to the fact that they became smaller as he proceeded north. He told them about the birds he had seen as a boy in Province-town, where his father had been a fisherman, how he had wondered where they spent the summer—and now he had found some of them right here in Mugford.

He explained his interest in the Eskimos, whose *tupiks* (tents) he could see from their deck, people whose ances-tors had lived on this coast for thousands of years. He wanted to know, he told the fishermen, more about the language, customs, and traditions of the Labrador natives; he wanted to see more of their stone-and-turf igloos, similar in every respect to those he had found among the Polar Eskimos.

Even in the dimly lit forecastle it was evident from their expressions that they thought he was not telling the truth. No man in his right mind would leave a comfortable home in America, a thousand miles away, to row along the coast of a rock-bound land, often swept by ugly seas from the North Atlantic, just to see flowers, rocks, stunted trees, and good-for-nothing Eskimos. There must be another reason.

Much later MacMillan learned that after he rowed away, they had talked it over and decided unanimously that he was either an escaped convict or was on his way to the gold mine in the Torngats, the big hills to the north, which they had all seen in the distance but never visited. It was diffi-cult for them to believe what he had said, for they had traveled little, and although every man aboard could find fish, box the compass, and make his way home in a gale, none could read or write.

At Hebron, Bishop Martin met MacMillan. The bishop, full-bearded and stocky, was a German as were nearly all the Moravian missionaries at that time. As at Nain, most of the Eskimo population came to see the new arrival for, as far as the oldest inhabitant could remember, Dan was the first ever to enter the harbor in such a canvas boat. The Eskimos looked at the little red canoe with delight and amazement; they touched it, lifted it to see how light it was, measured it a dozen times with everything from hands to harpoons, and acknowledged they had never seen anything like it.

To MacMillan's pleasure and surprise, the bark-rigged steamer *Harmony* which he had tried fruitlessly to follow three weeks before entered the harbor next morning. Captain Jackson was bound north to the tip end of Labrador with supplies for the last Moravian station on the coast, Killinek (the end or limit), which had been established in 1904. "Come on along with us, if you will," he said to Dan.

Within an hour MacMillan's canoe was lashed down on her deck, his gear tucked away into a snug cubbyhole of a cabin, and he was on the *Harmony's* bridge with the most expert skipper on the Labrador coast, a veteran of thirty years' experience, who skillfully threaded his way out to the open sea.

The old *Harmony,* with just enough horsepower to stem the tide in Hudson Strait, jogged along stubbornly. At times breaking waves tumbled into her waist over the low midship bulwarks, but she rose out of them like a tight cask and plowed on, water streaming out of her oversized scuppers. At length they rounded the last point and steamed in quiet water up to the mission, located in a snug harbor so small that anchors were dropped both ahead and astern to keep the ship from swinging onto the beach. They were in Killinek.

Learning from Captain Jackson that the *Harmony* was to remain awhile, MacMillan decided to take advantage of the opportunity offered for some exploration. From where he stood on the steamer's deck it was evident the nautical charts were inaccurate; shore lines were roughly drawn and many islands had no names. Jackson's chart revealed a cut through the mountains from Ungava Bay on the west side to the Atlantic on the east side, a distance of about eight miles. Although the Eskimos reported a good depth of water, all ships entering Hudson Bay had avoided it because of its evil reputation, due solely to the strength of the tide and a total lack of any safe shelter into which one could put a ship if required.

MacMillan wanted to attempt the passage in his canoe, which was equipped for rowing and sailing. When Dr. Paul Hettasch, the missionary, told the natives, there was a vigorous shaking of heads. "*Naga* [No]!" they said; the force of the tide was such that the canoe would be drawn under. Captain Jackson and his mate, Mr. Bush, also endeavored to persuade Mac not to attempt it, pointing out that the Eskimos knew this country far better than he, and he should listen to them.

But he did not. Calling to Captain Jackson, "I'll be back before you leave," he rowed out of the bight in front of the mission station and turned south to search for the entrance of McLelan Strait, known to the Eskimos as the Ikkerasak.

Seals were numerous, and there were birds everywhere, the fulmars, both light and dark (*Fulmarus glacialis glacialis*), being most prominent. Where do they breed? The Eskimos didn't know; they had never found their eggs. And there were thousands of kittiwakes, old and young. And what tremendous tides! Judging by the high-water mark on the shore, he concluded the rise and fall must approach forty feet; that, he reasoned, must account for the turmoil of waters against which they had warned him in the strait.

After rowing on for about five miles, he turned into an extremely narrow passage leading to the east. It dwindled to a point among the big hills; he must have made a mistake. There was another wide passage leading southeast between what is now Goddard Island and the mainland. It looked good, and away he went into a nice wide inlet leading southeast. This must be it, he said to himself, yet it lacked one positive sign of identification—no current, no rapid flow in the direction of the Atlantic. He sailed on for five miles right to the head of the inlet. No opening.

He furled his small sail and rowed slowly back along the northern shore, searching for an exit, for he now concluded that the narrow inlet he had first rejected must be the very one for which he was searching. Upon arriving at a low plot of ground, it occurred to him to walk over the tundra northward; it might lead him to the strait. In so doing, he discovered a narrow stream of water rushing eastward. Surely this must be it. He hurried back for his canoe and camping equipment.

The distance between Tunnusaksuk (Black Inlet) and

his discovery, which eventually proved to be McLelan Strait, was about a half mile. Returning to camp, he packed up his equipment, swung the canoe over his head, and plodded over the land north to the edge of the inlet. It was ebb tide, that is, the tide was running from Ungava eastward to the Atlantic, and there was a fresh westerly breeze. Why not sail through . . . sit aft, and let her go?

Once afloat, he made wonderful progress, blown by the wind and carried by the tide. There were whirlpools, although not as large or as violent as described by the Eskimos. It was not the swirling or rapidity of the current that bothered MacMillan but rather the increasing strength of the fair wind.

He now found himself in what amounted to a funnel, being blown rapidly out into the North Atlantic. With his mast stepped well forward and the boom on his jib-headed mainsail, owing to the strength of the wind, pointing forward of the mast, he knew well that if he attempted to go forward to lower sail or unstep the mast, he would capsize his fragile command.

He was now out of the narrow passage and had passed two large islands at the entrance. He was apparently bound for Europe! This would never do, for with every yard of progress the seas became rougher, and with every yard the swim back to land was longer. He knew already that in such cold water he never could make it to the shore.

It was an emergency, and he knew even a delay of a second or two could be serious. Clutching the rails of his bouncing, lurching boat with both hands, he crept forward gingerly on his knees, wishing fervently at that moment for a companion to assist him. At what seemed to him the most opportune moment, he lifted the mast out of its step and threw it overboard, sail and all, in one swift motion. Just as quickly he slid aft again, to prevent capsizing. Shipping his oars, he rowed back to the floating mast and sail, pulled both aboard, and started back for land.

Under the lee of the first island he rested and then pulled across for the second one. Rounding its northern end, he was astounded to find the entire crew of a fishing schooner lining the rail. They had seen him being blown out to sea and were prepared to go after him in a trap boat when one of the crew at the masthead had yelled, "He's comin' back!"

MacMillan had not even known they were there; otherwise he might have directed his course within reach of help. He noted: "Prior to that day, I had no knowledge of a Newfoundland schooner ever going so far north on the Labrador to catch fish, and I doubt if any schooner has ever been that far north since for such a purpose."

Leaving them, he pulled away for the land, deciding to return to Killinek by the way he had come, taking advantage of the flood tide now flowing westward into Ungava, and this he did, without incident. Within hours he reboarded the *Harmony,* sailed with her to St. John's, Newfoundland, and there journeyed across the island on the puffing narrow-gauge railroad to Port aux Basques. From there, via Sydney, he caught the night train to Boston for another winter of anthropology at Harvard.

# 10

IN 1906 PEARY, high in the hills on the western shores of Grant Land, had reported sighting snow-capped peaks far out over the ice of the Polar Sea, lending support to the persistent belief that there existed large areas of undiscovered land in the Arctic. Eskimos, with keener vision than the white man, also had reported sighting such land, and it was known that brant, hardy birds of the Far North, migrate regularly in a northwesterly direction from Grant Land, surely not to nest in the snow, it was argued, but on some undiscovered land mass.

In 1912 MacMillan wanted to mount an expedition to seek out this "lost continent." George Borup, then assistant curator of geology at the American Museum of Natural History in New York, urged him to postpone the trip a year, at which time the museum would support the venture and Borup would be able to come along as co-leader of the party. Mac was delighted at the prospect, which was marred, however, by abrupt tragedy.

Headlines soon after in a Boston newspaper read:

148

"George Borup, postgraduate student at Yale University, drowned off Crescent Beach, Connecticut." MacMillan was stunned, and shortly after, at a meeting of the executive committee of the museum's board of trustees, it was resolved to postpone the departure of the "Crocker Land Expedition" for one year and then to undertake it as a memorial to George Borup.

In preparation for the expedition, Dan had ordered, as part of the equipment, construction of a husky twenty-one-foot power boat at a boat yard in Medford, Massachusetts. With the summer ahead of him now without demands, he decided to go North in this little craft as far as time and ice conditions would permit. For a companion he invited Jonathan (Jot) Cook Small, a boyhood friend from Provincetown who was expert at handling small boats in any kind of weather, possessed great mechanical ingenuity, was a fine cook, had served as surfman at the Wood End Life Saving Station for many years, and whose persistent conservatism, as Dan noted, "served as kind of a balance wheel to my rather impetuous nature. I can still hear Jot's voice imploring: 'For Christ's sake, don't do that!' "

Now a word more about this Jot Small, who became on this and other voyages MacMillan's mate. For on a vessel if the captain is thought of as the wheel's hub, then certainly the mate is the king spoke, with one end at the hub, the other at the rim, and the job of keeping all the lesser spokes in their proper places.

Some mates insist on being called "Mister," but not so with Jot, who had neither the inclination nor the physical appearance for formality. The Smith Sound Eskimos said he was the homeliest white man they ever had seen, and the sight of him would send them rolling into a snowbank, doubled up in arctic mirth. Such a man had better prop up his personality with stronger stuff than formality and stouter words than "Mister."

Jot did. Actually he weighed about a hundred pounds, "soaking wet," as the expression goes alongshore, because everything, including fish, wood, and a forestaysail, is heavier when it's wet. He didn't have much hair, but it had been red. His face was wizened, and his eyes had the squint that comes from having looked too many years at sun on water. His movements, like his language (which was profane), bore less the stamp of grace than of an accustomed awkwardness which was not unpleasing.

He believed, did Jot, that you "can't learn nothin' if you don't argue" (which he pronounced "arger" so that it sounded like a buzz saw chewing through a pine knot), and he argued well, being keen enough to win when possible and philosophical enough to lose when necessary.

Jot was perhaps more the pepper than the salt of the earth. Asked to speak at a formal dinner at which Admiral Robert E. Peary presided, Small stood up, flushed and uncomfortable, and piped, "I ain't much to look at, but I'm a dam' sight worse to listen to," and sat down. The applause lasted several minutes.

Yet in the sanctuary of a neighbor's kitchen, or the lee side of a fishhouse, he could spin yarns more beautiful than truth and more dramatic than life, in which all the heroines were prettier than any you ever saw and the men could lift more, spit farther, jump higher, and lie with a steadier gaze

150

than anybody you're likely to meet nowadays.

The day the power boat, the *George Borup,* was launched, a Boston newspaper reporter strolled into the boat yard.

"Where are you going with her?" he asked.

"Mr. Small and I are going to Labrador," Mac replied.

"Labrador! Isn't she pretty small?"

"She's plenty big for two. She's iron sheathed for'ard against ice damage and her twelve-horsepower engine will burn either kerosene or gasoline. We're also carrying a mast and sail in case the engine lets go. We'll be all right."

"I hope so," said the reporter doubtfully. Evidently he thought the incident not worth reporting, for Dan and Jot found no mention of it next day.

They steamed north along the Maine coast in leisurely fashion, experiencing fine weather, and anchoring in deep-water nooks and crannies at night. The *George Borup* made good time and at length they swung north and east and ran into Grand Manan to see if they had any mail. There wasn't any, but when Mac remarked to the old man in the weathered building, "I'd like to live here!" the native retorted dourly, "You would? I guess you hain't been here long."

The *Borup* was comfortable, a good sea boat with a snug cabin. At Sydney they replenished the food supply, filled the water tanks, and loaded their lockers with canned beans, peas, peaches, pears, and evaporated milk, for this was the last chance. For the remainder of their diet they could catch fish and shoot ducks.

Soon they were away for Cape Smoky, a bold headland

south of Ingonish, rising a thousand feet from the sea, and within a few hours anchored on the west side of St. Paul's Island in what the chart designated as Trinity Cove.

At daylight, they shifted to a small easterly cove, for the wind was shifting to the west. Here they decided to wait until conditions were favorable for the 56-mile run to Newfoundland across Cabot Strait.

Their anchorage was beneath a towering cliff. Black guillemots, known to fishermen as sea pigeons, were constantly darting from cracks and crevices, and knowing that their eggs were palatable, Mac suggested they lay in a supply. The prospect of bacon and eggs in the morning sounded fine; they launched the tender which was carried across the stern and rowed into the beach.

At the bottom of the cliff, at least two hundred feet in height, the talus—a mass of rocky fragments—offered good climbing for a few yards, but then their troubles began. Jot said, "To hell with it," and started back, but Dan went on up, gathering eggs from the many openings betrayed by the hasty flights of the females as he approached. The eggs he tucked carefully into his shirt, next to his body, working higher and higher on the cliff, intensely interested in the task of getting something for nothing.

Suddenly he discovered that he had reached an impasse. It seemed incredible. He reached to the right; the rock crumbled beneath his fingers. To the left, another piece broke readily from the cliff. Above his head the overhang prevented further climbing; below, feeling gingerly, he could find no secure footing. He was caught and helpless.

"Jot," he called, humiliated, "I'm caught. I can't get up

or down. Throw a rope from the top of the cliff, and help me up."

As Jot went below for the new coil of three-eighths-inch manila, a boat with two men at the oars entered the cove. They were, they informed Small, members of the crew of the Canadian Government Lifesaving Station. They had seen the boat and came out of curiosity.

Small pointed up the cliff face. "Who is he?" said one of the Canadians.

"MacMillan. Went north with Peary," said Small.

"Give me that rope," said the Canadian. "He and Bartlett had dinner at my house on St. Paul's Island three years ago. Let's go!"

Dan, meanwhile, much ashamed at the commotion, was trying to help himself. He inched to the left, found a knob that supported his weight, and exchanged places. Too late, he found there was room for one foot only, and there he was, spread-eagled in a worse position, unable to move, and with his face and body pressed against the cliff. There was nothing to do but wait; a misstep now could mean death.

Within a few minutes—swish! The rope dangled ten feet to his left. Too far away. They couldn't see him from above, but one of the lifesavers had remained on the beach, and he signaled to Jot and the other Canadian, named Ross, to move to the right. The end of the rope disappeared. Another swish. The end now was dangling within two or three feet. Mac was tired now and trembling from the constant strain on one leg. Two feet never had seemed so far. Carefully he moved his body closer to the rope, an inch at a time, touched it with his fingers, finally clutched it with one

153

of his hands. Now to push the end of the rope between his body and the face of the cliff so that he could get a bight of it around himself; on one foot it was almost impossible.

Suddenly there was a vicious jerk on the rope! It was too precious to lose and he did not have the strength to wait for them to lower it again. He grabbed it with both hands, tumbling off his perch, swinging and dangling over empty space. He wrapped his legs about the rope as well as he could.

Ross and Jot passed their end of the rope around the stump of a spruce. Ross, a powerful man, sat on the ground and yanked MacMillan up the cliff inch by inch, while Jot took up the slack and held what had been gained. So they lifted Dan to the top, where he arrived with face and body covered with dirt, moss, and debris, and with broken guillemot's eggs running out through the legs of his pants. Even to the last moment the outcome was uncertain, for the small manila line was fraying on the cliff edge, which neither Ross nor Jot dared approach for fear of dislodging a rock that might have crushed MacMillan. When all three finally stood on top, conscious of the nearness of tragedy, Dan noted that, "I was almost peeved to discover they were amused by my general appearance."

They ran next for the Newfoundland coast and Cape Anguille, spending the night in snug Lark Harbor where the farmers had mutton to sell and blueberries covered the hillsides. That evening, with two big lobsters bubbling on the little coal stove, they watched the coast line, wondering whether this was indeed the first land seen in North America, five hundred years before Columbus sailed from Palos, as the Norse sagas relate.

Bound for Turnavik, they fell in with four or five Newfoundland schooners and ran with them from Bateau through the islands to Domino Run and on to the good harbor at Gready, protected from northeast gales by a low, flat island, where they lay over one night. The suffix *vik* in an Eskimo word means "the place of." Turnavik could, therefore, mean the place of the Tunit, who probably were a race of people inhabiting the North before the Eskimo. This reference may be to the Vikings or Norsemen who came to Labrador in large open boats and who were known as Tunit to the Eskimos.

Bob Bartlett had told Mac of a cave on Turnavik, and Bartlett said his father, and the older men generally, believed it had been inhabited by Vikings. When the *Borup* arrived there, Dan went looking for it, guided by a native, Tom Evans.

They worked their way slowly up a rocky valley, arriving at a mass of debris at the base of an inferior cliff. This was not part of the talus slope but evidently boulders brought to the island during the last glacial period. Beneath two huge rocks, on which and about which lay numerous smaller stones, there was a very good natural cave, about eight feet in diameter and roughly five feet in height, hardly large enough even for a small family.

There were unmistakable signs of its having been inhabited. The roof, which was the bottom of a large boulder, was black with soot, and the floor bore evidence of many fires.

Vikings? Who knows? Jot and Mac concluded that if

they were shipwrecked, it was the kind of shelter they would build or seek out, especially if they happened to be stranded on a bleak island such as this, utterly devoid of trees and without sufficient soil into which one might dig to construct an underground dwelling.

Any shipwrecked crew, and there had been many during the last five hundred years, might have done this. It could even have been the shelter of Gaspar Corte-Real, who sailed from Portugal for "Terre Neuve" in 1500 and never returned, or that of his brother, Miguel, who sailed in search of him and suffered the same fate. It seemed unlikely that anyone would purposely live in this barren place when there are bays and inlets covered with thick spruce forests almost in sight of its shores that would make much better home sites.

They headed next for the Moravian mission at Hopedale, called Aivilik (whaling place) by the Eskimos, arriving on a Saturday in time for church service, for devotions are held on Saturday evening and twice on Sunday. The church organ was played by an Eskimo, and the congregation sang the hymns with obvious pleasure, many of them in four-part harmony. One of the hymns contained in the book which they were using referred to *"Guduvaptingnepok"* . . . and *"Heilig, heilig, heilig, engelingiy imgerput."* The use of the German words for God and "Holy, holy, holy," interspersed with the Eskimo, indicates that the Eskimo language contains no equivalents for these.

Jot and Dan endeavored to take part in the responsive reading but gave up after encountering:

*"Tagva merngoerserviksarsiniarpose tarnipsingnut."*

156

It stumped Mac. Jot whispered hoarsely, "What in hell does that mean?" MacMillan withered him into silence with a glance.

The Lord's Prayer was somewhat easier for Dan, although there is an interesting idiom in the Eskimo version. When the Moravians first arrived in Labrador, they failed to find a word for "bread" in the passage reading, "Give us this day our daily bread." The Eskimos had never had or known bread; they had no word for it. Thus some important article of food must be substituted, so that the essential meaning of the prayer would be clear. As agreed upon by the original Christianized Eskimos, the word must be *pipsit,* dried trout, found in nearly every Eskimo home. Now the prayer reads: *"Uvlome pipsaptingnik tunitsivigitiguk* [Today give us dried trout]."

Under way again, they went on to the Hudson's Bay Company Post at Davis Inlet. MacMillan, describing the post in his journal, wrote: "The whitewashed buildings were decidedly old, judging from the method of construction, the size of the beams, and width of the boards. But more ancient than these even was the smell . . . nothing quite like it. Indian mocassins, snowshoes, caribou-skin coats, beautifully soft and of varied colors. And heavy with the bewitching odor of the soft-wood campfire.

"The merchandise on the floor, under the counter, hanging on the walls, and on the shelves, fully as interesting. Fox traps, bear traps, shotguns, rifles and ammunition, Hudson Bay blankets, 'dicky' (hooded jacket) material, Eskimo sealskin boots, blanket slippers, flour, corn meal, sugar, salt bacon, lard, and canned goods. I wondered if certain articles had not been there for a century."

The "inside run" from Davis Inlet to Nain was so intricate that no one at the post could describe, define, or even draw it on paper. The islands, varying from a nubble the size of the *George Borup* to several that were ten miles in length, are virtually numberless. With the engine rumbling happily, off they went; some of it Mac could remember, and some he had never seen.

On the port hand there was a wisp of smoke, and that did stir a memory . . . Tom Geer's home, unpainted, the color of the cliff behind it, a dwelling that knows no visitors for months on end.

They came to the landing. "Tom," said MacMillan, "what on earth do you do here, you and Mrs. Geer?"

"I catches trout, sir, and we is happy."

Maybe, reflected Mac, and then again, maybe not.

Still, they were all happy that night in the tight little house. His wife, with black shawl over her head as protection from the hordes of mosquitoes, had cooked a couple of the trout out in the back yard—fresh out of the net, each weighed ten pounds. Now the four of them drew up to a plain board table before a dish of the steaming red fish, cooked over a slow wood fire in an old black kettle. "A layer of salt pork, a layer of trout, and a layer of pork and so," she said as she ladled it out, hot and fragrant.

Off for Nain, they made their way among the islands, staying on the proper track generally, until they saw to port the mission's boundary stone with the letters "U F," Unitas Fratrum, indicating one corner of the 100,000 acres of land that was theirs by act of Parliament as long as they kept the church doors open for the Eskimo. They were ushered into the harbor by the shrill cries of the Eskimo children, always the first to spot the approach of anything, flying, walking, or afloat.

In due course they sailed for Finger Hill, west along the shore from Mugford Tickle, and Mac had a particular reason for so doing. On this island, according to legend, the Norsemen made their last stand against their inveterate enemies, the Eskimos. Only a year before an Eskimo friend had told him that on the summit of this island all the "strangers who came from the sea in open boats" had died of starvation and that their skulls were still there and could be seen. He warned, however, that no one should climb to the top, that no one ever had, and if he did, he never would return, for there was a mighty eagle at the peak which would avenge the death of the men who had died there.

Anchoring the *Borup* in the lee of the island, MacMillan told Jot not to worry and that he would be gone for not more than an hour. Actually it took somewhat longer, for the perpendicular cliffs fringed by finger-tip columns, which give the island its name, made the ascent difficult.

Once on top, however, he walked the entire length of the island over a fairly flat surface covered with sand, stones, and boulders. Here and there were patches of moss, and even a stray pink or white flower lent color to a generally dreary scene.

No ferocious eagle. Not a single skull.

They sailed north on the final leg, arriving at the Hebron mission where they were welcomed by Bishop Martin. In his journal MacMillan noted, "We had reached our objective. Our time was now running out. We had learned much about what Dr. Grenfell has termed 'one of the most dangerous coasts of the world,' and I felt confident that I could do it again in a much larger ship and without the use of the crude charts available, in some of which we had discovered many serious errors. I noted with surprise the date on one chart we had used . . . 1811! It was high time for a new edition and a new survey of the many beautiful harbors, bays and inlets."

Fall gales were imminent. Upon leaving "Cutthroat" on the way south, Dan questioned the *Borup*'s ability to weather the Kiglipait in a rough sea and strong wind from the northeast, the most dangerous wind on the Labrador. Off Port Manvers, huddled under the windshield with solid spray flying across the top of the cabin house, he studied the mass of white water near the entrance; the sea was breaking constantly on the ledges that nearly block the narrow channel.

"You ain't goin' in there?" Jot said.

"We've got to get out of this," Mac yelled back. "It's getting worse all the time, and this is the only harbor I know."

"Then I won't stay in the cabin and watch that engine. I'll be damned if I do." And Jot popped up through the forward hatch, crouched down and sat huddled and drenched with spray, figuring probably his chances of survival would be better topside than in the engine room.

Actually it worked out well. The *Borup* could go anywhere there wasn't breaking sea. They wallowed, pitched and rolled and took some solid water, and if the engine had quit they would have been done for, but it didn't. Finally they slid down the landward side of the last breaker and glided into a quiet and beautiful harbor. They caught a fat codfish and ate their supper, awed by the beauty of the spruce forest and the mountain range, its dark valleys already sprinkled with new snow.

Southbound again, they fell in with eleven schooners, deep laden with salt cod for Newfoundland, with whom they left Indian Harbor. Mac was still concerned about the weather. The wind was east with a falling barometer and there was no harbor for fifty-five miles. They were making seven and a half knots, keeping up with the fleet, which was carrying all the sail it had to take advantage of the fair wind. Jot was worried, too; the question was whether they could make Gready Harbor across Hamilton Inlet, a course virtually open to the rough water of the North Atlantic.

Finally Jot said, "Mac, you better get out of this."

It was good advice. Some of the schooners already had doused their mainsails and were now running before the wind under foresails and jibs. The *Borup* was riding like a duck and purring like a kitten. Quite frankly, Mac didn't want the Newfoundlanders to think that two Americans in a husky power boat were quitters, and that probably was what they would think if he ran for some sheltered inlet at the head of the bay.

Jot popped up out of the forward hatch again. "Mac, it's blowin' like hell. Let her go to the west'ard. We can git behind an island."

He was right. And to make matters worse, it was beginning to rain, even as the wind increased in strength. The storm already was shutting out their view of the low coast

161

line ahead.

Worried a bit and yielding to Jot's good sense, Mac put the wheel hard over and headed for the nearest island to starboard. There was a little cove on the southeast side; it would be better to grab it while they could and not waste time scouting for something better. A house within a few yards of the beach and a boat anchored off seemed to indicate that the cove would offer some shelter in an easterly.

Both men had had considerable experience on the water; neither had known it to blow and rain harder than it did that night. Jot spent part of the evening making flapjacks and smoking his pipe. Dan, mindful of the wind's roar and the rain pelting on top of the cabin, read Packard's *The Labrador Coast* and expected to hear the anchor rode part with a twang any minute.

If it should break—brand-new, three-quarter-inch manila, the *Borup* would be a total loss, smashed to bits against the ledges to leeward. Twice during the pitch-black night he crept forward on hands and knees to test the strain on their only hope of safety. It was as taut as a fiddle string.

Daylight confirmed their belief that the gale had been unusually hard. Wreckage of all kinds drifted past the mouth of the cove throughout the day, and some of it was painted green, fairly good evidence that at least one of the Newfoundland schooners had been lost.

It continued to blow all day, the following night, all the next day, and all that night. There was such a hard surf on the shingle beach in the cove that it would have been foolhardy to try to go ashore. Nothing to do but make more flapjacks, play the harmonica, and listen to the wind and rain. As the second night of blackness came on, Mac looked through the porthole and caught a feeble glow of light ashore. He wondered at it, particularly since it was visible all that night and the next.

Two days later, when they finally reached the beach, they walked up to the house and met the occupants, an elderly husband and wife. Yes, said the woman, they had seen them in the little boat and they were much worried for their safety, and so she and her husband had kept the light burning in the window each night so that it might encourage the men in the boat for they would know that someone had them in mind.

They were, it appeared, on the south side of Newfoundland Island; Cape North, their objective, was about twenty miles east and south. When they left, it had moderated, but the sea was still running heavily on the projecting reefs and rocky shores. Approaching Cape North, they passed a schooner on her beam ends, which is to say flat on her side, knocked down by the gale and drifting toward the beach. She had been abandoned as she dragged at her anchors several miles north.

There was worse news to come. Arriving at Gready, which Mac had considered one of the safest shelters on the coast, they found no dock to tie to and several buildings missing as well, all destroyed by a "tidal wave" that rolled into the harbor through the narrow eastern entrance at the height of the gale and swept away everything in its path. The first man to come aboard the *Borup* shook his head sorrowfully and said, "It were bad, zur, real bad."

Nor was this all, for what had happened in Gready was a

drop in the bucket. They learned next morning that every schooner in the fleet that had left Indian Head with them was a total loss in Mullins Cove, three miles beyond Gready. Despite rain, wind, mist, and heavy sea, the fleet had succeeded in "fetching" Cape North and on they went through the Run between Gready, Black Island, and the Mainland. With night coming on and the wind increasing, Mullins Cove on the starboard hand was the only possible refuge although it was wide open to an easterly.

The drubbing those heavily laden little schooners must have taken during the next two days probably would beggar description. As customary, when it became obvious that the vessels could not be saved, the crews packed their bags and went ashore, leaving the schooners, loaded with their summer's catch—and their winter's security—to the mercy of the storm. Mac went into the cove to take a look and it was a pitiful sight, its shores lined with the wreckage, not only of vessels, but of men's hopes, for those who had pulled ashore here at the gale's height had toiled all summer as men rarely toil and now had nothing but the clothes they stood in to show for it. It would be a hard winter for them.

Jot and Dan arrived at Battle Harbor in late September, stored the *Borup* with John Croucher, to be ready for the Crocker Land Expedition next year, and left for home by mail boat from the Bay of Islands on the next day.

# 11

ON AUG. 30, 1913, the ancient sealing steamer *Erik* blew her whistle, dipped her flag, and was soon out of sight beyond Cape Alexander, leaving the members of MacMillan's Crocker Land Expedition at Etah, on the northwest coast of Greenland, where they were to be picked up in two years.

MacMillan, whose expedition was supported by the American Museum of Natural History, the American Geographical Society, the University of Illinois, and friends who had contributed $10,000, had three goals on this trip.

Principally he sought to determine whether Peary actually had seen land approximately 120 miles northwest of Cape Thomas Hubbard. In 1906 Peary had named these "snow-clad summits" on the Polar Sea Crocker Land. Whether they existed was a subject of controversy, although Peary did not stand alone. Eskimos, whaling captains who had sailed to Bering Strait, and scientists such as Dr. R. A. Harris, of the U. S. Coast and Geodetic Survey, were confident of Crocker Land's existence.

During the second year of his expedition MacMillan

planned to explore the area of the Polar Sea northwest and west of Axel Heiberg Island, including King Christian Island, pictured on the map by Captain G. J. Isachsen as being sixty miles long and fifty miles wide, but still unvisited and unknown, as was much of this territory between Alaska and the Pole.

Lastly, in rounding up Eskimos from the Smith Sound settlements, among those who wanted to go along were Ahpellah and Etukasuk (spelled Ahwelah and Etukishook by Dr. Cook), both of whom had accompanied Dr. Frederick A. Cook on the trip during which he claimed attainment of the North Pole. MacMillan intended, if time and weather permitted, to retrace Cook's route with the two Eskimos, in an effort to shed new light on the continuing Cook-Peary dispute.

Dan felt it was fortunate that Etukasuk was one of the two concerned, for he was recognized as being an outstanding Eskimo both by his own people and the white men. The son of a tribal seer, he was intelligent, highly respected, and reliable, and after more than four decades of arctic work, MacMillan described this Smith Sound nomad as "the best I ever had."

The white men who made up MacMillan's first major expedition team were an interesting lot. The scientist was W. Elmer Ekblaw, a geologist, botanist, and ornithologist from the University of Illinois. Although heavily built, he possessed extraordinary energies and pursued his professional interests so constantly that he earned the reputation of being a "steam engine in pants."

Maurice Cole Tanquary, also from the Illinois staff, was

a zoologist. Of them all he probably was the best disposi-
tioned, a man of even and gentle nature, of quiet courage,
who had a fine voice and liked to sing.

Ensign Fitzhugh Green of the United States Navy was a
physicist and seismologist. A graduate of Annapolis, he
combined a high degree of intelligence with a concept of
strict discipline. He was not a "mixer," and he did not seek
to establish intimate relationships, either with the members
of the expedition or with the Eskimos. MacMillan always
believed that "if an Eskimo says it's going to storm, you
better listen . . ." but Green, more exclusively conscious
of the great intellectual abyss between Smith Sound and the
Naval Academy, had no such faith in the natives.

The wireless operator, Jerome Lee Allen, reportedly then
the "best in the Navy," had had little formal education but,
according to Dan's evaluation, "an inordinate ambition to
make something of himself." If something did not work,
trying one remedy never was enough; he would try six, and
not only had the keenness to think of them, but the patience
to apply them all. He sat up frequently until one or two in
the morning, studying—anything from algebra to English.

Harrison J. Hunt of Bangor, a Bowdoin graduate, was
the expedition doctor, an outdoorsman in splendid physical
shape. He was best qualified to make the long trip with Mac
to Crocker Land, but to select him would be to leave the
expedition without a physician at the home base, and that
was not prudent. Hunt was an excellent shot, handled a
kayak well for long distances, and was of the temperament
that "wanted to get in a boat and go somewhere"; that was
why he had come north.

Finally there was Jot Small, listed as "cook and raconteur."

At Provision Point at Etah they landed all their provisions and equipment, including forty tons of bagged coal and lumber for a "large, comfortable house." Mac had wanted to be landed on the Ellesmere Island coast, since his work was on that side of Smith Sound, but the master of the *Erik* had feared the ice pack in the sound and refused.

The most direct route to Crocker Land—if it existed— lay westerly across Ellesmere Island, then north to the tip of Axel Heiberg Island. By December 6, with the house constructed, complete with electric lights and a telephone to the nearby igloos—a source of amazement to the Eskimos because the wire had no hole in it for the words to go through—they had begun establishing food depots along the route ahead. The temperature was thirty-nine below, and Smith Sound, over which they must cross, was frozen.

Word had spread that the white men had built a big house at Etah, and throughout that winter of preparation they had many visitors. The Eskimos came in groups, whole families at a time, from as far away as Meteorite Island, well below Cape York, listening, transfixed, as the hand-wound victrola played the music of Caruso and Schumann-Heink. On Christmas evening fifty-four native visitors received portions of three large fruit cakes donated by MacMillan's good friend, Jerome Look, who was at that time general superintendent and chief engineer in charge of the construction of the Ashokan Dam and Reservoir, New York City's water supply, at Brown Station, New

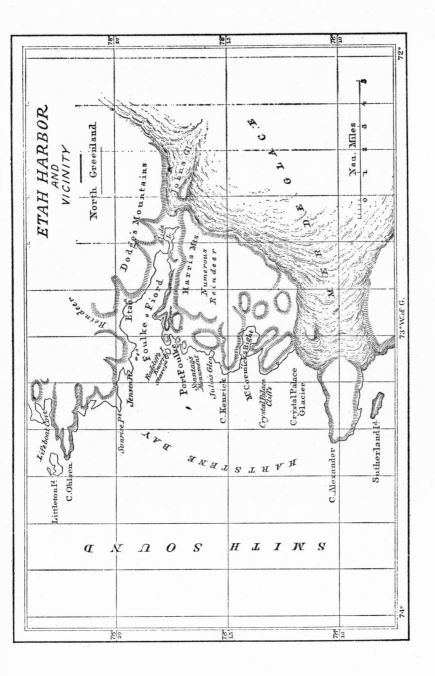

ETAH HARBOR
AND
VICINITY

North Greenland

Dodge's Mountains

Harris Mts.

Numerous
Reindeer

Etah

Foulke Fiord

Reindeer

Jensen Pt.

Sunrise pt.

Radcliffe
Emerald
Starr I. Fd.

Port Foulke

Sontag's
Monument

Julia's Glen

C. Kenrick

M°Cormick Bight

Crystal Palace
Cliffs

Crystal Palace
Glacier

C. Alexander

Sutherland I?

Littleton I?

Lifeboat Cove

C. Ohlsen

HARTSTENE BAY

SMITH SOUND

MER DE GLACE

Joins G.

73° W. of G.

71°

Nau. Miles

0  1  2  3  4  5

York. *"Mamucktosuah* [Delicious]!" exclaimed the Eskimos, with their mouths full of cake.

Dan called "Jerry" Look "my best friend," and the feeling was mutual; their correspondence over the years ran into hundreds of letters. MacMillan had lectured at Brown Station shortly after returning from the North Pole trip and had been most warmly received, both by his audience and the Look family. Jerry, who also had a Maine background, became an immediate source of support, financial and moral, for MacMillan's work and displayed the strongest interest in every phase of it.

When MacMillan left for the Crocker Land trip, he wrote to Jerry, "We sail at 3 o'clock in the afternoon of July 2nd, and I must have you there. Go as far as Boston with me if you can." And in the first batch of mail received at Etah, Mac had more than sixty letters, of which several were from Look, promising supplies and expressing eagerness for details of life with the Eskimos. There also were notes from Look's small daughter, Miriam, who had taken Dan by the hand possessively from the time he first arrived at the depot at Brown Station; she was a vivacious youngster who wore hair ribbons and "skinned the cat" with agility in the birch tree "out front." When the children at Brown Station played "Discovering the North Pole," and they did often, Miriam either was allotted the role of MacMillan or she went home. She wrote a pencil-scrawled note to "Uncle Dan" at Etah, announcing that she had some new kittens and adding, "I wish you was my brother . . ."

Also in the mail was a letter from an unknown correspondent marked, "To be opened when everything has gone dead wrong."

Nearly a half-century later, this letter remains unopened. "I never wanted to break faith with whoever wrote it," Mac said, "and things just never have got that bad."

Mumps and influenza, about the last things MacMillan had expected, halted the whole expedition on the ice of Hayes Sound, and it was March 10 before they started off for Cape Sabine again, late in the year for a 1,200-mile sledge trip, three hundred miles of which would be over the Polar Sea drift ice. MacMillan decided to cross Ellesmere Island over the Beitstad Glacier, a vertical wall of ice fifty feet high and fifty miles long, rather than tackle the longer, boulder-strewn, wind-swept route through Flagler Pass. Peeawahto and the fat-faced Kaiota cut steps in the face of the ice wall, and Etukasuk started off the apparently impossible task of getting their gear up over it by putting a tumpline on his 125-pound sledge and hauling it up the glistening barrier on his back, smiling and sweating. In a single day they had placed four thousand pounds of equipment on top of the glacier.

Two Eskimos, with their sixteen dogs, quit and went home, not so much because of the hard work but because one wanted the wife of the other, who objected, and they both raced home to settle it. This made the loads of the remaining sleds so heavy that the dogs could be induced to move only by free use of the whip; it also cut down the amount of food that could be transported so that it was evident they would have to live off the land—musk oxen, caribou, bear, and arctic hare—wherever possible. Two days were required to reach the glacier's summit; here they built two snowhouses at an altitude of 4,750 feet, with the temperature at fifty below. From this point Ekblaw was sent back to Etah with frosted feet.

On their way across to Blaamanden a blue fox crossed in front of the teams. Had the fox been going their way, they would certainly have made a record march, but as it was he had the expedition's ill will for some hours afterward. To stop or control Eskimo dogs with the tail of a blue fox waving in their faces is like stopping the world from going around. The *komatiks* (sledges) fairly leaped through space. The unexpected lunge caught them all unawares, and pipes, tobacco, matches, meat—everything not tied on —were left spilled beside the trail. The fox trotted on slowly at first, looking back over his shoulder as if to say, "Are you after little old me?" But as the dogs approached, he quickened his pace a little, to tease them, and then to show what running really was like, he turned himself into a bounding black ball which quickly faded to a speck in the far distance. The dogs slowed down, tongues hanging, and looked foolish, turning their heads to the men as if to ask, "What on earth was that?" and not knowing that these foxes reputedly can even outrun the arctic hare.

The good sledging and good weather ended as they rounded Skraelingodden. The light wind freshened to a strong breeze and at forty below seemed to go right through them. Their clothes were driven full of snow; it was ankle-deep during the whole plod to Schei's Island, where they killed thirty-five musk oxen and spent four comfortable days in a snug snowhouse, with a snow-block windbreak for the dogs, for there was no natural lee.

Leaving a note in the igloo for Green who had been sent back to Hayes Sound for supplies, telling him to feed his dogs from the cache there and then come on to Cape Thomas Hubbard as quickly as possible, they started on for what Sverdrup called Hvitberget (White Mountain), its snowy head raised above the northern horizon. They passed a musk-oxen herd feeding on the hillside and left them undisturbed; no meat was needed now. The Eskimos, up ahead, rushed toward a little knoll and engaged in a friendly tussle over something on the ground.

*"Suna* [What]?" called Mac. "Pemmican. Emu tau. (Milk also)!" they yelled back. They evidently had uncovered one of Sverdrup's caches, established in 1902. They gnawed the pemmican (American) and cracked the frozen milk (Norwegian) in their teeth delightedly; both supplies were in good condition.

On April 14 they arrived at what they judged to be Cape Thomas Hubbard, the northern end of Axel Heiberg Island. Green's supporting party arrived later with everything needed for an estimated twenty-five days on the Polar Sea. If Crocker Land were only 120 miles from shore, as Peary had told MacMillan, the distance out could be covered in twelve days and the return in seven, at the most. The thirty-three days of continuous effort, during which dogs and men had covered 580 miles, or an average of 17½ miles a day, had wearied the teams; ten dogs had dropped in harness, due to stiff head winds, heavy loads, and insufficient food. Nearly all the sledge dogs had suffered from dysentery and weakness, which Mac believed due to salt in the pemmican. His plan now was to fill them up with all the obtainable musk-ox meat, double-feed them with pemmican on the long marches, and cover the 120 miles as quickly as possible.

They headed out over the blue ice of the Polar Sea, looking for a land that had already been named, which Peary claimed did exist, and yet which geologists and oceanographers declared could not exist. At the end of the first day's march from land they had covered fourteen miles northwest of the northern end of Axel Heiberg Island. MacMillan turned to Etukasuk: "How much farther did you go with Dr. Cook?"

The Eskimo looked back at their point of departure, surveyed his surroundings, pointed with his whipstock back on their trail toward a small pressure ridge. "It was about there where we made our last camp."

"Then what did you do?"

"I held a flag up over my head and Dr. Cook took a picture. Then he said, 'Now we'll go back.' "

This is the story told to MacMillan that day by the Eskimos when they were about ten or twelve miles northwest of Cape Thomas Hubbard, the northern end of Axel Heiberg Island:

Dr. Cook and the two Eskimos started back toward Axel Heiberg Island. Etukasuk went alone to a cache on its northern end to get a rifle which he had hidden there; then all three proceeded southward on the sea ice on a line roughly parallel with the western shores of Axel Heiberg Island. They continued southward to the eastern shores of

Amund Ringnes Island, discovering on the way two un-charted islands. At no time were they ever out of sight of land.

Thence Cook and the Eskimos moved southward to Jones Sound by the "Hell Gate" of the Sverdrup Expedi-tion, where they abandoned their dogs and proceeded by canvas boat to the northern shores of North Devon, estab-lishing a winter camp at Cape Sparbo. This habitation was located and photographed in 1910 by Bob Bartlett, accom-panied by Etukasuk. Dr. Cook was disappointed in not being able to get to an English whaler, on which he hoped to reach civilization.

The Cook party succeeded in living through the winter, when game was abundant. In the spring they began their long walk back to Anoritok and at this time they were often hungry, on occasion nearly starving.

"Dr. Cook pushed the sledge, Ahpellah and I pulled," said Etukasuk.

The Eskimo said an old seal under the rocks at Cape Sabine gave them strength to cross Smith Sound in May. Then Cook went south along the coast of Greenland by dog team, with the intention of catching the first steamer for Copenhagen.

Indeed, it was a wonderful trip, and Cook was unfortu-nate in not receiving honor for what he actually did. But MacMillan said, "The fault was all his own. Tempted to grasp the thousand miles of travel over the Polar Sea, he lost all."

Why did Peary say that Dr. Cook had not reached the Pole? In 1909 he and Matthew Henson, an expert in the

Eskimo language, questioned Ahpellah and Etukasuk, the two companions of Dr. Cook. At that time MacMillan also showed the two Eskimos the charts of all lands west of Etah. On these charts they drew their trail. The story as told by them then and again in 1914 to MacMillan was the same story told to Knud Rasmussen, Peter Freuchen, and to others in the northern part of Greenland. It never varied.

For MacMillan, the "Crocker Land" trail ahead was disturbing. Dan caught the Eskimo tongues wagging about it —"much water, sun high, not freeze, ice moving"—and he knew they were concerned. He bantered with them; go give the dogs a double ration of pemmican, he said, and remember the ice is better now than it was off Cape Columbia with Peary in 1909. They agreed it was and were cheered.

But the open leads gave them trouble. They had to wait for them to freeze over, and crossing on the rubbery ice was hazardous. Their dogs were having a bad time; two more dropped on the trail, and all were tired.

By dead reckoning they judged they were about fifty-two miles offshore, based upon an estimated advance of only three and one half miles per hour, although they felt their observations for longitude and latitude, to be taken later, would improve this figure. On April 20 they did their best, crossing nine newly frozen leads, and figured they had covered thirty miles by day's end.

April twenty-first was a beautiful day. All the mist had evaporated under the rays of a bright sun and the clear blue of the sky extended down to the very horizon. Green was no sooner out of the igloo than he came running back with the cry, "We have it!"

They ran to the summit of the highest mound. There could be no doubt about it. What a land it was! Hills, valleys, snow-capped peaks extending through at least one hundred and twenty degrees of the horizon! They had discovered a land one hundred times bigger than Crocker Land!

MacMillan was elated, as they all were, until he inquired of Peeawahto how they should direct their course and to what point of this new land. The Eskimo said nothing but continued to scan the horizon carefully. Then he said casually that he judged it to be *pujok* (mist.) Having great respect for the Eskimo's acuteness of vision, Dan nevertheless attempted to convince him that he was wrong. Mac turned to Etukasuk for encouragement. He shrugged. *"Immaha* [Perhaps]." Green, in any event, still believed it to be land.

As they proceeded farther, the landscape gradually changed its appearance. Its extent also varied with the change in direction of the sun. At night, with the sun in the northwest, their new-found "land" disappeared completely. They sipped hot tea, gnawed at their eight ounces of pemmican, and did some serious thinking. Was it possible that Peary, with all of his experience, had been mistaken? Was this mirage which had fooled them the very thing that had deceived him eight years before? If he actually saw Crocker Land, there was only one conclusion—it was more than 120 miles away, for they were now at least a hundred miles from shore, with nothing in sight but a limitless expanse of ice.

Their hope for clear, cold weather and good traveling

was fulfilled. The morning of April 22 was clear as crystal and the thermometer indicated thirty-one below zero. Green, an expert navigator, with artificial horizon and sextant, obtained a good sight: Latitude, 81 degrees, 52 minutes; Longitude, 103 degrees, 32 minutes, both of which agreed almost exactly with their dead reckoning. To increase their latitude, they set a more northerly course on the next two days, and further observations indicated they were 150 miles due northwest from Cape Thomas Hubbard. They not only had reached the brown spot on the map marked Crocker Land but were thirty miles "inland." There was not a thing in sight but ice; clearly they were in pursuit of a will-o-the-wisp, changing, receding, but always beckoning.

Recalling that seven years before Peary, tired and conscious of his age, had written of Crocker Land, "My heart leaped the intervening miles of ice [from Cape Thomas Hubbard] as I looked longingly at this land, and in fancy, I trod its shores and climbed its summits, even though I knew that pleasure could be only for another, in another season," MacMillan was saddened. In his journal Dan wrote, "He [Peary] left his discovery for younger men to prove or disprove. This we had done.

"How I disliked to return and tell him, and the National Geographic Society, the American Museum of Natural History, and the world, that the land did not exist, that it was a mirage of the rough and rugged surfaces of the Polar Sea . . ."

They struggled on for one more day, covering about six difficult miles and finding nothing but jumbled masses of broken ice. The elusive mountain peaks toward which they had so laboriously directed their course now had disappeared completely.

MacMillan, knowing that it was getting very late in the year for traveling on the Polar Sea, hoped to "double march" back to the land, that is, cover the distance in half the time required to come out. This is often possible because dogs and men are going "home," more than half the food has been consumed and the sledges are lighter, and the party is following a well-marked trail.

The dogs, frightfully thin, were getting double rations of pemmican and working hard. The men rose as early as three in the morning, made long marches each day, with only brief stops for rest, hot tea, biscuits, and munching of frozen meat. From their "Igloo No. 3," that is, what had been the third stop outward, they decided to strike for the land in a single march, for the leads were opening up. MacMillan wrote: "When within a mile of the land, a cairn was visible on the summit of a low, projecting point to the southward. Since Peary was the only man who had ever been there, I knew it to be the one described by him as being on the 'low foreshore' beneath the cape. Although we had walked some thirty miles, I felt that we must take advantage of the good weather to ascend the hill and secure his record . . . absolute proof that he had been there and, incidentally, the only proof.

"I shall always remember that walk. Evidently Peary wanted the man who secured that record to work for it, and Green and I did, breaking through a heavy crust with nearly every step until we reached the top . . . We climbed one crest after another, but finally the last one was mounted, revealing, outlined against the blue sky, a large, well-built cairn enveloped in a blanket of snow.

"A short stick projected from the top. At the base of this, I discovered a cocoa tin. Removing the cover, I found within a piece of the American flag, containing the red, white, and blue and one star. With it was the notation, 'Peary, June 28, 1906.' We replaced this with a small silk flag and a record of our arrival there.

"We now turned eagerly to an examination of the Polar Sea. Peary stood here and from this point saw what resembled land lying to the northwest.

"The day was exceptionally clear, not a cloud or trace of mist. Yes, there it was! Extending from southwest true to north-northeast, hills, valleys and snow-capped peaks . . . which we now had proved to be a mirage, or loom of the sea ice."

Three days' food remained upon their sledges. It had taken them thirty days to reach this point from "home." How many would it require to return, and would the land support them? Those were the questions they faced as they turned in that night, grateful to be, at least, off the treacherous sea. They had covered 725 miles in fifty days.

MacMillan instructed Green, with Peeawahto, to proceed down the coast two marches and back in one, to make a southern survey. Dan and Etukasuk headed north, realizing that the immediate concern was meat. In ten hours they had two caribou, small and nearly perfectly white, unlike the caribou of Newfoundland and Labrador; this new species had been named in honor of Peary the *Rangifer pearyi.*

May 2 and 3 were typical of the northern end of Axel Heiberg Island—strong winds and drifting snows. On the morning of the fourth Mac began to worry about Green and Peeawahto. Six days had elapsed and he had given them only three days' food. Late in the afternoon a black dot appeared on the ice foot, and MacMillan, concerned, hastened out to meet the team, which he recognized as Peeawahto's by the way the dogs were distributed. Seeing only one man, he was about to call out, "Where's Green?" when he saw that it was Green.

"This is all that's left of your southern division," he said to MacMillan.

"What do you mean?"

"Peeawahto is dead. My dogs were buried alive. My sledge is under the snow forty miles away."

Green said that shortly after their leaving the weather had become increasingly bad. He and Peeawahto decided to take shelter and built a snowhouse. The Eskimo, as is the usual practice, when ready to tether the dogs for the night in a driving snowstorm, selected a spot swept clean by the drifting. Green, a novice in arctic work, and fond of his dogs, staked them out in the shelter of huge cakes of ice.

Following their evening meal, they were conscious of the increasing darkness of their igloo and realized abruptly that, due to the depth of the drifting snow, they were being rapidly buried alive. With snow knives they cut into the ceiling, permitting it to fall, thus increasing the thickness of the floor and also the height of the snow bed on which they lay. They continued to do this throughout the night and in the morning emerged approximately fifteen feet higher than their former entrance of the night before. Where Green had hitched his dogs there was only a mound of snow; all had perished, unable to free themselves.

Green suggested that they continue south and complete the survey with the one remaining team. Peeawahto reminded him of MacMillan's order, "Go down in two marches and return in one," and said that since they already were overdue he was going back to MacMillan, knowing full well that if they failed to reach the western shores of Smith Sound by a certain date, they might be compelled to remain at Starvation Camp at Cape Sabine and suffer the same fate there as did Greely's men.

MacMillan wrote in his journal: "The Eskimo hitched his dogs to the sledge and started north on the return trip. Thereupon, Green grabbed my .22-caliber, high-powered rifle and took up his position in front of the dogs, commanding Peeawahto to follow directly behind him; this in spite of the fact that Peeawahto had suggested Green ride on the sledge and that he had promised to bring him back to me.

" 'Twice,' said Green, 'I discovered that he had left my trail and was directing his course to the right. The third time I discovered that he was whipping his dogs and leaving me. I dropped on one knee and shot him through the head.' "

"What did you do with the body?" MacMillan asked.

"I carried it with me on top of the load."

"And what did you do with it that night?"

"I slept with it on the couch in the igloo."

"What did you do with it the next morning?"

"I dragged it out of the igloo."

"Where is it now?"

"I left it lying on the ice."

MacMillan wanted to go back and give the Eskimo a decent burial. He knew, however, that if he did, Etukasuk, who had not understood what Green was saying in English, would go with him. In this case Green might not suffer punishment, but his friends, according to the practice of the Smith Sound Eskimos, might all be killed.

Dan concluded it would be best to leave Peeawahto where Green had left him and let Green tell his own story. MacMillan recorded, however, that "his [Green's] assertion that if he had permitted the Eskimo to escape with the sledge, dogs and food, he would have starved, is not a sufficient reason for killing one of the best Eskimos I have ever known . . .

"It was, indeed, a long walk alone and without food, but Green knew perfectly well that I never would have left him to starve, that I would have been on my way in search of him immediately following Peeawahto's arrival at the dugout."

They started for home. Etukasuk killed four caribou, and they fed a whole one to each weakened team; the men steam-cooked the hearts, tongues, livers, and tenderloin in a tin kettle. Three of the brains were set aside to be frozen for breakfast.

Through the haze of the sixth, white-capped Hvitberget could be distinguished, at least thirty-five miles distant. Etukasuk led all day long, setting a good pace with the help of a large square sail rigged ingeniously to the back of his sledge in the manner of the English explorers of a half-century or more before; most of them did better than he, however.

Setting his square sail bravely to take advantage of a strong fair wind, he entered upon a long lane of glassy ice. The sledge, under pressure of canvas, ran amuck, with its captain, courageous to the end and ashamed to abandon ship, gripping the upstanders and blowing like a porpoise. The sledge plowed through the dogs, scattered them right and left, jibed, wheeled crazily, and capsized. The expressions on the faces of the dogs were indescribable. They had never been overtaken and charged by a sledge before; standing about it, they eyed it with suspicion, ready to attack if it showed the slightest sign of life.

Saturday, May 9, was the sixtieth day, a long, fast run with a gale at their backs and so thick that they did not see each other all day.

On the fifteenth they attained the summit of the glacier, after an eleven-and-a-half-hour struggle and an exciting run along the eastern slope during which Green overturned and smashed his sledge. A white wolf followed them throughout the day and at night sat on his haunches at a respectable distance, interested in their preparations for making camp.

The Greenland coast was now in sight through a heavy bank of mist, and the nineteenth gave them their last real going-over from weather. Nothing would have tempted them to round Cape Rutherford that day but the can of jam that Ekblaw had promised to leave under the Svendson cross at Sverdrup's old winter quarters in Rice Strait. Explorer Sverdrup and his men erected the cross in memory of the expedition doctor who was found dead in his tent in May 1899.

Arriving at the shore, they peered beneath every suspicious pile of rocks, ascended the hill, looked beneath the cross. No jam. They finally sat down to the same old menu —tea, pemmican, and biscuit—and were tired enough to be thankful for that.

From this point a rapid run brought them to Peary's old hut (a cabin house taken from S.S. *Windward*) at Payer Harbor. Here Ekblaw was to have left two cans of beans buried in the northwest corner, but praise be, there was instead a box containing tinned peaches, pears, and marmalade. With hands and faces smeared with the unexpected sweets, they failed to hear the approach of two galloping dog teams.

Upon leaving Etah, MacMillan had arranged with Akpoodashaho and Ooblooya that if he failed to return by the time of the coming back of the little auks, which is to say, May, they were to drive over the ice of Smith Sound and hunt for him on Ellesmere Island, for the party might be without dogs, making its slow way home on foot. Now they were here, as arranged.

MacMillan's journal notes: "I was very much interested in the way in which these two received the news of the death of Peeawahto. Naturally they looked about for him at once. I was perfectly willing to let Etukasuk explain his absence, which he did in Eskimo and with gestures. A part of it I could understand, and a large part I couldn't. But this I gathered . . . Peeawahto was under the snow, buried by an avalanche which came thundering down the side of the mountain. Green had emerged from beneath it all by digging with his hands, but Peeawahto could not do that.

Etukasuk and I were far away at the time and only knew what Green had told us. Green had returned alone with Peeawahto's dogs. His own were buried beneath the snow.

"I could easily understand Etukasuk's version of the whole sad affair. Green had described to him with his few words in Eskimo how the snow from the hills had slowly buried their igloo and, at the same time, had buried his dogs, which was true, but the men had not been buried by an avalanche."

All of their belongings were transferred to the sledges of the "rescue party." Their dogs, lean shadows of their former selves, wagged their tails upon being relieved of their loads by their fat brothers from home. Within six hours they were on the Greenland shore, headed south through light, soft snow.

Near Cape Hatherton one of Mac's dogs staggered from side to side and then dropped. He had covered his 1,400 miles with head and tail up. Now, nearing home, it was as if he said, "Well, I think you can make it now without my help," and he gave up. Mac slipped his harness, stroked his head, and left him, knowing that he would follow when he had renewed his strength.

The dog was curled up with the team in the morning, ready for the last leg home, the end of a long and hard journey which, like so many of man's efforts into the unknown, had produced no new lands but, instead, new truth.

185

# 12

NOW THAT Crocker Land had been proved nonexistent, MacMillan deemed it necessary to inform the American Museum of Natural History that the expedition's scientific and geographical work should be completed by the end of the summer of 1915 and that a relief ship should be dispatched to arrive at that time.

Their precious wireless communication at Etah, with which Allen had done so well and in which they had taken so much pride, now had failed. There was only one way of contacting the States, by letter from South Greenland, and Dan decided he did not want to trust such an important message to anyone else but would make the thousand-mile moonlight trip, crossing Melville Bay himself in December and January, in company with Peter Freuchen.

This Freuchen, factor of Knud Rasmussen's trading post at Umanak on the Greenland coast, who eventually became widely known as an author and television personality, was probably the best authority in the world on the Polar Eskimo. He lived and starved with them for years; he married one; he understood what they thought and felt.

Freuchen was a good writer, an easy talker, but you had to watch what he said, not because of any malicious intent, but because he liked a joke and he would fool you just as long as you could be fooled before he would break into a roar of laughter.

Freuchen, who had been going to make the Melville Bay trip anyway, promised to make all arrangements for both dogs and men, including Tanquary, who, though no lover of the out-of-doors, had expressed a desire to go along, somewhat to MacMillan's surprise. Etukasuk would go, too, and they planned to leave in the middle of the arctic night.

The trip to Umanak (the heart-shaped place), now less appropriately named Thule by Freuchen and the U. S. Government, was reached without event. Here Freuchen gave them a warm welcome and wanted to start at once, but the Eskimo girls at the post insisted on a farewell dance. To the strains of a squeaky victrola and a few deeply scored records they stepped through the plain quadrilles with a missionary and three South Greenland belles, one with child, one just married, and the third with her cap set. The latter, with eyes for Etukasuk, pushed him and his bearskin pants from corner to corner, for obviously he was helpless and bewildered. Seated on his sledge, cracking his long whip over the backs of galloping dogs, he made a picture . . . but in dancing he was hopeless.

Having obtained dogs for Tanquary, they were on the sea ice and ready for the start on January 31. One thing Peter had forgotten. "Wait one moment, please." In a short while he returned. "Well, I have done it."

"Done what, Peter?"

"I have married them."

"Who?"

"Two Eskimos."

"Really! What did you say?"

"Well, he said he wanted her. I said that was all right. Now we will go."

No courtship, no wedding bells, no ring, no license, no promise to love and obey, no honeymoon, no minister or justice of peace. That was matrimony reduced to the lowest common denominator.

They drove to Akpat on a cold, clear night and the stars seemed within reach. Towering cliffs guard the entrance to this village, the name of which means "place of the murres." Koolatingwa was their host, and being one of the best hunters of the North, his larder was full. He hitched up his dogs, sped away to a cache in the moonlight, and was back in a halfhour, his sledge loaded with delicacies—frozen murres (*Uria lomvia lomvia*) and fetid seal, items from the harvest of the summer months. Although the birds were not exactly fresh, having been packed away uncleaned and warm in sealskin bags five months before, they were banquet fare in the North. After the evening meal Freuchen discoursed at length on politics and government, and thus the old year went out and the new one came in.

Heading easterly, they stopped off at Kikkertak Island, where they stayed with Ooblooya and his wife, Kasahdo. In a bad year shortly before Kasahdo's three children were starving and so hungry that one of her breasts was nearly destroyed by their teeth. She finally resorted to slitting the ends of her fingers, thus permitting her children to suck her blood, and mother and babies all survived.

The Eskimos were attempting to outdo each other in entertaining their white guests, and Ooblooya offered them a dish that none of the three white men had had previously. What resembled a fat, frozen seal was squeezed up through the small round hole in the floor, the one entrance to the winter home. With a sharp knife a slit—about a foot in length—was made in the belly. The host then removed his bird-skin shirt, plunged his hand and forearm into the seal's belly, and withdrew it, smeared with grease and clutching several black strips of meat. It was strips of sun-dried narwhal, packed in narwhal oil. MacMillan noted: "Was ever anything better! Long we ate and swelled and slept and ate again, and praised our host . . ."

It was at this point that MacMillan had his first misgivings as to the probable success of Freuchen's plans, if the latter had made any. Peter had negotiated this same trip six times; he planned to cover the 132 statute miles (actually more because of necessary detours over the ice) in three marches. To do this, he was obviously counting on ideal weather, no leads, and good going. Mac felt the amount of food and nature of the equipment was barely sufficient, and events proved that he was right to entertain such doubts.

To begin with, the temperature was about forty below, the bay was full of mist, and there was no snow suitable for making a house at the end of a day's march.

Then Hendrik, Freuchen's South Greenland assistant,

left a bag of biscuit on the trail and lost a can of oil. Within a few days they found themselves virtually without food for men or dogs, with wet boots and mittens they were unable to dry for lack of fuel or shelter, and lost in the mists of the bay for want of a compass. In addition, Hendrik became ill and had to be lashed to his sledge; Freuchen also was sick, coughing a great deal, but still on his feet.

After eight days the mist lifted and Mac located the Great Square of Pegasus in the southern sky at about four or five o'clock in the afternoon; he directed their course to the left of that, looking for land.

For a meal the men had tea and a mouthful of biscuit. At night they slept in an enclosure of five sledges with one man on guard against the hungry dogs. They removed the dogs' harnesses each night to keep the creatures from eating the sealskin traces, for that would have left all three men facing possible death; in the deep snow travel would have been impossible with only one pair of snowshoes. Several times the dogs rushed the sledge "stockade," trying to get at the harnesses, and Mac, standing watch, beat them off with a whipstock.

By January 14 they were down to dog meat. They killed three, cooking one for themselves and feeding two to the pack. MacMillan wrote: "The dead had hardly finished breathing when they were gobbled up by the living. All biscuits gone. Hendrik remembered somebody had two pounds of biscuit and a little sugar in the mail bag, addressed to a girl in Upernavik. We all agreed this should be utilized for the good of the party. Out it came, as quickly disappeared."

They stood another all-night watch to save their harnesses, skins, and sledge lashings from the dogs. At five the next morning MacMillan broke through the ice and fell into the water, catching himself to keep from going clear under, but at forty below, half immersion was bad enough.

After this mishap all three decided they must be close to land and should make a dash for shelter while they still had the strength. They threw virtually everything off the sledges to lighten the load for the weakened dogs, cracked the whips, and started, driven by hope and determination.

Mac's journal records: "My black lead dog, running loose, picked up a trail and his dropped tail—a sure sign of discouragement—snapped back into its usual curl on his rump. He quickened his pace and then came that prolonged howl of welcome from dogs tethered up ahead.

"We rounded the cape, and there were the igloos!"

They rested eight days, during which the dogs consumed thirty seals and became bright-eyed and bushy-tailed again, giving that characteristic bass growl of affection typical of them whenever one of the men approached. In addition to the letter to the American Museum, Mac wrote to Jerry Look at Brown Station, telling him he intended to remain in the North another year, alone and independent of any relief ship.

He wondered whether Look would send him provisions, providing the museum was unable to do so, adding, "I am not in the least concerned over the possibility of being able to reach home, for I am sure I can do so by dog team via Ellesmere Island, Baffin Island, and Hudson Bay, whenever I care to. . . ."

191

Tanquary and Freuchen went on south with the mail. Mac started back to Umanak with Etukasuk; heading north across Melville Bay for a quick run up the coast, they had nothing on their sledges but frozen narwhal meat, a gallon of oil, and a little tea. Dan felt he had to return to Etah because it now was so late in the year that, should he go with Tanquary and Freuchen and be delayed in getting back, all the expedition's plans for spring work would be jeopardized. He was particularly eager to study the geology of Ellesmere and Axel Heiberg islands.

The return trip is evidence of the haste he felt. This sledge journey from Cape York to Umanak, a distance of seventy-five miles, made on a cold arctic night, was undoubtedly the longest in his entire career of northern work. According to informed writers of arctic travel, it probably was one of the longest ever accomplished. Freuchen, who had lived in the area six years, declared he never knew of anyone, even an Eskimo, to make this trip in one march, as did Mac and Etukasuk. Thus they returned to Etah and to work.

The Eskimos agreed that early 1915 was the hardest season they ever had experienced. It was spring, when according to custom the families move to Peteravik to kill seals and walrus. But neither was plentiful, food was hard to find, and at Kiete, thirty miles to the south, the Eskimos had been compelled to eat their dogs and burn their sledges for fuel.

The white men went hunting with them, for with times so hard, one could not expect the Eskimos to provide all the meat for the expedition.

192

This is what hunting walrus is like, and it has not changed in the last thousand years for the people of Smith Sound:

One works far out to the edge of the ice, watching the black, smoking leads. Tether the dogs well back, for their whines and howling may disturb the quarry. Cautiously creep to the edge of the wide crack in the ever-shifting pack, where great, black, fierce-looking heads occasionally break the surface, emitting peculiar grunts and calls, their gleaming white tusks in marked contrast to their dark necks and heads. Fur-clad hunters, with harpoons in their right hands and coils of rawhide line in their left, crouch on the ice and emit deep grunts in imitation of the herd.

Then the walrus head toward them, and disappear, and the hunters know by this action that they are coming closer. Crouch at the edge of the lead then, and as the heads break water, there is a swish of flying harpoons and trailing lines. The walrus snort and splash, the hunters drive their iron-pointed "togues" deep into the ice through a loop at the end of the harpoon line, and then the struggle begins that may last for hours.

Anglers are thrilled by a thirty-pound salmon on the end of an eight-ounce rod. Here is a two-thousand-pound mass of fighting energy on a quarter inch of humming, twanging rawhide line. And this is not for sport but for the life of starving dogs, for the existence of the pinch-faced wife and crying children, snuggling for warmth under caribou skins in a cold snowhouse beneath the cliffs of Peteravik.

Even when the struggle is over, and the huge beast is partly dismembered, often there comes a cry of warning, for there has been a wind change and the ice is crumbling ominously. Then the trail actually rises and falls ahead of them, ice waves buckling and bending in what once was a rigid surface. And the hunters do not always gain the shore; many a man and his dogs are carried off to the south, never to return, and once an entire village of men, women, and children from the Baffin Island shore was lost in this manner.

One day, during the summer, a large herd of walrus came slowly along the shore, feeding right in front of the camp. Jot, Esayoo, and Mac launched their kayaks, sixteen feet long and eighteen inches wide amidships, and prepared to attack them, supported by Hunt in the punt with his rifle.

When walrus are feeding at the sea bottom on clams, as these were, one is at a disadvantage, for they may rise to the surface facing in any direction. Eskimos never attack under such conditions, since a walrus may very likely come up directly under the kayak. But having failed to make a kill on two previous attempts under perfect conditions, Dan was anxious to show the Eskimos that he could do it.

One bull walrus, probably about three quarters of a ton in weight, remained apart from the others by ten yards. Dan placed the kayak so that when this bull surfaced again, the creature would be headed away from him.

The walrus soon emerged, breathing heavily and in a perfect position for MacMillan's attack. Dan dug his paddle deep into the water and jumped the kayak ahead at full speed, so rapidly, in fact, that in nervousness he dropped his harpoon on the deck of the kayak and found himself alongside the mammoth brown body before he was prepared for the attack.

The walrus was lying on the surface with head down in the water, probably munching a mouthful of clams. Mac could not place his paddle in the water between the kayak and the walrus without alarming him. He could not reach his paddle over the walrus into the water. He was helpless, and any second the walrus would lift his head, make his own attack, thrust his tusks down through the deck of the kayak, which would then roll over and drown MacMillan before he could get out.

Dan figured his only hope for survival was to surprise the walrus and throw him off balance, even for a second. Grabbing the harpoon from the deck, he lifted it high above his head and with all his strength drove it deep into the walrus's back. The whole great body lunged with pain; the creature roared and whipped his head around almost under MacMillan's arm, then raised up high above him, ready to charge. Mac whacked him with the paddle as hard as he could, a blow which surely made no great impression on a beast that has been known to ignore rifle bullets.

To Dan's surprise, the walrus fell over on his back and disappeared beneath the surface. The sealskin float attached by a line to the harpoon was bobbing along the surface so rapidly that Hunt was unable to overtake it for several minutes. When he did, he fired six shots at the walrus, leaving it still very much alive. During the melee MacMillan had backed off, yelled to Jot to bring out the dory; Small arrived on the spot with Esayoo who had one cartridge in his pocket that ended the fight.

To the astonishment of the Eskimos who cut up the walrus, MacMillan's steel-tipped ivory harpoon point was found deep inside the chest wall, indicating the strength with which the blow had been delivered. They had never known of anyone to do such a thing before, they said, and from that time on he attained a certain local distinction for being the man who had stabbed a walrus in the back and lived.

Several of Mac's Eskimos, arriving from the region of the Humboldt Glacier, where they had been hunting polar bear, brought to him two interesting gifts. One was a yellow, faded record of the Elisha Kent Kane Expedition of sixty-one years before, bearing the date of August 24, 1853. The other was an old cap lining on which was marked, apparently with a sharp object, the letters "O.K."

Kane had written in the book on his arctic travels, a best-seller in its day: "At Rensselaer Harbor I erected a small beacon cairn on the point and, as I had neither paper, pencil nor pennant, I burnt a K with powder on the rock, and scratching O.K. with a pointed bullet on my cap lining, hoisted it as the representative of a flag."

Mac now had the historic cap lining. Years later he discovered that the O.K. on it did not mean "all right," but that the family name originally was O'Kane rather than Kane.

Dan decided to make a trip up the Greenland coast to the Humboldt Glacier in search of bear and to stop at Rensselaer Harbor to discover whether further signs of the Kane expedition might remain. He actually found the first sign even before they arrived there; by the end of the second day's march from Etah they arrived at Bancroft Bay, and at the entrance, after much searching, Dan was thrilled to discover a large letter "K" carved on the vertical face of a rock. A few feet from it lay the remains of a demolished stone cairn, the contents of which were gone.

Rensselaer Harbor, long the most northern habitation of man, yielded more evidence. Standing on the top of Observatory Island, Mac remembered that Kane had written: "On the highest point of the island . . . is a deeply chiseled arrow mark filled with lead."

He looked down at his feet and found himself virtually standing on the arrow! In the middle of the area was a deeply chiseled hole. Kane had recorded: "Near this [the grave of two of his men, Schubert and Baker, which Mac-Millan also discovered] a hole was worked into the rock and a paper, enclosed in glass, sealed in with melted lead." Lead, paper, and glass, however, were gone.

In memory of America's first arctic explorer, MacMillan inserted his ice lance in the hole of the "deeply chiseled arrow mark" and to the top of it fastened the American flag entrusted to him by the Kane Masonic Lodge of New York City. Sixty years had gone by since the Stars and Stripes had flown over these cliffs, whitened shores, and islets.

One morning at Etah there was a hail at the window, "Hello, Mac!" and Tanquary had arrived from the south where he had gone to purchase dogs. He was cheerful but had badly frosted feet. He thought he would be as good as new in a few days, but MacMillan took one look and knew better and turned him over to Dr. Hunt. Tanquary, he figured, was out of the sledging game; he was crippled. Eventually Hunt had to amputate both big toes, and this he did with a pair of surgical shears and without anesthesia, while Tanquary gritted his teeth and held onto the bedposts.

Conditions did not improve. Sledges were arriving and departing every day, reporting caches empty; because of the unusual extent to the southward of the sea ice, walrus were scarce and hard to secure.

As the fall of 1915 came, waiting for the ship that would take them home proved nerve-racking, too, for some. It was not so for MacMillan, who did not intend to go home anyway, who was "busier than ever" preparing for the expedition to the little-known and unvisited King Christian Island. But others of the expedition had scanned the bleak horizon for months, their hopes periodically raised and dashed by innumerable strange shapes in the distance that proved to be not vessels of deliverance, but only nature's ice architecture, the forms of which are virtually endless.

MacMillan noted on September 1: "In our meeting today, we discussed the safety and welfare of the expedition, conscious of the fact that it is forced to be longer than was intended, and that, therefore, one must think in terms of readjusting to the additional demands. We feel that it is absolutely essential to open communications with South Greenland and this by dog team leaving here about November 24.

"From now on, each man will stand a twenty-four-hour watch, from 3 P.M. one day to 3 P.M. the next.

"It is growing colder very rapidly. The temperature today is at 28. I have given up all hope of a ship this year. Hunt and Allen, however, are still hopeful. That she has tried to reach us, I have no doubt. She may have been blocked by ice, or wrecked on the Greenland coast.

"We have food enough, but not much of a variety. The boys, a week ago, were very much worried and decided that we were in a rather serious situation. They feared that my management of the food, especially in my sharing it with the Eskimos, who have really provided us with meat for the last two years, was not wise.

"All of the geographical work done thus far can be attributed to the Eskimo dog drivers, without the help of whom Peary could never have reached the Pole. That this concern on their part was uncalled-for is clearly shown by the list of food supplies handed me by Ekblaw today."

Three days later he noted that "a majority of the boys" had given up the ship, although "a few are still watching the open spaces between Knorr and Starr Islands." Allen was ill; he thought it was from eating the whole-wheat biscuit that did not seem to agree with some of them. Green had a toothache and Hunt put in a temporary filling of rubber. Tanquary, at length, was up again. Mac, realizing the importance of establishing a hunting station in hopes of getting fresh meat for the winter ahead, left for Nerke, thirty-five miles south of Etah.

While at Nerke on September 15 Dan wrote in his journal: "The cry of 'fire!' or even of 'murder!' could never have startled me more than the loud yelling coming out of Arklio's tent this morning. In a few seconds, I realized that something was coming and that it must be a ship. It proved to be Peter's [Freuchen's] power boat, puffing along the shore.

"Imagine my surprise to hear Jerome Allen yell: 'Dr.

Hovey [Edmund Otis Hovey of the American Museum of Natural History] is here! The ship is at Umanak!' The long looked-for ship had come at last.

"Within a few minutes, Dr. Hovey shouted, 'How is it for going home?' This was my last wish. I could not go home with so many plans for the next year, but I was glad for the boys who were apparently very homesick and who really had no reasons for remaining. . . ."

The American Museum had chartered the three-masted auxiliary schooner *George B. Cluett* from the Grenfell Association, and finally the vessel had succeeded in reaching Umanak in North Star Bay, having had a long and tedious trip from New York due to head winds, ice in Melville Bay, Dr. Hovey felt they must not delay going back, particularly since the *Cluett*'s captain did not wish to go farther north and was impatiently awaiting their return. But if Mac wished to remain, the provisions for another year's work would be taken off the *Cluett* for him.

MacMillan recorded: "As Dr. Hunt was away with the Eskimos hunting caribou, I could not think of leaving him alone in the North. I told Dr. Hovey that I would not go home but would remain with Hunt, furthermore, not to be concerned about our safety; we could go home in the spring by dog team down the Greenland coast and catch a steamer for Copenhagen. . . . Thereupon Jot declared that he preferred to remain with me rather than go home on the *Cluett*, even if he were to receive no salary.

"I dashed off a few lines to my sister in Freeport, telling her of my decision and not to worry. Leaving us our mail and a half box of oranges, off they went toward the south.

"All seems well at home in our family. The war is the one great topic of interest right now, but from here it seems so far away that it is not a part of our life. With so much to do, we rarely think of it."

Abruptly MacMillan realized that he faced an immediate local emergency. Before leaving Etah for Nerke, he had told the Eskimos they were to have the house if he did not come back there to live.

Knowing nothing of white man's stoves, he could visualize them moving in precipitately and burning down the carefully built shelter that he still was going to need. No dog team was immediately available, and the shore traveling was bad anyway, but he had to get back, and within a matter of hours!

He launched a somewhat battered twelve-foot flat-bottomed punt, got down to the oars, and rowed, covering the forty-five miles to Etah in eighteen hours of steady pulling that left his hands cramped and numb, his back and legs stiff from the same position for so long. Nor was the distance the only difficulty; his day-and-night row took him around Cape Alexander, favorite walrus-hunting ground for the Eskimos, and through much of the trip these creatures—weighing from three quarters of a ton to a ton—were breaking the sea all about him and threatening to come up beneath the little punt and capsize it. He had left Nerke at 4 P.M.; at ten the next morning he arrived at Etah, weary, but overwhelmed with relief to find that the house still stood.

As it turned out, five of Mac's expedition, desiring to go home, since the two years were up, went to the *Cluett,* which was still 120 miles short of Etah because of an inexperienced skipper and a faulty engine. Eventually they gave up hope of getting home on the *Cluett* and sledged down the Greenland coast to board a steamer for Copenhagen.

Meanwhile the *Cluett* also suffered from having two captains, one in charge of the ship and the other, experienced in northern navigation, engaged as ice pilot. The latter, Captain Comer, finally left the *Cluett* and with Dr. Hovey came to live at Etah with Mac and Jot Small. In the spring Dan engaged an Eskimo driver to take Dr. Hovey, not in the best of health, to a port where he, too, could take a vessel for Denmark.

MacMillan was mindful that in more than a half century, his was the only expedition to winter in this area which had not lost one or more of its men through hardship, scurvy, and lack of proper food. Dr. Kane, the first to winter nearby, had lost three. Dr. Isaac Israel Hayes also lost three. Charles Francis Hall, the leader of the Polaris North Pole Expedition, failed to return. Adolphus W. Greely lost nineteen out of a total of twenty-five. Otto Sverdrup lost his doctor and a sailor. Peary lost one man in 1892 and a second in 1909.

MacMillan could not know, but in nearly four decades of leading exploratory trips into the Arctic, including this one, which would be of four years' duration, he was never to leave a man in the icy wastes.

Even now, whether or not a ship could get through the ice to them, life at Etah was both orderly and productive. Dan and Jot and the Eskimos killed ptarmigan, arctic hares, and even some caribou. They went to McGary's Island and opened up a cache of eider-duck eggs made the previous

June and brought back some of them, "frozen as hard as rocks," and in excellent condition.

"They can be compared, appropriately, to nuggets of gold, for such they are to us now, and have that appearance when chopped in half with an axe," MacMillan noted.

Some of the Eskimos moved into the Etah house, where the white men had been quartered, and Mac employed Wewe, the daughter of Hans Hendrik of South Greenland, to keep house. As with all well-run households there were occasional domestic problems, as he noted:

"Wewe's baby boy has been annoying her by stealing raisins out of a tin can in the pantry. It has been a problem what to say or do to prevent him from doing this. Finally Jot solved the problem. He placed a large picture of President Woodrow Wilson on top of the raisin tin. I note that the youngster starts confidently toward the raisins, sees that man looking right at him, lets out a yell and backs out of the pantry."

Jot was finishing a new, small sledge, weight thirty-six pounds; Ahtuksungwah was cleaning caribou skins for new *kooletahs* (outer garments) for the men, and Mac was "busy making notes, compiling words of the Eskimo language, and jotting down items of interest found in my reading."

This was, indeed, for MacMillan, home, sweet home.

# 13

ON THE THIRD day of spring MacMillan began his 1916 expedition to King Christian Island, leaving Etah with eight sledges, seventy-two dogs, and seven Eskimos on March 22. It was relatively warm, twenty below, but they were hampered at the start by heavy drift and a strong southerly wind that made traveling "a regular smother and a fight all the way into camp . . ."

By April 17 they were at Cape Nathorst, the southern tip of Ellef Ringnes Island, and on the next day at five o'clock King Christian Island was clearly visible on the western horizon, offering the first view of their objective.

In general, they had done well at finding game for much of the journey, but for the past several days there had been only "a number of bear tracks, but no bears, which causes me concern over my pemmican supply." The dogs were tired and very poor for lack of meat, and Dan was considering sending the Eskimo boys into the high hills for hare, caribou, and musk oxen.

It was an unattractive country, land so low that at times

they could not tell whether they were on the shore or the sea. By its appearance they thought it good grazing ground for caribou, but not for musk oxen, which prefer somewhat rockier ground because this offers them better protection against wolf packs, their only enemy.

On April 19 Dan noted: "King Christian Island is mine. I know of no one who has ever been here. It was seen in the distance by members of the Sverdrup party in 1900, but never visited. The land hereabouts has the general appearance of Ellef and Amund Ringnes Lands, rather high at some distance from the shore, with a gentle slope toward the water's edge.

"We are 485 statute miles from Etah. Our pemmican supply is such that we must return soon if we do not succeed in finding game. Tomorrow we must find meat or we are through."

As they plodded along behind their sledges, not at all happy, a big male polar bear popped out from behind an iceberg. Nukapingwah and Mac were ahead, and almost before the latter could reach for his graflex, hanging from the upstanders of the sledge, they were in the middle of the mixup which followed.

They had learned from the experiences of the last few weeks not to permit their dogs to attack a large, lively bear. It was not a healthy thing to do, and they could not afford to lose dogs. Nukapingwah "popped" the bear at once, with his Winchester .35, a powerful rifle. The animal dropped, rolled, and was on his feet almost instantly; he then made hurriedly toward an iceberg, knowing, as did the men, that there is always a hole or ditch at the base caused by wind and swirling snow.

Into this the bear tumbled, momentarily lost from sight. As is the practice, Nukapingwah immediately unhitched his dogs from the bounding sledge, and Mac attempted to do the same, but failed, due to the confusion. In the next instant Dan found himself on the brink of the snowbank and beheld there below him a stirring picture—a bloodstained polar bear with glistening white teeth, in a half-crouching posture, knocking the dogs right and left with his huge paws.

As the sledge plunged down on top of the bear, Mac pointed the camera at him and snapped the shutter, hoping that the creature "was on the ground glass." (He was.) Abruptly man, bear, and twenty dogs were rolling around together in the hole in the snowbank, a melee which ended with a report that left Mac shaking his head, ears ringing. Nukapingwah had arrived with his Winchester and administered the *coup de grâce*.

"The bear has saved us forty-three pounds of pemmican. North Cornwall is a certainty now, a land which I had not planned to reach," Mac noted.

En route to North Cornwall, he concluded that "the North Magnetic Pole, discovered by James Ross in April 1830, to be in 70 degrees, 5 minutes, 17 seconds north and 96 degrees, 46 minutes, 45 seconds west, is no longer there.

"When I am on the 96 degrees, 46 minutes, 45 seconds meridian west of Greenwich, England, my compass needle should point due south, that is, if I happen to be between the North Magnetic Pole and the North Geographical Pole, as I am. However, I find that the needle does not until I have arrived at a point west of that meridian. This is absolute proof that the magnetic pole has moved to the westward. Why? I venture to state that as yet no one really knows."

Camped at Ellef Ringnes Island, he built a cairn on Easter Sunday, April 23, 1916, and enclosed a record which said, in part;

> Arrived here yesterday on my return from Findlay Land (King Christian Island) to Etah, North Greenland. I shall leave here tomorrow for Cape Ludvig. From there I shall proceed to North Cornwall, where I hope to find musk oxen enough to enable me to map east coast as far as Gordon Head . . .
>
> Thus far, we have killed thirteen bears, thirteen seals, sixteen hare, two ptarmigan, and thirty musk oxen. Have three days' supply of pemmican on our sledges . . .
>
> All well.
> MacMillan.

Three months later this record was discovered by explorer Vilhjalmur Stefansson who had traveled north from his base in Alaska.

Such records are important since they are the only proof that the writer has actually visited the spot. Furthermore, if an expedition fails to return, as did Sir John Franklin's expedition of 1845, such records aid in the search for the missing explorers. If Franklin had left a record on Beechey Island in Lancaster Sound, the site of his first winter quarters, all might have been saved. Fourteen years after his disappearance a record was found at Cape Herschel revealing the fate of the entire expedition—129 men!

On April 26, 1916, MacMillan and his Eskimos left the south shore of Amund Ringnes Island and headed across Hendriksen Sound for North Cornwall. He was the first in sixty-three years to step on this island. Its northern, eastern, and much of its southern shores had never been visited by man. In 1853 Sir Edward Belcher, searching for Sir John Franklin and his men, had landed on its southern shore, touching for a few hours only at two points.

Upon the summit of its northern shore, rising to a height of 1,200 feet, MacMillan constructed a cairn five feet high and four feet in circumference and placed within a record in a small bottle. This record was found recently by a Canadian aviator and is now in the Archives at Toronto, Canada.

When Mac returned to Etah, there were busy times. Jot bagged a big *ookjuk* (seal) at the ice edge, and Dan decided to have it prepared as a specimen for the American Museum. He also tried recording Eskimo singing on the phonograph, and although Ahlnayah "did her best," he had doubts whether a woman's voice "can be transmitted to a wax cylinder with such a machine as I have."

They all went to McGary's, or Eider-Duck, Island, the Eskimos in their kayaks, to get duck eggs for the winter. In one hour Dan had collected three hundred, and together they accumulated a thousand, a number equal to that cached two years before. Many of the nests contained as many as five eggs, most of them perfectly fresh. The eggs are large and olive-colored; the ducks prefer to nest on islands to get away from their worst enemy, the foxes, which will eat both ducks and eggs. But still the ducks do not get away from the ravens, often seen flying with an egg on the end of their bills, heading for a high crevice on the bold escarpment of Dodge Mountains where their young await a morning meal.

"Only six hours sleep last night," MacMillan noted on July 3. "There is too much to do to remain longer in bed. I was never so much in need of an airplane as I am right now. As Peary predicted seven years ago, the airplane will surpass the dog team and the ship in a very few years. We are 'speeding up,' so to speak. I should be at Ittibloo for the eggs of the herring gull (*Larus argentatus*), a bird not listed as breeding in Greenland. In fact, I know of no ornithologist with a statement to that effect. I would like to be at Hakluyt's Island during the nesting season of the murres, to find out if both the *Uria troile troile* and the *Uria lomvia lomvia* are there. This is the 'akpah' of the Eskimos and the 'noddy' which I used to see on cold winter days at Provincetown.

"I hope to find the eggs of the ivory gull. I doubt if the museum has a single one. I understand from the Eskimos that it nests up near the Humboldt Glacier . . ."

By July 10 they were blowing eggs, that is, removing contents from the shell, for the American Museum. When it was high water, they walked over to Provision Point to "salt down" some walrus skins for preservation.

Mac's Eskimo sealskin *tupik* (tent) had been completed and would be pitched in a few days. He had had this summer shelter made, quite different in shape from any other in the world, as a specimen for the museum, feeling that

209

both anthropologists and ethnologists would be interested in its design. It was not conventionally A-shaped but had a nearly vertical front with a rather long sloping back held to the ground by a ring of rocks. The rocks are used because there is no wood in the Arctic for tent pegs, and even if there were, they could not be driven into the frozen ground.

The small boy, Kahdah, happened to hear Dan say he would like to obtain one of the sculpins which, surprisingly, frequent Etah harbor. This horny-headed fish is well known on the New England coast. Kahdah borrowed a kayak and in a few minutes was back with a fine specimen, caught with hook and line at the outlet of the brook that flowed into the harbor east of the house. Its markings were greatly different from those caught off the docks of Provincetown, and it probably constituted the most northern species of this fish (*Acanthocottus groenlandicus*) ever caught.

In midsummer they shot the squareflipper or bearded seal, the *Phoca barbata,* largest seal in the North, valuable because its skin is in great demand for boot soles. They found trout in the stream leading from Alida Lake—fat, firm-meated, and succulent. Moved by sudden nostalgia at the sight of walrus feeding on the clam beds, which recalled "clamming" in boyhood days, Mac and Jot went alongshore at low water and dug a "mess" of the *Mya truncata,* the clam of the North, which he had never seen before going to the Arctic and which is some kind of cousin of the Cape Cod "hen clam." Dan continued to photograph Eskimo hunting equipment, including fish spears, bows and arrows, harpoons, and killing irons; he also had begun compiling an Eskimo dictionary.

In August he rowed up the fjord to the "bird cliffs," the Dodge Mountains, so named by the Hayes Expedition, and attempted to record with the dictograph the musical notes emitted from the throats of thousands of little auks. With regard to these birds, he injected, in the midst of a notation to the effect that he was "packing and photographing" specimens, the comment that "the Eskimos are having a banquet tonight . . . their Thanksgiving . . . the main course, the *pièce de résistance* consisting of very old and absolutely rotten dovekies, one fetid feast to which all look forward. The aroma, no the smell, in the vicinity of their conclave is pervading and also leads to the conclusion that there must be something better somewhere. The banqueters are off again tonight to the cliffs."

With each day that went by the expectation of a ship arriving at Cape Alexander dwindled, and Dan began to prepare for another winter at 78-20 North Latitude. By the end of August 1916 they were lighting the lamps, the first they had allowed themselves to enjoy for five months. With only two lamp chimneys left, they obviously would be down to candles long before the winter was over.

The harbor ice was now 25.5 inches thick. It was now very dark even at noon, especially if the day was cloudy and there was a good deal of wind and drifting snow.

Late in November all the Eskimos came to the house, the men dressed in women's clothing and the women in men's. They thought it an uproarious joke; old fat Inahloo looked like Humpty Dumpty and Kakotcheeah (Jimmie) looked like a beautiful girl. After the white men had

211

laughed sufficiently, the Eskimos asked for a *kilaute,* the only musical instrument they have (Mac had one, packed away for the museum, and brought it forth), and they became very excited and frolicsome, making almost frenzied motions with the head, body, and legs.

On December 7 Arklio, Etukasuk, and Tauchingwah sledged in with the mail from Umanak and a report that a ship was there. She was the Danish vessel *Danmark,* with orders to transport the Crocker Land Expedition to St. John's, Newfoundland. She arrived at Umanak on September 23, after battling six weeks with the Melville Bay ice, finally broke through and tried to reach Etah without success. Having failed, and realizing that the summer was gone, the captain had put her into winter quarters.

MacMillan decided that his fourth year's work was to be the exploration and survey of Ellesmere Island from Cape Sabine to Clarence Head, particularly since this stretch of land, as laid down on the latest maps, was portrayed inaccurately because all information regarding it had been acquired from a ship's deck, several miles from the shore.

Of this area Sir Clements Markham had declared, "Next to northern Greenland, the most interesting part of the unknown region is the land on the western side of the northern part of Baffin Bay, between Smith Sound and Jones Sound . . . No one, so far as we know, has ever landed [here]."

On March 25, 1917, MacMillan left Etah with four sledges, the Eskimos, Etukasuk, Arklio, Akpoodashaho, forty-two dogs, and about 2,400 pounds of gear and supplies.

On April 1 they were at Cape Isabella, which was obviously impassable, for strong current and violent wind had driven the smashed drift ice to a height of nearly sixty feet over the ice foot on which they were traveling. Mac surveyed the cape's gullies, filled with hard snow, which made ascent dangerous. This was the spot where the British North Pole Expedition of 1875–76 had landed and of which Sir Georges Nares had written: "Commander Markham landed . . . on the south side of the extreme point of the cape. After an extremely rough scramble up one of the gullies, a cairn was erected on the outer spur [of the cape] 700 feet above the waterline, a cask for letters and a few cases of preserved meat being hidden away on a lower point . . . magnetic west of the cairn."

It was too tempting to pass up. There are few thrills in arctic work equivalent to the discovery of records left by those who came before. To find in these frozen wastes the words of men, living or dead, who also were willing to go cold, hungry, and alone to the world's frontiers, was like listening at firsthand to the voices of history. Where, Mac wondered, was the cairn?

The Eskimos were not enthusiastic, so he left them in camp. Cutting footholes in the hard snow, he edged up the cliff face alone, finally reaching the windy summit, and there was the stone pile he sought. He rolled away the heavy boulders, but there were no records.

He would try the lower cairn. Climbing down to the three-hundred-foot level, he scanned the rocks carefully and finally spotted what he sought, a barrel, marked on the head, "Alert." Within it there was a copper tube, containing a statement written by Captain Nares, including the record of four deaths from scurvy and "exhaustion."

Hopeful of finding other documents, Dan went back for his sharp-eyed Eskimos. Within a few minutes they dug out of the snow a tin wrapped in heavy sailcloth, containing a letter addressed to Captain Nares and reading in part:

> Pandora, August 24th, midnight 1876
>
> Dear Captain Nares:
>
> I have tried to get northward, but have not been able to reach beyond Cape Hatherton this side, or Latitude 78 degrees, 45 minutes on the east side . . .
>
> After a heavy southerly gale yesterday, we have succeeded in getting through the S.W. pack and if I succeed in getting back into clear water, I proceed homewards at the end of this month, having cruised here all the navigable season in the event of your sending a boat party to Littleton Island.
>
> Trusting that you are well and have succeeded in your arduous work. Yours truly, Allen Young.

The existence of the letter now was ironic. Captain Nares had been here and had stood within twenty feet of his mail, yet had failed to find it.

As they worked south, they observed the second largest glacier in the Smith Sound region, roughly twenty miles along its face, and this Mac called the American Museum Glacier, noting that the ice surface was a "perfect network" of bear tracks. The dogs eagerly pursued the *nanook* (bear) for four hours, at the end of which time, scrambling through the rough ice, Arklio shot him in a pool of water where the "the tiger of the North" had chosen to make a

214

In sealskin boots and kooletah (parka), Miriam takes her trick at the wheel as *Bowdoin* threads its way northward through the icebergs of Melville Bay, Greenland.

MacMillan endeavors to persuade a baby musk-ox that men can be friendly.

If anyone is going anywhere, this Eskimo pup wants to go, too.

ABOVE: Her rugged bow thrust into a niche among islands at Frobisher Bay, Baffin Island, *Bowdoin* takes refuge from dangerous drift ice. BELOW: In serious trouble, *Bowdoin* is stranded on a ledge at low water in Refuge Harbor, North Greenland. Once termed the strongest wooden vessel in the world, the Mac-Millan schooner was floated virtually undamaged.

These uneasy musk-oxen are in customary battle defense formation, tail to tail in a circle, waiting for MacMillan to move a
step or two closer before charging.

All arctic life is not ferocious. These baby eider ducks are snug
and peaceful in their nest made of down plucked from the
mother's breast.

stand. The Eskimo had taken care to harpoon him first, for polar bears sometimes sink when shot.

On the latest map, "Polar Regions, Baffin Bay to Lincoln Sea," issued by the Navy Department in 1911, there appeared nine tidewater glaciers from Cape Sabine to Clarence Head. MacMillan discovered and mapped forty-two, including one on Boger Point that he named in honor of the American Geographical Society.

Saunders Island, he found, does not exist, even though it had been shown on all charts for the last century and many navigators, including Mac, had tried to locate their ships' position by it. Evidently, some time in the early days of 1850, an iceberg had been in that latitude and longitude; in the Arctic icebergs often are mistaken for islands and islands, when snow-covered, for icebergs.

But time was running out. On May 18 they heard the note of the first glaucous gulls of the season; already there would be much open water ahead and they must push along for home.

On June 4 they received mail at Etah. Dr. Hovey was well on his way home, sledging south toward a Copenhagen-bound ship. Peter Freuchen wrote, as of October 4, that the war was still on, that Rumania had joined the Allies, and that Germany had made no advance. In fact, he had heard that the war was over, that the Germans had attempted to cross Holland, the populace had turned on the water and drowned the whole army.

Captain Hansen of the *Danmark* requested MacMillan to have everything ready for "quick delivery" upon his anticipated arrival about August 1. He apparently was worried over weather conditions and the shifting of the ice pack.

On July 22 Mac wrote: "I pack away for shipment my sleeping bag, a duck's nest, an old Eskimo soapstone lamp, and develop and file away the last of my negatives.

"The relief ship, either the *Danmark,* in the ice in North Star Bay, or a ship from home, can come at any time now. The boxes are packed and ready to go on board. I must confess that I am really sorry to leave what now, after four years, seems very much like a home. I hope that the relief ship does not arrive until September 1, or even two weeks later."

It did arrive before that, however. The S.S. *Neptune* arrived at 3:30 P.M. on July 31, 1917, under the command of Bob Bartlett. At the time she was sighted by Inahloo, Mac was busily cranking the motion picture camera, trying to get a film of the falls at the rear of the camp. Inahloo leisurely picked her way from rock to rock, as if the coming of a ship were an everyday occurrence, and asked Dan if he had seen it. When he said no, she looked surprised.

He went to look at the steamer, bucking a heavy sea and head wind, and still far off in the southwest, but he knew she was not the *Danmark.* Off Provision Point she blew her whistle and Captain Comer thought she might need a pilot, so Dan jumped into the punt and rowed off across the harbor. At first he did not recognize either ship or skipper until Captain Bob Bartlett's face appeared on the bridge and in a voice long remembered yelled, "Hello, Mac!"

At Cape Parry, Bartlett had overtaken the *Danmark*

216

stuck in the ice, with engine-room fires out and the crew refusing to go on, claiming that they did not ship to go so far north. Bartlett went alongside, showed the *Danmark*'s skipper his orders from the American Museum to proceed north for the rescue of the Crocker Land Expedition, and they transferred all the expedition boxes from the *Danmark* to the *Neptune*. Leaving the *Danmark* locked in the ice, Bartlett came on to Etah through the pack; he was twelve days crossing Melville Bay and said he encountered more ice this year than on any of his previous trips. The *Neptune* bore evidence of this: a huge canvas patch was draped across her bow, covering ice damage.

Finally aboard the *Neptune* with four dogs, "good friends which I cannot leave behind," Mac noted in his journal: "At 3:15 this morning, Captain Bob signaled to the engine room that we were ready to leave for home. Our four years are now a thing of the past. To lean over the rail and say good-by was one of the hardest things in my life. The Eskimos, men, women, and children, continued to wave until they were mere dots on the horizon. I can never forget them . . . loyal friends, every one.

"As Bob turned the bow of the ship toward the south, I happened to think, to realize for the first time, that we were being 'rescued,' if it can be called that, by the *Neptune,* the same ship which had attempted to reach Lieutenant Greely and his twenty-four men in 1882, thirty-five years before. That year she had failed. This year she had not."

The first two steamers that might have brought the expedition back to the States within the scheduled two years had been hampered as much by personnel or mechanical shortcomings as by ice conditions. The engine of the *Cluett* was unpredictable; her master was inexperienced in ice navigation. The *Danmark* never had been across Melville Bay and those operating her did not want to go.

After four years a ship and a captain as used to bucking ice as eating breakfast reached Etah and the "rescue" was effected.

# 14

IRONICALLY, ALTHOUGH MacMillan rejected an Army commission in 1918 and signed up as a Navy enlisted man because he wanted to go to sea, he did not get there during World War I.

Eventually commissioned, he found himself, as a lieutenant junior grade, assigned as assistant to the chief of the naval experimental station at Hampton Roads, Virginia. As such, his principal duties were to fly in various types of aircraft—including biplanes and triplanes—and make reports on their assets and liabilities.

At this distance in time any assessment of his brief period of active duty points in one inevitable direction: Everyone with whom he flew was killed, and it probably was during this 1918–20 interlude that the legend of "MacMillan luck," in which several of his intimates believe firmly, was born.

On one occasion he was urged to go aloft with five colleagues from the Virginia flying field and declined because he had to go into Norfolk to pick up a pair of shoes that were being soled. This errand was important since he wanted to wear the shoes on the following morning when he had an interview scheduled with Gilbert Grosvenor, President of the National Geographic Society, to discuss the possibilities of a trip North as soon as the war was over.

Arriving in Washington the next day, he bought a paper at the newsstand—the plane had crashed, and all five were dead.

Shortly after the war's end, in the spring of 1920, Navy flyers from Virginia were ordered to go to New York to welcome the fleet home from Europe. On the way back, with Louis Barron at the controls, the entire side of one of their two engines blew out, a propeller shattered and a large chunk of it struck the plane directly behind MacMillan's head. They were forced down into the sea off the New Jersey coast. Barron ordered them all out onto a wing tip to counterbalance the weight loss of the missing engine and taxied ashore. A Navy cruiser eventually picked them up. Barron, an excellent flyer, was later killed by a rookie pilot as he sat in his cockpit, his plane on the ground.

With the war over, Dan participated vicariously in a brief skirmish with the Hudson's Bay Company. A prominent Boston businessman conceived the idea of establishing three or four northern trading stations in competition with the H.B.C. He acquired the three-masted Newfoundland sealing steamer *Thetis,* once bark-rigged but now a fore-and-after, a vessel best known for having rescued the Greely Expedition in 1884 while under the command of Commander Winfield S. Schley of the United States Navy. The Boston firm engaged MacMillan to sail north in the *Thetis* and compile a report for them on whether such a venture was practical and, if so, where the trading posts should be set up.

As soon as he joined the ship at Montreal and the skipper found out that Mr. MacMillan was seagoing, Dan was made second mate. In that capacity he assisted in taking the vessel down the St. Lawrence River and up the Labrador. Much of this voyage covered territory with which he was unfamiliar, including stops at Chesterfield Inlet and Fort Churchill in Hudson Bay. Of particular value, the trip gave him an opportunity, close on the heels of his studies in anthropology at Harvard, to observe the Eskimos and Indians of the Hudson Bay area, even though it did not last long. At its termination Mac recommended that the redoubtable Hudson's Bay Company could not be bucked, but the Boston interests decided to do it anyway, a venture that proved to be unsuccessful and short-lived.

MacMillan was convinced by this time that in the choice of ship lay the key to successful arctic exploration. He had had a good chance to watch the performance of the *Roosevelt, Neptune,* and lastly the *Thetis,* all vessels with extensive arctic histories.

Peary had said to him, "Hiring a ship at $15,000 is what consumes valuable funds that should be used for other purposes."

Obviously, then, what he should do, since he had firmly decided to become an explorer, was to have a ship built expressly for the work and own her himself. At Etah, with plenty of chance to think about what such a vessel should be like, he had come to these conclusions:

221

The nineteenth-century arctic explorers Elisha Kent Kane and Isaac Israel Hayes both had used small sailing ships with success. Use of sail, with minimum auxiliary power, would reduce the amount of necessary fuel and result in great savings in money and cargo space.

In order to protect the propeller from ice, such damage being the greatest danger to an arctic ship, the vessel should be widest just aft of amidships, rather than just forward, as is conventional. This would force the flow of ice away from the stern as it passed the ship.

The underbody of such a vessel should not be wider than the exposed hull, as is true with many steamers, for that prevents them, when squeezed in the ice, from rising up out of it. Instead, his ship would be deep and narrowing; if squeezed, she ought to be able to "pop up," fall over on her bilges if necessary and right herself again when the ice broke up.

She would be small and of shoal draft, enabling her to hug the shore line and avoid the heavy ice.

Remarkable work had been done in the past with small ships, where larger, heavier vessels had been crushed to pieces. The first ship to work her way between the huge icebergs of Melville Bay was the little *Discovery* of fifty-five tons, and with no gasoline or diesel power. She was so small, in fact, that her story of epic discovery was not believed for more than two centuries. The largest of Martin Frobisher's three vessels was of "thirty tons burthen," the next in size was of twenty tons, and the smallest, of ten.

By having a vessel small, the Eskimos could bury her in snow, a perfect insulator against extremely low temperatures encountered during the long sunless period beyond the Arctic Circle.

MacMillan also decided she should have two watertight bulkheads, so that if "I broke her stern off, she would float, and if damaged for'ard, she would still float, and if pressure of the ice pack broke her in half, both ends would float." And knowing that in those days neither diesel oil nor gasoline could be obtained after leaving Sydney, Nova Scotia, he decided her motive power should not only be small, but that her engine should be able to burn a mixture of whale oil, seal oil, and kerosene.

His ship would draw about ten feet, since this is roughly the rise and fall of arctic tides. This would enable him to run her ashore at high water, work on her bottom or propeller between tides, and float her off again at the next high tide. Most steamers in northern work, such as Peary's *Roosevelt,* had drawn too much water to make this possible.

The ship he wanted must be strong, so that if she did ground in uncharted waters or strike an ice pan, rugged construction would prevent anything other than local damage.

Naval architect John Alden said, "If I could get them, I'd never let anyone but the Hodgdon brothers in East Boothbay touch a boat of mine." And William H. Hand of New Bedford, whom Dan had asked to design the new vessel, said the same thing. MacMillan went to East Boothbay to see the brothers Hodgdon, Charles, Will, and George, whose family was famous for building ships up to and including three-masted schooners.

He wanted a schooner, he said, and he wanted them to

build her. What did they think she would cost? They listened to him and ventured to suggest it might amount to $35,000 to do what he wanted done. He did not say to them expressly that he had only two or three thousand dollars but that he had some good friends, Jerry Look among them, who would help him raise the money. He did say that he would pay each of the three brothers $10 a day for work on the schooner until she was finished. Would they? They would, and they did, and without any contract, either.

The result was the *Bowdoin,* named for Dan's alma mater, a pole-masted, gaff-headed, spoon-bowed schooner that some marine authorities have suggested is the strongest wooden vessel in the world. Of sixty tons, equipped with a forty-horsepower engine, and sheathed with ironwood up to the waterline as protection against ice, she aroused the admiration of everybody who worked on her and since then of everybody who ever sailed aboard her. Deep enough to stand up stiffly in a half gale of wind, her lines were nevertheless so "easy" that she was comfortable butting into a head sea, efficient under limited power either ahead or astern, and would turn on a dime. She was paid for by "friends" from all over the country, who purchased shares in her, and incidentally in the future of arctic exploration, at the going rate of $100 apiece.

MacMillan already had his objective selected: the first expedition would go to Baffin Island, to the Foxe Channel on its western shores. Foxe had looked into it in 1631; Parry had sailed up its western coast in 1821, but its eastern shores were virtually unknown. Vague reports of the natives, and of a German, Bernhard Hantzsch, the first ever to cross it, had resulted in the rough delineation of two large lakes known as Nettiling (Place of Little Ringed Seals) and Amadjuak. MacMillan believed that there must be hundreds of lakes in such a land which is barely above the level of the sea.

Nor had he forgotten an incident which occurred as he stood on the bridge of the *Thetis,* anchored in Erik Cove near Cape Wolstenholme in the fall of 1920. Old and young blue geese (*Chen caerulescens*) were alighting in the harbor. They were arriving from a northerly direction. Was it not reasonable to assume, he asked himself, that the blue geese were breeding on Baffin Island?

Arthur Cleveland Bent of Taunton, Massachusetts, a noted ornithologist, had written: "To find the breeding resorts of the blue goose is one of the most alluring of the unsolved problems in American ornithology." By wintering with the new *Bowdoin* in Foxe Channel for a year, MacMillan believed it would be possible to solve this problem.

Learning of the destination of the *Bowdoin,* the Carnegie Institution of Washington, D.C., expressed a desire to cooperate by establishing a scientific station on Baffin Island for the study of terrestrial magnetism and atmospheric electricity.

Mac chose Jot Small for his mate on this trip. Harold Whitehouse of Boothbay, Maine, long employed at several east-coast shipbuilding plants, was the engineer, and Thomas McCue, Newfoundlander, who began his career at the age of eleven when he ran away on a square-rigger bound for China, was signed on as cook.

Ralph Robinson, whom Dan had known since the former

was a student at Worcester Academy, was general assistant for the expedition. Since they expected to do extensive work in terrestrial magnetism and atmospheric electricity, their "magnetic observers" included Richard Goddard (now Professor of Astronomy at Dartmouth College) of Winthrop, Massachusetts, Navy ensign, son of a marine engineer and grandson of a whaling captain, and Dawson Howell of Boston, a Navy lieutenant who had served on transatlantic convoy duty and in North Russia.

When they sailed from Wiscasset—selected as a departure point because it was away from the city's hubbub and comfortably cool to work in even in the summer months—the hold was crammed full. Every locker, shelf, and sea bag was bulging. In addition to the ordinary stores they had dolls galore for Eskimo children, contributed by American school pupils, fruit cakes, chocolates, salted peanuts, chewing gum, grape juice, and a deckload of lumber, oil, coal, kerosene, and drummed gasoline. The schooner was "below her marks" had there been a Plimsoll line, and her ironwood sheathing was six inches below the water line —which made it useless—but Dan knew that fuel, food, and coal consumption between Wiscasset and Hudson Strait would lighten the *Bowdoin* materially before they came to "ice country."

By August 23 they were north of the Arctic Circle. From the crow's-nest a "water sky" could be seen to the north, but there was no break in the ice pack either north or west. Mac decided to retreat south and east and attempt to circumnavigate the field; seven hours of steady work under power finally placed them in open water and he set the four "lowers" (jib, jumbo, foresail, and mainsail) and let the *Bowdoin* go northeast under sail.

Suddenly there appeared dead ahead a "growler," a compact mass of very old ice, black with dirt; these are to be avoided religiously if one thinks anything of his ship. Due to the helmsman's confusion, however, the schooner hit, dead center. If Mac had not been well down in the bottom of the crow's-nest, he would have been thrown out, headlong, by the impact. The engineer off watch and asleep, leaped from his bunk and sprang for the companionway, sure that they had hit the face of a cliff and would go down in a few minutes. Tom, also asleep, muttered "God!" and turned over for another nap. As for the *Bowdoin,* she bounded off the ice like a rubber ball and went serenely on her way, but for the remainder of the night at reduced speed. She had had her baptism under fire and emerged triumphant; the *Bowdoin* was sound and solid.

They finally rounded what they decided was King Charles Cape and discovered that what appeared to be mainland at first sight actually was a large island partly blocking the mouth of a deep-water harbor that would hold a hundred such vessels as theirs—a perfect sanctuary safe from whichever quarter the wind might blow. In they sailed, finding themselves in what was virtually an inland lake, save for the single narrow entrance. Their engine exhaust started an arctic hare and flushed ptarmigan feeding in a mossy spot near the beach. Here, Mac decided, was sufficient depth at low water, freedom from ice pressure and strong currents, an abundance of game, and a good water supply. Here the *Bowdoin* would remain for the winter.

This harbor, which MacMillan discovered, was not on the chart and it now is known as Schooner Harbor. The Canadian Government suggested that it be called Bowdoin Harbor, but Mac said he preferred to have the name Bowdoin given to a beautiful harbor which he had found in northern Labrador, an excellent refuge for anyone rounding Cape Chidley or Killinek, one of the danger spots of the North. This was done; it now is on the charts of Labrador, which MacMillan helped to edit in 1943–45.

They stripped the *Bowdoin* of her running rigging, ran out their heaviest anchor, heading her in the direction of what they believed to be the prevailing winds, ran a stern line to a rock on the beach, and took all the deckload, all provision and camping gear to the shore, well above the high-water mark. In the arctic night at fifty below they could not risk a ship fire and the possibility that home, food, and clothes might all be destroyed, without even wood left for shelter or fuel. Peary's *Roosevelt* was afire in 1905; Amundsen's *Gjoa* caught fire in 1903 and again in 1905, and the U.S.S. *Rogers* was burned at Siberia, and her crew retreated to an Eskimo village to avoid perishing.

The hunting parties immediately began to bring in ptarmigan, old squaws, and eider ducks, all very acceptable, for a supply of fresh meat is a sure preventive of scurvy, so prevalent among earlier arctic expeditions which subsisted largely on salt beef.

American whalemen in the North recognized this nearly

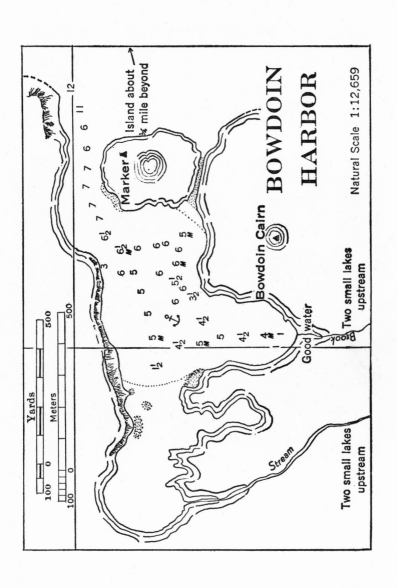

# BOWDOIN HARBOR

Natural Scale 1:12,659

Island about → ¼ mile beyond

Marker ▲

Bowdoin Cairn

Good water

Brook

Two small lakes upstream

Two small lakes upstream

Stream

Yards

Meters

500

500

100   0

100   0

a hundred years ago through association with the Eskimos. If a sailor showed scorbutic symptoms, he was sent immediately to the igloo of an Eskimo for "treatment," that is, to live on the Eskimo diet. Essentially this is meat, at least half of which is raw and half of that in a putrid condition. The total amount of vegetables, rockweed or green leaves, consumed by an Eskimo would certainly be less than two pounds per capita per year—and scurvy did not show up among the Eskimos until they began to eat the white man's food.

On an island at the mouth of the little harbor he had selected for winter quarters MacMillan erected a boat's mast as a flagpole, from the top of which fluttered a pillow-case, to let the Eskimos at Cape Dorset know where they had finally decided to stay. This small Eskimo population soon would be on its way to the Hudson's Bay Company Post at Cape Dorset.

On September 13 they heard two shots at the harbor mouth and a few minutes later four Eskimos were seen outlined against the sky on the hill crest west of the anchorage. It was Kavavu (Bee) and his brother, Nipatchee (he who stands upright), and their wives. They had come to help and within an hour came sailing back to camp with a polar bear jammed into the schooner's sixteen-foot sponson canoe. They had found the bear swimming at the harbor mouth when they went to set the trout net across a small stream.

Without mortar or cement the expedition erected a building twenty-three by eighteen feet and six feet high, out of morainic stones which they hand-carried on breasts, shoulders, and heads, one by one, for distances of twenty to four hundred feet. They wore holes in mittens, boots, and shirts, but the "dry dyking," led by Robinson, was eminently successful. Inside this rock wall they built a "double house" of beaverboard with a two-inch air space, through the floor of which projected cement pillars, firm bases for the magnetic instruments. The *Bowdoin*'s trysail was stretched as a flat roof for both buildings and held to the top of the rock walls by heavy bags of sand. Over this Jot constructed a regular A-roof of heavy canvas. Later, when snow was available, the Eskimos covered this with snow blocks.

An observatory was built by pitching a regular tent and building over this a snowhouse. Briefly, the work of the two observers was to determine the horizontal and vertical intensity of the earth's magnetic force; thus the observatory had to be "nonmagnetic"; it was, however, lighted with electricity supplied by the power plant aboard the *Bowdoin*.

This observatory really was a darkroom containing three instruments, each mounted upon a cement pier and containing a magnetic needle; two of these were suspended by quartz threads, the third swinging upon delicate bearings. Mirrors attached to these needles reflected a beam of light upon a drum covered with sensitized paper and revolved by clockwork once in twenty-four hours. The slightest deflection of the needle caused a ray of light to strike the drum at varying heights, which, upon development and measurement with reference to a horizontal line, revealed the local magnetic intensity.

Ice continued to pack around the *Bowdoin* and by October 10 she was clearly frozen in for the winter, which in this case meant they might not be able to break her out until July or August. It was comforting to know that her steel anchor chain had been tested for 20,000-pound breaking strength and that she was well sheathed with "greenheart," so that her planking would not suffer seriously.

No special provision was made for exercising personnel, for Mac believed "the benefits derived from compulsory gymnasium exercise are questionable and I think practically negligible." Instead he encouraged the men to go hunting and trapping, the latter "always with the hope there was a white fox at the end of the line for their sister, sweetheart, or wife, several of whom were well supplied the first day, for the men returned with a total of ten!"

As always, Mac spent a great deal of time studying the sky. An arctic winter can never be monotonous to one interested in astronomy, for nowhere is there more beautifully displayed than in the North sun pillars, parhelia, paraselenae, halos, coronae, glories, mirage, looming, fata morgana, and purple lights, all of which fairly run riot.

In December, Kavavu and Nipatchee, now hired as assistants and dog drivers, brought their wives, children, sisters, and old parents, Mac having given them permission to do so. All arrived on the seventh, the older people walking and the three little ones wrapped in caribou skins and bound with rawhide to the top of the loaded sledge, their snapping blackeyes and red cheeks deep within the warm covers, where they laughed and prattled. For the white man's goods the men would hunt, work, and drive sledges; the women would sew warm skin clothing, indispensable for winter travel.

231

At ten below zero the Eskimos decided to pass up an invitation to winter in the *Bowdoin*'s hold and to build their own snowhouses. They knew they would be warmer on a snow bed than on coils of rope in the frost-covered interior of the schooner. Within a half hour after they had begun their work on the houses the superiority of their craftsmanship over the Smith Sound Eskimo was apparent.

Building a good snowhouse is an interesting bit of work, for the Eskimo actually is constructing a twelve- and even eighteen-foot arch with apparently no support and yet so strong that when once completed the whole family can stand on the roof.

As they worked, all building material was cut from the inside, enabling one man to build his home and be independent of help, for all snow blocks are under his feet and need not be passed over the growing wall by an assistant. Snowhouses consist of about fifty blocks, roughly three by two feet; they are from twelve to eighteen feet in diameter and are constructed spirally from right to left, each block so beveled on edge and bottom as to be supported by the last in place. This enables the builder to hold the blocks with the left hand and to fit them by cutting with the right. In the meantime his wife is chinking the joints on the outside with loose snow.

Within two hours their winter homes were complete, both opening into a common porch and a single snow entrance. The snow beds were raised two feet from the floor and covered with skins. The next day large windows, made of blocks of clear ice from the neighboring pond, were fitted into the sloping walls. Many might doubt that such a

232

home could be comfortable, yet when lined with sealskins or an old tent, with seal-oil lamps lighted, pot boiling, and a weary victrola going, it is a palace to an Eskimo and a wonderful refuge for a white man from "the south" who has had a long march through rough ice against a cold and biting wind.

They encircled the igloos with a five-foot wall of snow which served as protection against drifting snow as well as being a nonconductor of cold, enabling the occupants to maintain an even temperature within. A hole in the roof, four inches in diameter, insured a plentiful supply of air. It is interesting to note that prior to the advent of the white men, tuberculosis was unknown among these people.

Once settled in their snowhouses, the Eskimo neighbors began daily (and nightly) visits to the cabins of the *Bowdoin* which were mutually enjoyed. Mac noted that "so much that is far from the truth has been written about these people. That they eat blubber, devour the oil of the stove lamp, eat soap and candles, abandon and even murder their old people, weep when the sun sets in the fall, and have a 'very rapid subcutaneous circulation' et cetera are all contrary to my study of them . . .

"Innuit they call themselves and should be called by us, for our term 'Eskimo' is one of contempt and of Indian origin, meaning an eater of raw meat. Innuit is the plural of innuk, meaning man, and may even justify the translation of some authorities into 'the people' or the 'real people' or the 'only people,' depending on the temperament of the reader. The word root 'innua' implies that which man has, the inner man, himself; therefore, his soul."

At Christmas all the Eskimos were invited to dinner with the white men and they had heaping plates of turkey (cooked and canned by a Boston firm months before) and vegetables, topped off with nuts, raisins, and cigars. When their dinner had settled, they went out on the ice for fireworks. Possibly the Roman candles preferred the snugness of their warm wrappers to a freezing whiz through space, for many of them uttered only feeble protest and died on the spot. But those that did go off brought forth startling yells from the audience, especially from old Ooktookhe, who vigorously waved his candle and crowed like a rooster.

After the Eskimos had unwrapped their gifts, they prevailed upon Mary, wife of Nipatchee, to play a few selections on her new accordion—purchased recently for two fox skins at the Cape Dorset trading post—and she obliged with a couple of tunes picked up by listening to the victrola.

They all were looking forward to warm weather, especially to May, when the seals—a source of meat, boot soles, and boat bottoms for the Northlander—would enlarge their breathing holes and emerge to lie in the bright sunlight on the surface of the harbor ice.

The Baffin Island method of killing seals (*Phoca hispida*) differs little from that of North Greenland. A screen, measuring about five feet by three, is made of white cotton cloth, obtained in trade from the Hudson's Bay Company. When attached to its frame, a cross of wood, it resembles a boy's square kite. Grasping this in the left hand and rifle in the right, the Eskimo searches the harbor on a bright sunny day looking for a basking seal, whose dark form is in striking contrast to the white of the snow.

Holding the screen low (the Eskimo contends the seal cannot see above the height of a man's knees) the hunter boldly approaches to within one hundred yards of his quarry. He then crouches low enough for the screen to conceal his whole body, cautiously peeping over the top of it, watching the seal's every movement.

When the seal lifts his head following a short nap, the Eskimo halts and hides behind the screen. When the seal drops his head, the Eskimo advances. At thirty yards he props the screen firmly on the ice, sits down, takes careful aim around the right-hand end of his shelter, and fires. Not more than 25 per cent of all shots fired succeed in stopping the seal dead on the ice, for the creature is generally within two feet of his hole, and even when mortally wounded, manages to roll over and slide down the incline into the sea where it sinks to the bottom and is lost.

Generally speaking, the rifle probably has done more harm than good in the Far North because of the Eskimo's love of shooting at every living thing, regardless of the fact that it may be utterly impossible to secure the wounded or dead animal. MacMillan on several occasions suggested to them that such acts might spell hard times and possibly starvation in the future. They admitted the possibility and seemed to repent temporarily, but the very next day would bring the same sort of behavior, apparently a manifestation of the primitive love to kill.

Birds were becoming more plentiful every day. Arctic owls were seen on almost every knoll, evidently migrating northward from Canada and northern New England. To Mac's surprise, several pairs of duck hawks (*Falco pere-*

*grinus anatum*) began building their nests on the high cliffs bordering Schooner Harbor. This species is the "noble peregrine of falconry," and the Eskimos termed it the most fearless and strongest bird of the North; even the owl and white gyrfalcon feared its attack.

In late June, MacMillan witnessed a convincing demonstration of this. A flock of white and blue geese flew over the ship, heading north. With the suddenness of a flash of lightning there was a downward rush of an apparently black ball from a clear sky, right into the midst of the birds. A white goose fell from the flock to the harbor ice, closely followed by the duck hawk. Mac ran toward them both; the hawk hovered over his head for a few minutes, turned, and flew directly for its nest on the north side of the harbor. The snow goose, dazed by the shock of attack and the fall, managed to take wing and escape in a few moments.

Dan reasoned that the hawk, with a short, curved bill, could never strike a blow strong enough to stun a six-pound goose. Could he possibly do it with his feet? Yes, said the Eskimos; the blow was delivered with the hawk's talons knotted into "fists."

Examination of the females of several birds shot at this season revealed a very interesting fact. The ptarmigan generally lays eight eggs and begins incubating. To MacMillan's surprise, in every bird examined they found from seventy-five to ninety eggs. By thus holding in reserve until needed eight and ten times the number of eggs laid, nature insured perpetuation of the species and made up for the tremendous loss of eggs due to the depredations of ermine, fox, and man. If not needed, these eggs are absorbed in the body. He examined several other kinds of birds to find out if this condition prevailed and invariably found clusters of minute eggs resembling small bunches of grapes.

Bumblebees, flies, and mosquitoes also appeared in June, with the blossoming of the first flower in the North, the purple saxifrage. Just how far north these insects go Mac still does not know, but he recorded mosquitoes 7½ degrees from the Pole and caterpillars even farther north. He constantly urged his party to endeavor in every way to add to the collections of insects for science. Some were more diligent than others. Bromfield was especially interested; McCue, the Newfoundlander, would rather shoot polar bears. They passed each other one day back among the hills, Bromfield returning from the hunt shouldering a big .38-caliber Winchester and Tom McCue carrying a Savage .303.

Tom shouted across the valley, "What did you get?"

"Two spiders and three flies," replied Bromfield.

McCue picked up his rifle and plodded on, now and then looking back over his shoulder and shaking his head in amazement.

Late in June, MacMillan sledged out of Schooner Harbor, bound for the only Eskimo encampment on the western coast of Baffin Island, a village of about thirty persons, living in sealskin and cloth tents. Evidently the natives had seen him coming from a long way off, for all were scrubbed and shining with hair combed and seemed glad to have visitors. Nearly all were women who came out to greet Mac and his drivers; most of the men were away hunting in the North.

One of the women remembered Captain Spicer, for whom the Spicer Islands in Foxe Channel were named thirty years earlier for she and her husband had lived on the ship for several winters with the Americans.

In the village they were shooting ptarmigan with bows and arrows, evidently not caring to waste their ammunition upon such small game. They were astonishingly accurate, often sending the small arrow directly through the head of the bird; it was the first time MacMillan had seen such primitive hunting in any tribe he had ever visited.

On June 22 they passed the fresh tracks of a polar bear and two cubs, the first seen that year. The tracks told an interesting story. The mother had stationed the two cubs behind a block of ice. She then started out toward a seal, evidently sunning himself at an ice hole. The little ones, impatient, had dashed out from behind the block and started toward their mother. The mother turned back and had plainly punished her children, for there were signs of a scuffle in the snow. She led them again back to the block of ice and once more crept out toward the seal. The tracks stopped abruptly and led back again toward the cubs. The seal, probably initially disturbed by the cubs and their "spanking," had slipped back into his hole and escaped.

By the time they had returned to Schooner Harbor the warming July weather made it clear that they should get ready for departure. The harbor ice was still about four feet thick, and to hasten the melting process they sprinkled forty bags of sand all about the ship and to a distance of thirty yards ahead of the schooner, leading out to the big anchor. The sand absorbed the warm rays of the sun and began to "eat down" into the ice; within three weeks it had cut a channel almost as perfectly as one could do it with a saw.

They steamed ahead, picked up the anchor, and moved the *Bowdoin* into a small bight on the eastern side of the harbor entrance. At low water Mac picked out a place free of rocks and on the next tide ran the schooner up onto the beach. The tide ebbed and over she went, so far in fact that his crew declared she never would come back.

The engineer went to work on the propeller, which had been bent on the trip up, pounding it back into perfect shape.

Then they watched the tide returning in the afternoon, wondering whether the *Bowdoin* really would float upright with such sharp bilges. They had "battened" (fastened down) all hatches and "secured" all companionway and other openings. The water crept slowly up her side, went in through the scuppers and started up the deck, toward the main hatch, but only for six inches. She slowly righted and, on the high water, floated. "Billy" Hand had done his work well.

They backed the *Bowdoin* off, anchored her in the little harbor, and started for home the next morning. The new schooner had proved her worth and borne out MacMillan's theories on what an arctic vessel should be by successfully wintering in the ice and being the first ship to circumnavigate the difficult Foxe Channel.

Although ice conditions and lack of snow on the land for dog teams had prevented the expedition from visiting the nesting grounds of the blue geese, MacMillan was certain they were nesting about the shores of the lakes in the interior.

Accordingly he directed the factor of the Hudson's Bay Post at Cape Dorset, to send an Eskimo into the interior to obtain a clutch of the eggs. This was done in the winter of 1922–23 and the eggs now are in the Museum of The Historical Association of Provincetown, the first ever brought out of the north.

# 15

FOR FIFTEEN MONTHS in 1923 and 1924 MacMillan commanded an expedition sponsored by the Carnegie Institution and by the National Geographic Society, which wintered at Refuge Harbor, North Greenland.

The expedition established a "nonmagnetic" scientific station, conducted tidal and meteorological observations, and performed extensive work in botany, geology, ornithology, and anthropology. Mac himself sledged two thousand miles along the shores of Greenland, Ellesmere Island, Bay Fjord, and Eureka Sound.

It is not, however, for any of these reasons that the 1923–24 trip aboard the *Bowdoin* was singular; rather, it is because of what happened in the categories of communications and shipwreck.

By August 6, 1923, Dan had realized a dream of six years, to visit Greenland in "my own little ship," for they arrived at Cape York, North Greenland, at 11 in the morning, after picking their way between the ice and land for more than thirty miles. Five Eskimos immediately came off

241

in kayaks, men whom he had known for fifteen years.

Two days later they had reached Etah and anchored overnight in front of "the site of our old home of 1913–17," and Mac rowed in to see what was left. Every particle of wood had disappeared, "but a mass of heterogeneous articles, all useless, lay scattered about the grounds, bringing up a flood of memories of our four happy years . . ."

On August 17 they steamed into Refuge Harbor, where to Mac's delight they found four fathoms (twenty-four feet) within fifty feet of the low-water mark, which meant the schooner could lie in close to the beach, and he decided to winter there "because all conditions are so ideal." He did not, however, know when the harbor froze or how early in the year it "unfroze," but the other factors, good hunting grounds, fresh water, and proximity to Cape Sabine by dog team, were too important to reject.

By the nineteenth they had unpacked the scientific instruments, and here—against the lonely background Mac knew so well, including solid ice to the horizon—they introduced the new communications factor. Don Mix of the American Radio Relay League was aboard, and they proposed to establish Station WNP (Wireless North Pole) and to make the first radio contact from the Arctic to the United States. As early as the nineteenth Mix had broadcast a report of their safety and given the location of the expedition in hope that someone might pick it up.

It was not, however, until September 9 that Mac was able to log: "Don succeeded in reaching home last night through a man in Prince Rupert, British Columbia, on the Pacific Coast, distant over three thousand miles. He sent him half of my message (to the press), also telegrams to Lettie (Mac's sister) and to Joe Cook of Chicago, requesting that he express my appreciation to the Central Graduate Association of Theta Delta Chi for the bronze tablet." (He had found it only the day before, where someone had tucked it in the *Bowdoin*'s lazarette for safekeeping shortly before sailing.) It was "in appreciation of [MacMillan's] service rendered to his fraternity and all mankind . . . as educator, scientist, explorer, author, and man."

This radio contact was a historic "first" in communications, and it worked both ways, for the first news the MacMillan expedition received was of the "terrible disaster in Japan and the death of a half million people in Tokyo, Yokohama, and other cities." It was a great step forward from the days when the Crocker Land Expedition had spent virtually an entire war in the Arctic, without knowing much about it.

Excerpts from the radio log, almost grotesquely interspersed with Mac's journal notations on sledging and polar-bear hunts, reveal graphically how well the expedition's equipment succeeded in bringing civilization to the threshold of the Arctic:

From Chicago, September 28—"Dear Mac, from October third on we will broadcast messages from your families and will endeavor each week to have one of your friends or relatives talk to you. American newspapers already have carried one million lines on your expedition . . . E. F. McDonald, Jr."

MacMillan noted on November 27: "Left Etah at 4 A.M. Reached the ship at noon. Hard sledging over rocks and bare ground on Cape Ohlsen."

A little later, on January 1, 1924, the radio brought to him and his expedition party, "The best wishes with all compliments of the holiday season . . . the whole American people join me [in wishing] for the health and safety of you all and for the success of the expedition. Calvin Coolidge."

February 3: "Your observatory work and copy of radio reports on satisfactory character of building conditions of instrumental installation and progress of observations aroused much interest . . . (in Washington)."

February 11: "MacMillan why in the world no stories coming back from you for North American Newspaper Alliance? They are hungry for material."

Meanwhile the Arctic was continuing to be its old rigid self, radio notwithstanding, and Mac noted that "conditions were miserable in the house (ashore): with both primus stoves going and also an Eskimo lamp, we could not raise the temperature to zero."

On March 25, he wrote from Nerke, "Here just after midnight after a fifty-mile march over the icecap. We sledged down to Cape Alexander and partly over the glacier. Etukasuk thought we had better go over the icecap to Peteravik [because] we could see open water all along the coast.

"Possibly forty below zero. Abram Bromfield, the interpreter, froze one wrist badly. As I walked ahead of both teams practically to the summit, I was dead tired, with cramps in both thighs and covered with sweat.

"When we finally reached the sea ice at the foot of the

A strong snowhouse, warm and comfortable, is welcome at the end of a rugged day of exploration; three Eskimos can construct a dwelling like this in an hour.

Formed by the rise and fall of tide on the face of every cliff, the icefoot often is the only arctic "highway" for Eskimos and their dogs.

**Protecting** her young, the mother's raised paw suggests there is substance to the legend that polar bears are "left-handed." MacMillan took this striking photo from *Bowdoin's* deck.

Frozen in solidly for eleven months, the schooner *Bowdoin*, most northern ship in the world, lies in lonely Refuge Harbor, North Greenland. *(Photo by Professor Richard Goddard, Dartmouth College)*

ABOVE: This colorfully-beaked Northerner is an arctic puffin (Fratucula artica naumanni), one of the few birds which nests in a hole in the ground. BELOW: Thousands of these dovekies (Alle alle), known as little auks, nest in rock debris at the base of Etah's cliffs in North Greenland, with Brother John's Glacier in the background.

Clements Markham Glacier, to my surprise, the Eskimos wanted to keep right on to Nerke and to warm Eskimo igloos there, which we did.

"The village was deep in sleep when we drove in, but was instantly all astir with excitement. Naturally, I was expected to sleep in the big igloo of Ahpellah, the same who went with Dr. Cook. I chose that of his brother, however, Arklio and his wife, Alnaghito, because it was free of children, most of whom had some kind of a skin disease. We talked until three in the morning.

On April 18, "in a tent for the first time this year," he was camped with his Eskimos at the foot of the Sutherland Island Glacier which they had crossed in the hopes of a good run to Sulwuddy. He wrote: "I had a mishap today which resulted in a broken sledge. The south side of the glacier is generally swept clean and the snow compacted by the wind into a hard, flinty surface. The dogs are generally excited at this stage of the journey and always begin a mad gallop.

"The Eskimos all used skin drags, that is, heavy rawhide line wound around the smooth runners of their sledges to increase friction. I had often been down before with no drags and away I went. Kakotcheeah stood at the bottom with his whip to stop my dogs, but when he realized the terrific rate at which they were coming, he ran to one side.

"I would have arrived safely had it not been for a slippery spot at the slight turn. It was exactly a snap-the-whip effect. The sledge went bodily sideways, completely overturned two or three times. I don't remember when I left the sledge, but was well ahead of it, striking on the back of my head and rolling over several times.

"The sledge was a wreck, one side being split in three places. This, although apparently serious to a white man, was made light of by my Eskimos. They always repair my lashing. We had no drill, therefore they shot holes through the side of the sledge with my .22-caliber rifle and soon had her nearly as good as new. To draw the crack together, they used the twisting method—a dog trace and the handle of a hatchet."

Early in May, Mac decided to go to Cape Sabine and put up a Greely memorial tablet near Starvation Camp; this had been one of the objectives of the expedition. He left the ship about noon on May 6, with Ralph Robinson, Richard Goddard, and John Jaynes and three Eskimos, immediately running into a thick snowstorm. They had no compass but could now and then see a faint sun, the direction of which, when checked by their watches, gave them a rough course to go by.

With very little food on the sledges for seven men, they could not face the possibility of a two- or three-day storm out in Smith Sound, so they plugged along for twelve hours, finally hitting Sabine "right in the eye, just north of Brevoort Island." It was so thick when they reached Starvation Camp that Mac decided to bed down on the ice and take the sledges through the pressure ridges to the shore in the morning; it was impossible to see well enough to pick the best route at night.

The next day, having arrived at the site of Greely's Camp Clay, which is marked by the four walls of the rock hut, they examined every boulder in the immediate vicinity as a possible base for the bronze tablet, which measured four by three feet. They finally decided upon a large stone at the sound end of Cross Lake, three quarters of the way to Cemetery Ridge and distant from the house one hundred and seventy-five yards; it had a natural, flat sloping surface, and Mac felt it "would serve admirably for our purpose." Jaynes and Robinson worked all the afternoon and evening, drilling holes for the expansion bolts.

On May 8 MacMillan wrote: "Put the finishing touches on the tablet this morning and took motion pictures of the unveiling, which we did by drawing aside a large American flag. Both Eskimos and my own party stood by the rock."

The tablet reads: "To the Memory of the Dead Who Under Lieutenant A. W. Greely Here Gave Their Lives to Ensure the Final and Complete Success of the First Scientific Cooperation of the United States with Other Nations, 1881–1884. Erected by The National Geographic Society, 1923."

Thus was honored, at the instigation of the National Geographic Society, one of America's foremost arctic heroes. Greely and his party had lived in a well-built home at Lady Franklin Bay, some 235 miles northeast from this site. There they had stayed for two years, accomplishing scientific work, taking meterological observations, even breaking the world's record of "farthest north."

But a ship from home failed to reach them in 1882 as promised, and failed again in 1883. These army men of the Greely party obeyed their orders and retreated south in open boats to try to meet a ship at the edge of the ice. Fifty-one days over a zig-zag trail of 500 miles of difficult travel, their journey was one of the most arduous ever undertaken in arctic work. Imprisoned by ice, they finally made their way to Cape Sabine, expecting to meet a Government vessel there. Instead, in a rock cairn, they found a heartbreaking letter informing that the rescue ship had gone to the bottom within sight of their camp and the crew had gone home in small boats.

Greely's men were, by bitter circumstance, condemned to a fate that would mean death for most of them by slow and agonizing starvation. These were the men whom the tablet honored, this the spirit of scientific zeal which was commemorated by the tablet on the stone at Cross Lake.

In the following days motion pictures of musk oxen were taken (a maddened bull charged within six inches of his tripod camera, forcing him to abandon it momentarily)— incidentally, these were the first movies ever taken of musk oxen—magnetic observations were completed, specimens of birds, rocks, and eggs were carefully packed away. Past Victoria Head, up Flagler Bay, they had discovered the remains of an Eskimo village possibly a thousand years old, for they were then on the old migration trail of the Smith Sound native, evidence of whom was found by the Norsemen in South Greenland as far back as 986.

They had driven their dogs over the hills of Ellesmere Island, down into Bay Fjord, on to Eureka Sound and Axel Heiberg Island, where they found coal in abundance, a leaf-bearing Tertiary deposit of a hundred million years before.

Now they thought of going home.

June is the melting month in the North. Snowbanks disappear; water trickles down the faces of cliffs, and brooks run merrily through the valleys. In June pools and puddles appear on the surface of the sea ice, followed normally by a rapid breakup of harbor ice and a drifting away of the floating pans, large and small. Blue water can be seen then, and one knows summer has come.

But no such change occurred at Refuge Harbor. By the latter part of July, when the *Bowdoin* had been locked in the ice more than three hundred days, MacMillan grew somewhat alarmed. Was it possible that Refuge did not break out each summer? He asked Etukasuk, who said that he thought some years it did and some years it didn't, and that was no comfort at all. It was not wise to let time answer the question, either, for they were not provisioned for two years; if caught, it would be necessary to abandon ship and retreat south to the winter igloos of the Eskimos.

Dan decided to do what he could to help himself. For days they strewed parallel lines of ashes from the galley stove upon the harbor ice from the bow of the *Bowdoin* to the nearest point of land dead ahead. Ice can be easily but slowly cut by placing dark material on its surface, which absorbs heat from the sun's rays. The black path of ashes led to a margin of open water bordering the shore—a narrow lane leading to the harbor entrance, now their only exit.

Mac spent days sounding every foot of the way and believed he had located every ledge and boulder that might bar their progress. There was one particularly dangerous spot on the north shore, a granite ledge which projected under the water nearly to the edge of the harbor ice. This was visible on the mean low water and partly exposed on the spring tides. The rise and fall was ten feet. The *Bowdoin* drew ten feet; there obviously was no margin here. A strong northerly wind, for which he hoped, might be of help in blowing the ice sheet away from the shore, thus widening and deepening the channel.

On the night of July 29, at dead high water, he decided to make the attempt, wind or no wind, Mac himself took the wheel, figuring that if anything went wrong, he would rather be personally responsible. They crept along at dead slow speed, "smelling" their way past the ice sheet.

The schooner's spoon bow crunched the ash-strewn lane into smithereens and they gained the open water along the shore. So far, so good, but now came the real test. Thirty yards ahead was the ledge, exactly ten feet below the surface. Ordinarily the *Bowdoin* would require the same amount of water; maybe, Mac thought hopefully, relieved of much of her cargo during the winter, she might draw only nine feet tonight.

He ordered full speed ahead, figuring that if she caught, maybe he could bounce her over it. This was it, and he held his breath, as did the mate McCue in the forerigging, watching the water depth.

Bang!

She had hit hard. He jingled the engine room for "full ahead" again. A puff of black smoke poured out from under her counter and the water churned astern. She refused to budge. He rang for reverse at full speed. No movement, not even with all the crew—weighing more than a half ton—mustered aft in hopes they might raise her bow enough to ease off.

They were caught solidly on "dead high water," which is to say that the tide was falling and there would be a lot less water there before there was as much again. They were hard and fast aground at the top of the world, with no help.

They took soundings forward and aft and discovered the only shoal spot was exactly amidships and apparently directly under the schooner's keel. She was caught on a pinnacle rock, and when the tide went down she would be flat on her side. There was a good chance that her back might be broken from the strain of supporting her whole weight at one point. It was equally possible that she might crush her bottom lying on her bilge or that she might fail to right herself with the rising tide and be filled with water through the hatches and companionways. If the latter happened, she would be submerged and a total wreck.

There was one course available to them—to try to keep her on an even keel and, as for breaking her back, hope for the best. Mac ordered the peak halyards run out to a huge rock on the side of the cliff and the throat halyards to an anchor in the harbor ice. This gave him two block-and-tackle rigs, one out on either side, which he could tighten or slacken in order to keep the vessel upright. With a spirit level on the chart table in the cabin, he watched the bubble move slowly from right to left, meanwhile yelling instructions to his crew to tighten up, now starboard, now port.

Concerned, he ordered the cook, who was seventy, the oldest man aboard, to leave for a safer place on the harbor ice. Fastening a rope about his waist, the mate lowered him to an ice cake alongside, on which he paddled off some distance.

When the *Bowdoin* was half out of water, the crew was whispering and tiptoeing about the decks and cabins as if afraid of awakening her from sleep.

Since the harbor ice was afloat and, under sufficient strain, could be pulled bodily toward the ship, it was Mac's plan to have the cliff sustain most of the weight by slacking off slightly more on the lines on that side. He dropped over the vessel's side on a rope and, taking up a position directly aft of the vessel, decided that her slight heel away from the cliff was exactly what he wanted. Four men now remained on board.

At that instant they all heard the rattle and thud of falling rocks on the hillside and the unforgettable "twang" of manila parting under great strain. Both lines to the cliff had snapped, and the schooner fell with a tremendous splash, flat on her port side, with the rail from the fore-rigging to the quarter bitt aft completely submerged.

Aboard ship, everything not tied down slid across the deck, into the bilges, off shelves and bunks, with a tremendous conglomeration of bangs and rattles, crunches and smashing noises.

Mac recalled: "Mix, Goddard, and Jaynes happened to be on deck, standing on the starboard side. Hearing the snap of the lines followed by a slight movement of the ship, Mix and Goddard sprang for the rail, straddled and gripped it with their hands and knees. Jaynes evidently tried but failed to mount and found himself in the air. Down he went and disappeared into a mass of water and rubble ice. Robinson was below in the after cabin. He felt the tremor of the ship and rushed for the companionway. Upon gaining the

252

afterdeck, he endeavored to save himself by grasping the four-foot binnacle. His hands slipped from the polished brass top, and away he went, flat on his belly, into the water, well clear of the rail."

The mate was with MacMillan, on the ice. Mac sang out to him to help Jaynes while he ran along the ice edge to get Robinson. In a few moments they had pulled both of them out, shivering, wet, and breathing hard, but with nothing broken; they got them both aboard again and wrapped them in blankets in their bunks in the after cabin. Jaynes swore that the schooner "went out from under him."

As the tide fell, it could be seen that the schooner's keel was caught on top of a ledge and that three planks on the port side were crushed and splintered. There was no great cause for optimism; it seemed very likely that when the tide came back the vessel would fill from the top and that would be the end of her. Yet to give up was unthinkable, for to lose the schooner was to jeopardize the lives of all of them.

If she would float on the flood tide, there was a chance. If she would not, they were lost. She had to be lightened, to give her every advantage. Working hurriedly, they first took off everything that would be necessary to sustain life if they had to proceed south in open boats—tents, camping equipment, blankets, weapons, and provisions. Next they went to work in the vessel's behalf, emptying all water tanks, dropping both 600-pound anchors over the bow, and letting out most of 180 fathoms of chain. Then they calked all hatches and portholes, turning her into the equivalent of a corked bottle.

They had done all they could. They went back to their

meager camp on the ice to wait.

It was a grim show. Inexorably the tide returned, crept up the slanting deck toward the midship hatch. Had they calked it sufficiently tight? Now the water was playing along the sides of the cabins, beginning to lap at the portholes—and now, now it had reached the cabin doors!

Suddenly it seemed as if the *Bowdoin* became conscious of what was happening to her, realized how unbecoming it was for a vessel to allow herself to become submerged. Inch by inch, while they held their breath lest some of her gear might carry away with the great strain, she righted herself, until she floated on even keel once more as the tide neared its crest.

"Everybody aboard!" Mac yelled. "John, start your engine."

Jaynes started the engine. Mac jingled for full ahead, full astern. It was the same story. The *Bowdoin* was not going anywhere on this tide. "Well," said MacMillan with a forced smile, "that was a rehearsal. Now we'll do the thing all over again, only better." Soundings had revealed that the tide had not risen as high as it had twelve hours before; the only real hope was that it would next time and that their supporting lines to cliffs and ice pan would hold on the second try.

They ran out the halyards again, fitted out with brand-new line, and this time Mac decided to let her list toward the cliffs, allowing her to settle into a bed of rocks. This she did, but slightly too fast and too hard, cracking another plank. The planking, however, was of minor concern to him; the builder had poured twenty-one tons of concrete into her bilges as inside ballast, molded into her frames, and that would help a great deal.

Twelve hours later they got a break—a foot more water than the previous high tide. At exactly "dead high" Mac jingled for slow ahead, the diesel rumbled, the clutch went in, and she was moving! Quickly he rang for "Stop!" blew the air whistle impatiently to signal the eleven Eskimos and seventy dogs to hurry aboard, complete with tents, kayaks, pots, and killing irons. They scrambled, boosted, grunted, yipped and scratched, and finally were all aboard, disheveled and in heaps.

Now, surely, they were off. But it was not to be so. During the slight delay to take aboard the Eskimos a small iceberg, driven by a southwesterly wind, popped around the corner of the bluff and, like a stopper in a jug, completely closed the only exit.

From the ice barrel Mac studied the situation. On the starboard side the berg pressed against the shore. Not even a kayak could squeeze between. But on the port hand it might be done, where part of the old winter ice impinged against the berg—if the *Bowdoin* could just crack that ice and shove it to one side.

"John," he yelled to the engineer, "I'm going to back her to the end of the channel. Then we'll give her full ahead and hit the ice up there and see if we can bust it. We may be able to split it and sneak out through the broken pieces before the berg slides to leeward and closes it up again."

Dan slid down the halyard to the deck to take charge.

First at half, then at full speed, the schooner charged down upon the ice "gate" that they must open or stay North another year. All hands were on deck and hanging on, waiting for the inevitable shock of collision. The *Bowdoin,* all sixty tons of her, stopped short and everything aboard, below and aloft, animate and inanimate, went skittering forward in a heap.

Mac was chagrined. The ice must be thicker and heavier than he had thought. He went forward to inspect damage and found, to his great relief, that her steel-shod oak stem was not even dented but that wiggling away from her bow was a fine, threadlike crack through the middle of the ice pan.

"Give it to her!" he yelled to the engine room, running aft.

The little schooner leaned into that crack, churning up a magnificent wake with her efforts, opened it up to a yard, then two, and finally wide enough to squeeze through. To windward the big berg pressed threateningly against the pan, but with full speed ahead they shot out into open water, a strong southwesterly and a heavy sea, bound for home, the *Bowdoin* slightly battle-scarred but totally unvanquished.

# 16

ONE GREAT AREA of the Polar Sea remained a mystery in 1925—roughly that section between Alaska and the Pole and northwest of Axel Heiberg Island. At least twice land had been reported here and tidal experts had predicted that it would be found. The quest for this land had been the primary object of the Crocker Land Expedition, and Mac-Millan had concluded that since the area is "inaccessible by ship and extremely difficult to reach with dogs, it awaits exploration by air."

Since no one ever had visited this territory in summer, the amount of open water at this period was unknown, but it was assumed that in the late part of the season there would be a number of large open leads which would permit the use of an aircraft capable of landing on water.

The National Geographic Society sponsored the expedition of 1925. MacMillan's four assistants were Lieutenant Benjamin H. Rigg of the U. S. Coast and Geodetic Survey, as magnetic and tidal observer; Dr. Walter N. Koelz, from the University of Michigan, ornithologist; and Maynard

Owen Williams and Jacob Gayer, correspondent and photographer, respectively, of the National Geographic Society. The first natural color photographs of the Arctic were taken on this trip.

The United States Navy co-operated generously, assigning to the expedition a unit of eight men and three amphibious planes, Loenings, which were the best available at that time. This aviation unit was under the command of Lieutenant Commander Richard E. Byrd, Jr., of the Bureau of Aeronautics.

The expedition was to be a two-ship affair; the *Bowdoin* was to be accompanied by the steamship *Peary,* which was the former steam yacht *Rowena,* built on the lines of a French trawler, purchased by MacMillan from a sports editor of the Hearst newspapers and renamed after Mac's former commander, Robert E. Peary. The *Peary's* skipper was Captain George E. Steele of Gloucester, an able master mariner. Lieutenant Commander Eugene F. McDonald, Jr., second in command of the expedition, was in charge of radio equipment, for it was intended, via the code operators of the American Radio Relay League, to remain in day-to-day contact, not only with the United States, but even farther points. The *Peary* carried the naval unit and the three planes; the smaller *Bowdoin* had stowed aboard spare parts, three plane engines, and 1,500 gallons of gasoline.

After some difficulties with ice and minor groundings the vessels arrived at Etah in a snowstorm on August 1. The schedule was tightly arranged because the crews of the ships numbered thirty-nine men and they had provisions only for three months; MacMillan planned to depart about August

25. The task of landing and assembling planes, of establishing food and fuel stations on Ellesmere Island, and of flying at least two thousand miles must all be done within this allotted time.

The *Bowdoin*'s men at once began work on the landing beach, removing all stones and boulders and smoothing it up until it was acceptable to Commander Byrd and his crew. The wooden sides of the boxes in which the wings had been crated were laid on the ground as runways to the water's edge, their ends weighted with rocks.

Within two days all three planes were assembled and in the air. At nightfall MacMillan was piloted on the first flight over Greenland, but the engines were not running satisfactorily.

On the sixth two planes were loaded to the limit with gas and supplies, with the intention of establishing a substation across Smith Sound. They failed to get off the water. Rain, fog, and low-lying clouds did their worst.

On the eighth, two Eskimos came walking over the stony hills from Anoritok, nineteen miles away, to see the "giant birds" of the white men. They had heard the roar of the Liberty engines and had seen the black dots in the sky.

That evening the aviators flew to Cannon Fjord, on the western side of Ellesmere Island, hoping to establish a substation which might help them to Cape Thomas Hubbard, 250 air miles. Smith Sound was virtually covered with large sheets or pans drifting out of Kane Basin, the surface of which made a safe landing impossible either with skids or wheels. Narrow lanes of open water offered possible landing places in case of emergency, but once down, there would be no way of rising out of these leads until they had widened.

Dan wrote in his journal, "Imagine with what pleasure I looked down from a height of 5,000 feet upon big hills over which we laboriously pushed our sledges in 1914–16 and in '24. Stripped down to undershirts and reeking with sweat, we had wallowed in snow thigh-deep, yelling at our dead-tired dogs until our throats were raw and our voices gone.

"At that time, I looked up into the deep-blue sky of a beautiful May day and muttered to myself, 'Some day, the aviator will laugh at this!' The dream had come true, as dreams generally do if one persists in them."

He recognized old camping sites, recalled innumerable incidents of both suffering and triumph. There was the Reid Glacier, at right angles to the course of the valley, which it had blocked completely, forming a gigantic dam behind which was a lake large enough for them to have landed on if necessary. Alexandra Fjord, an inlet of Buchanan Bay, was inviting looking, with not a particle of ice and smooth as a mirror.

Now they headed out over the ice fields of Smith Sound for home. A few miles west of Littleton Island they saw a mother walrus and her baby sleeping on a pan of ice. As they dropped to an altitude of one hundred feet, the mother sleepily raised her head, roused by the thunder of the Liberty. She was plainly bothered by this strange creature, stirred uneasily, then prodded her little one, and away they lurched beneath the water, possibly refuting the theory that when animals encounter a new enemy for the first time they exhibit no fear.

As the waters of Beitstad Fjord had been found to be ice-free, it was decided to attempt to land supplies at its head, as such a station might be utilized on a return trip from Eureka Sound if food or fuel were needed. Two of the planes succeeded in reaching the mouth of the fjord but were unable to establish a station, owing to rough water and cross winds.

On August 12 the wind blew so hard from the south that nothing could be done. They spent the day watching the planes, to prevent them from going adrift.

Two planes got away on the fourteenth and succeeded in landing their first cache of supplies at the head of Flagler Fjord, 107 miles from the ship. They returned to Ellesmere Island in the evening but were unable to leave anything more because of drift ice. A realization of the fact that, because of prevailing ice conditions in the North, no dependence could be placed upon a supply station, once established, was a severe blow to the plans of the naval unit.

Mac conceded rather ruefully: "From my sledging experience and also from the reports of the natives, I had confidently believed that all of Flagler Fjord and Eureka Sound would be suitable for landing throughout the summer months."

By August 18, as a result of eighteen days' work, two small deposits of food and fuel had been advanced only 107 miles. One plane only was now available for flight, and her wireless equipment was not in working order.

Could they possibly fly two thousand miles in the remaining ten days? Yet this distance must be covered if airplanes were to accomplish the work left undone by the

Crocker Land Expedition's dog teams in 1914–17.

MacMillan, increasingly dubious about the cruising radius of the planes, even eliminating all possibility of accident and breakdown, felt there was no way that the task could be accomplished before September 1. They might even have reached Axel Heiberg Island and the edge of the Polar Sea, but nothing was to be gained by that, for Mac himself had sledged all over this area. Nothing, apparently, could be gained by remaining longer at Etah, and Mac-Millan therefore requested Byrd to give up all plans for further flights across Smith Sound and make ready to re-turn home.

MacMillan concluded, "Our decision to terminate the flight work seemed to be justified. The planes simply could not do the work required of them, at least not until the conditions so new and trying to planes had been studied and corrected."

MacMillan left for the Eskimo village of Kahna, twenty-five miles to the southeast, to visit his old dog driver, Etukasuk, and bring him back by plane if he cared to come.

The waters of Inglefield Bay were so filled with ice that for a few moments Mac doubted whether the pilot could make a landing in such rough water, for the wind was blowing at least forty miles an hour. But he dropped handily between the drifting ice pans and taxied up to the rocky shore, enabling Dan to land from one wing.

Etukasuk was there, all smiles. "Get your mittens on and come on!" Mac yelled to him. Without even inquiring where they were going, the Eskimo turned and ran into his *tupik* (sealskin tent) for the mittens. He reappeared in a moment, followed by his somewhat bewildered wife (it would be interesting to know what he told her he was going to do), climbed into the rear seat, and they were off.

As far as one could detect from his actions or facial expression, the Eskimo might have been flying all his life. His complete trust in the infallibility of the white man's creation and in the man who was operating it was evident. He and Inugeeto, who flew at Etah, probably were at that time the only Eskimos in the world to have flown.

Although the expedition's experiments with aviation were less than successful, they still marked the first use of planes in that area and paved the way for further use of aircraft in polar exploration. Beyond this, the trip also made possible the first practical use of short-wave radio by the U. S. Navy when the *Bowdoin* was at Etah, within eleven degrees of the North Pole.

The radio equipment was designed and built for the expedition by Zenith Radio Corporation, of which Lieutenant Commander McDonald then was president. On the other side of the continent, aboard the U. S. S. *Seattle,* flagship of the U. S. fleet then in the Pacific, was Fred Schnell, a young radio "ham" commissioned for the cruise at McDonald's suggestion.

As the U. S. fleet steamed west and the MacMillan expedition north, Schnell kept in constant touch with the *Bowdoin* by short wave. When the *Bowdoin* reached Etah and the fleet was off the Tasmanian coast, their short-wave communications were maintained with all parts of the United States, for the first time in radio history.

At this time MacMillan put a group of Eskimos in front

of the microphone at Etah to sing for Admiral Coontz of the Pacific fleet, sending the human voice almost exactly halfway around the world, a record that never had been approached in those days when most ship-to-ship communication and most amateur transmissions of any distance were tapped in code. Admiral Coontz commented that the Eskimos sounded like a college cheering section. MacMillan agreed.

The *Peary* arrived on the morning of the twenty-third at Igloodahouny and, leaving orders for her to follow the *Bowdoin* down the coast, the schooner proceeded to Kahna to land Etukasuk. Waters of this part of the North then were almost wholly uncharted. MacMillan wrote in his log, "Off the Redcliffe Peninsula (the tongue of land between McCormick Bay and Inglefield Bay). However, there is a dotted line indicating shoals. I might have known that this was put there by Peary and meant something definite, but a careful examination from the air on the day before failed to reveal any dangers.

"We were going at full speed about one mile off the beach when there came a tremendous crash, hard enough, it seemed, to rip the whole bottom out of our staunch little ship and sounding especially violent to me, since I was down in the cabin donning oilskins in anticipation of a heavy rainstorm."

Mac scrambled up the ladder to the afterdeck, and one glance was sufficient. The schooner was "high and dry," having run up on rocks so far that she obviously would be there until the next tide. Over the rail the gasoline must go, all thirty-nine barrels of it, and over it went into a choppy sea, but they fastened the barrels together and anchored them, eventually recovering all but two. The *Peary,* having received the *Bowdoin*'s signals, stood by to assist if needed.

At low water all hands walked around the rocks underneath her to survey the damage. They found the shoe (protecting the keel) almost completely gone and the keel itself so badly split and splintered that they trimmed off large sections with an ax. "Is she seaworthy enough to go home?" they asked Mac. "No question about it," he said confidently, and at high water they backed off, hoisted the lowers, and scudded down the wind for Cape Parry. They made one stop, working in through closely packed ice to stop at a small Eskimo encampment to leave some presents sent North by "Miss Miriam Look of Providence, Rhode Island," the daughter of Jerry Look who had evidenced a strong and continuing interest in Mac's arctic work.

One of the secondary objectives of the expedition was a survey of the Norse ruins of Greenland. Near Godthaab was situated the so-called "Western Settlement" of the Norsemen, consisting of about ninety farms and four churches, and Governor Simony appointed Borreson, resident physician, as guide for the MacMillan expedition to a Norse building, the best then standing in the settlement.

The Godthaab Fjord is sixty miles in length and as beautiful as it is long, presenting a composite reproduction of Norway and Switzerland—the fjords of the former and the snow-capped peaks of the latter. Within a few yards of the shore the *Bowdoin* nevertheless was sailing in water nearly two thousand feet deep, and some of the peaks rose from the water's edge to more than five thousand feet in height. More than nine centuries before the Vikings, in their high-prowed open boats, had traversed these same waters that must, in many respects, have reminded them of home.

As they approached the head of the fjord, crystal with glaciers descending from the Greenland icecap, they saw the Norse ruin, a square rock building standing in the center of an elevated plain a hundred feet above the water's edge. This was the fortress-church of the Norsemen at Ujaragssuit. About twenty feet square and ten feet high, it was made of uneven slabs with smaller rubble between, forming a smooth exterior and interior wall. The land about the ruin was a swamp covered with dwarf trees and bushes.

MacMillan wrote: "It was with a feeling almost of reverence that we stood at the open door of what had apparently been a church, a beautifully built and well-preserved rock structure. Its roof, probably of logs thatched with turf, undoubtedly had been long missing.

"If it did serve as a church, naturally arises the question, 'Why not windows?' In lieu of these we discovered small port- or peep-holes, for it is hard to conceive how anything, even arrows, could have been shot through such small openings. I am informed by some of the Danish officials that churches served the double purpose of worship and defense, and it is possible that the Norsemen went to service, as our Pilgrim forefathers in New England did, with weapons in their hands.

"Within a few yards of this structure were the remains of several buildings and also the rock outlines of their stockyards and barns for cattle, which we know they had

—sheep, goats, and cows."

It would not be surprising if the Norsemen did go to church with "weapons in their hands," for the oldest Eskimos consistently indicated to MacMillan that the only battles their ancestors ever had had were with the people who "came here long ago, rowing in boats without sails. And our people put skins on their feet to keep from slipping on the ice, and killed them all."

As they were working down the coast from Sydney, the wind whipped around from southeast to northwest with vivid flashes of lightning and driving rain. A nasty cross sea caught the *Bowdoin* from a half-dozen directions and she shipped tons of water over her bow and both rails, threatening to wash some of the crew overboard.

MacMillan noted: "We finally shortened down to a foresail alone, to ease ship a bit. In taking down our forestaysail [jumbo], one of my men was almost completely buried by a sea which swept over the bow, and another was taken off his feet. Working in the pitch dark, they did well to remain on deck.

"Fearing for their safety and not hearing a sound above the roar of the wind and rush of waters, I left the wheel for a moment and ran forward to learn if they were still there. I found them tugging on the sail, endeavoring to lash it down to the boom. I had no sooner reached the wheel again than the third member of my watch, our fifteen-year-old cabin boy, was knocked down by a sea which swept aft along the deck, flush with the low rail—a close call."

At this moment an ominous slatting and banging forward revealed that the lacing on the foregaff had given away; this could easily mean the loss of the foresail itself, which would be a serious handicap. Mac yelled down the companionway, "All hands on deck!" and they tumbled up with a rush, showing that every man had turned in "all standing," which is to say that they went to bed with their clothes on, anticipating trouble.

It is difficult for the landsman to know what a circumstance of this kind is like. There is the roar of wind, the surge and crashing foam of the waters, the thunder of canvas and the crack of whipping rope, dark forms in oilskins obeying commands less heard than anticipated and doing it in pitch-black night more by sense of touch and long familiarity than visually. And always one keeps a hand for oneself, for wave after wave bursts over the vessel, smashing with a thud against small boat or cabin trunk.

But the next morning was glorious, a beautiful fall day, and they "held" the good weather with them, finally steaming into Wiscasset Harbor with the *Peary* on October 12, to receive a typical Maine welcome. Governor Brewster and hundreds of well-wishers from the Pine Tree State turned out to welcome the "boy from Freeport," now Lieutenant-Commander MacMillan.

# 17

THE CHEMISTRY of a legend, in this case involving a white schooner and a man in faded blue shirt and knee boots, is easier to understand than to duplicate. Time, of course, is a principal ingredient, to which must be added enough of the understandable to make it palatable and enough of the extraordinary to render it delightful.

As for the time, consider the years from 1921 through 1940, during which many of those persons who know Mac-Millan and the *Bowdoin* first came in contact with them. This period can be expressed statistically, even though that is the lesser aspect of it.

In these years Mac made twelve expeditions to the North, including an eight-thousand-mile cruise to Newfoundland, Iceland, the east coast of Greenland, Baffin Island, and Labrador. He made the first survey from the air of the North Labrador coast in the area of Nain, discovered the remains of the Frobisher Expedition of 1576–78, explored the deep fjords of Greenland, and made a study of the Umiamako and Rink glaciers.

If, as has been occasionally suggested, the world really is a small place, certain circumstances appear determined to prove it.

The 1927–28 MacMillan expedition to the North, sponsored by the Field Museum of Chicago, was a two-vessel affair, the *Bowdoin* being accompanied by the chartered schooner *Radio,* the latter one of those "tender" vessels that rolled her dories under, as the saying goes, at the least provocation. The *Radio* was skippered by Jack Crowell and was loaded with house-building equipment, since they planned to establish a scientific station, complete with recording instruments, near Nain, Labrador.

Scientists with the expedition, representing the Field Museum of Chicago, included Dr. Duncan K. Strong, anthropologist; Dr. Sharat K. Roy, assistant curator of geology; Dr. Alfred Weed, zoologist, and Arthur Reuchert, artist of the museum, who hoped to record accurately the colors of live fish of the North, particularly the trout, whose brilliant hues fade soon after it is caught.

The trip was eminently successful; the station was established in Anetalak Bay, south of Nain; a dock was built; the snowmobile was put ashore, and the *Bowdoin* was sent North with the anthropologist and fossilologist aboard to visit Silliman's Fossil Mount at the head of Frobisher Bay, Crowell being in charge of this part of the expedition.

But the greatest human-interest aspect of the trip occurred at Anetalak, where Mac had remained with the *Radio,* which he had declined to send North because she was not as good a vessel in heavy weather as was the *Bowdoin.*

Dan had left word at the Hudson's Bay Company post, informing them that his anthropologist wanted to study the Nascapi Indians, and asking that when the Indians arrived, they might come to Anetalak where he could talk with them.

Sure enough, they showed up, and MacMillan, seeking to establish friendly relations with them, for otherwise they might not remain, approached one of their number. Dan recalled to the Indian that he had participated in the Cabot expedition to the land of the Nascapis in 1910.

MacMillan said to the Indian, "I met a little boy, who was with a one-eyed man, and they took us to the Nascapi village. I taught the little boy how to do some gymnastic tricks, including handsprings, and he held my hand and followed me about until the time I left. I have often wondered what happened to him."

The Indian man before him smiled, pointed his finger at his own chest, and said, "Me."

Out of this extraordinary coincidence science emerged the gainer. The Indian persuaded his fellows to stay; the expedition hired the whole lot; they pitched their tents nearby and remained with the expedition all winter, allowing Dr. Strong an excellent opportunity to study them at leisure.

On all of his expeditions MacMillan took North with him scientists from more than a dozen colleges and universities, whose efforts, together with his own, contributed to the sum total of human knowledge in the fields of ornithology, biology, anthropology, geology, archeology, botany, glaciology, icthyology, meteorology, and oceanography. In addition, he began taking with him on each voyage a certain number of young men, some college students, some not. For most it constituted a remarkable education in living; many who never had been to sea became members of the crew, learned navigation and seamanship, and gained new self-sufficiency and even courage. These "alumni" of the *Bowdoin,* now roughly three hundred in number, regard MacMillan as a largely self-sufficient combination of parent, sage, and likable human.

Also during this period he had delivered thousands of lectures throughout the United States, had written several books, magazine and newspaper articles, and his name had become synonymous with the Arctic, which America found a fascinating subject as it had been before and since the days of the Peary-Cook controversy.

There is a better way to understand this segment of time, however, and what it did to MacMillan or he to it, and that is to know a few of the events that occurred.

In Frobisher Bay, Baffin Island, in 1929, the *Bowdoin* lay with an ice anchor out to a mass of ice off the southern end of Loks Land; it was here that Martin Frobisher's expedition of 1578 lost one of its ships, a "barque" that was crushed by the ice. The man standing midnight watch was Frank Henderson of Provincetown. As he paced the deck, looking out over the white massive wilderness, deafened by the sound of pelting rain, wind, and crunching ice, he felt suddenly that the current was taking them rapidly northward against a light northerly wind. He jumped into the main rigging, took a bearing on an island off to port, slid down a stay, and hit the top of the main cabin with a thump which brought Mac up the companionway ladder three steps at a time.

"We're goin' north, hell-bent."

"Seems impossible," said Mac. "The wind is north." He took a bearing too. "You're right. Roust out all hands. Get every man on deck fully clothed, ready to abandon ship if necessary."

Suddenly there was a whirling mass of destructive power and sound, so noisy that the *Bowdoin*'s crew had to yell to each other, and all because the forty-five-foot tide had turned north abruptly, sweeping the schooner along with it.

Squeezed and punished by the mass of ice that the tide was shoving down onto her, the *Bowdoin* creaked and groaned as if every fastening would start.

Mac scrambled to the ice barrel at the top of the mast, and from there in the semidarkness he saw the real danger; a big iceberg, the size of a city block, was sweeping down on their quarter.

Of great concern to Mac was the *Bowdoin*'s beautiful Oregon-pine main boom, which projected far out over the stern of the schooner; this would be the first to feel the impact of collision with the berg.

If this seems a matter of small consequence to the landlubber, it is because one has to go down to the sea to understand that the true mariner, as sensitive as he is to the necessity of preserving life whenever and wherever, regards his command—the vessel—as a being, whose hull is a body, whose spars are limbs, and it is therefore to him virtually as great a cause of suffering that the vessel which has borne

273

him safely through sea and storm should be wounded as that he should turn his back on a friend or, worse, on the woman whom he loves.

All the crew came topside, knowing they might well have to abandon ship, except Tony Alexander, also of Provincetown, known as "Tom Boots"; he was the schooner's cook. Tom came up in boots and stocking hat, took one look at the weather and the prospects, and yelled, "I'm too old to die in the cold!" Whereupon he went below, stripped down to his shirt, propped his feet against the stove rail, took out papers and tobacco and rolled a cigarette, being thus prepared to meet his Creator in reasonable comfort.

Henderson wanted to go out on the floe and release the ice anchor—huge tongs stuck in the pan—but Mac wouldn't let him because of the danger involved. Instead, Dan kept the engine full ahead, swinging the ship from starboard to port and back, keeping her sides as free as possible from ice jams so that he might preserve at least minimum maneuverability. Every few seconds he looked astern at the approaching berg, grinding up pans in its path with deafening roar and sweeping down upon them at great speed with all the majesty of a full-rigged ship under sail.

At the last possible moment he swung the *Bowdoin*'s bow as far to port as the ice would let it go. The berg went by them so closely that it scraped the bulwarks amidships, and had its top not gone to a peak, it would have carried away the crosstrees. After it had gone by, Mac discovered an open pool of water in the lee of a grounded berg and hung on there until daylight. No vessel of such small size could have survived a collision with the berg.

MacMillan's knowledge of vessel handling in the ice was on a par with his knowledge of the approximately four hundred miles of uncharted coast line by which one approaches the Arctic from the east coast. Since he had learned this territory from the deck of small, shoal draft vessels, he knew it intimately, and each year traversing some of the same area, he picked up new knowledge—often from necessity. In the twenties Jack Crowell, a graduate of the Massachusetts Maritime Academy, and later mate of the *Bowdoin* on several expeditions, was captain of a sixty-odd-foot schooner, the *Sachem*. The two schooners cruised in company on a summer voyage to the Arctic Circle and beyond. On the way back, the *Bowdoin* leading, they went through the complex Port Manvers Run, and somewhere the *Sachem* fell behind. Arrived at Nain, MacMillan figured Crowell must have taken a wrong turn somewhere.

An Eskimo named Amantos came aboard the *Bowdoin* and reported he had seen the *Sachem* going the wrong way in the "Run." The two schooners had wireless communication and Mac opened up to talk to Crowell. Crowell answered and said he didn't know where he was and he couldn't seem to find a way out.

"What does it look like?" Mac asked.

"Trees to port and starboard and lowland up ahead."

MacMillan replied, "That's Ugpiktok [Bearded Seal] Bay. Take your first sharp right, then a left, then another right, and come on in."

Crowell did, and the *Sachem* came into Nain without further event. From that day the Newfoundland fishing schooners made a practice of following the *Bowdoin* through the narrow channels and many stretches of bad water.

Whether you are a sailor or whether not, understand this, that when a Dane or a Newfoundlander—and the world does not produce better sailors—looks at a man with admiration for his seafaring, it is for reasons which a man finds hard to put into any book, for it has to do, as the saying goes, with having salt water in one's veins, rather than blood.

That is the type of exaggeration for which colloquialisms are notorious, yet Dan MacMillan comes close to being such a man. It might even have been different had there been several vessels in his life, but the fact is that there was principally the *Bowdoin,* and in her, with her, he forged a life in which the two were, to a major degree, inseparable and indistinguishable. Particularly in moments of anxiety, it was difficult to say where man left off and vessel began, so closely did they share the challenge of circumstance.

Consider, then, that he sailed this schooner thousands of trackless miles, through waters unrecorded on any charts, unlisted, unnamed and undescribed by any—if any—who had been there before and that he faced with her whatever the whimscalities of nature provided, both cruel and gentle.

Even among sailors there are many kinds. In moments of crisis many are keen and competent, yet become profane and tense. He was not, and is not, such a man, for his greatest epithet would be acceptable in Sunday School. On the contrary, he seldom did more than pace and hum softly, never outwardly distraught or tense. In such manner, he would decide, as an outstanding attorney might sense in a courtroom crisis, the essence of truth and logic, wherein lay the proper answer.

In such manner he shortened sail or "held on," as sailors say, faced the gale, or worked his vessel off the foaming ledges. In such manner he refused to abandon his command, even when those natives who knew well the odds he faced disclaimed dourly, "You'll never get her off!"

In emergencies of storm or stress, he was a power unto himself—not solely through an uncommon knowledge of such things as logarithms and cosines—but because of a feeling for the workings of nature and the manner of a ship which he himself would be hard put to translate into words. This is the way of a man with a vessel, if he is such a man as this, and in considering this, remember that he had none of your modern devices of navigation which are supposed to replace, or supplement, the thinking of man. Consider, also, that the waters in which he sailed most often held not only the perils of shoals and rocks but also of the dreaded, and often tragic, ice.

And because of a limited water supply, there were times when, in order to refill water tanks, he was forced to push the *Bowdoin*'s bow close to a fresh water stream pouring down from the top of a towering iceberg or from the face of one of Greenland's glaciers.

Roughly three decades after the death of Ross Marvin, MacMillan's companion on the 1909 Peary North Pole Expedition, Dan sat in the after cabin of the *Bowdoin* beside the Danish official of the Greenland trading post.

An Eskimo looked down through the companionway for an instant. Mac recognized him immediately as Inugeeto (who had been known to the crew of the *Roosevelt* as "Har-

277

rigan") and who, with Kudlukto, had been with Marvin when the latter died on the Polar Sea.

Mac turned to the Dane. "Did you ever hear a report being circulated among the Polar Eskimos that Marvin did not drown but was shot?"

"No, I never have."

"Well, there is one of the boys who was with Marvin—the one peering around the corner of the companionway. Ask him about it."

The Dane went topside and was gone only a few minutes. When he returned, his face reflected both surprise and seriousness. "That report must be correct. This boy on deck, Inugeeto, says he was a cousin of Kudlukto and wanted to ride on the one sledge. He was tired from walking many hours. Marvin would not permit him to ride. Kudlukto became angry, grabbed his rifle and shot Marvin, afterward pushing his body out on the young ice."

Why had it taken so long for the story to emerge?

About 1915, missionaries went from South Greenland to North Greenland, building a Lutheran church at Umanak. Eventually, these northern Eskimos came to confess their sins to the ministers, and Kudlukto revealed the burden of conscience that he had carried for years. Time, with Eskimos, as with most peoples, apparently makes confession possible, if not inevitable.

In 1935 Mac married, and it is essential to understand how this came to be, for it, too, is a basic part of the legend.

Ever since Jerry Look's daughter, Miriam, at the age of five, had sat on Dan's knee and listened in wide-eyed wonder to his stories of the sea and the Arctic, MacMillan had been her hero. When he sailed on the Crocker Land Expedition, the little girl was on the dock with her family to bid him farewell.

In retrospect, there appears to have been considerable determination and imagination in a letter she handed to him, marked, "To be opened at the North Pole." In it she wrote wistfully, "I wish you was going to be with us all the time you are gone and all the rest of the time. When you come back I will be down to the Brooklyn Navy Yard." The letter was signed with ten rows of X's which she marked "kisses" and five rows of circles entitled "hugs."

When Dan returned from those four arctic years, Miriam went with her father to meet him. And ever after, though she spent a roving childhood, moving from one dam site to another, and later, moved by a mature spirit of adventure within herself, roamed the world's far corners, she always managed to be at the cap log to welcome Mac home from his northern voyages.

With a background similar to Dan's—a long line of Maine and Nantucket sea captains—she was as much kin to the sea as he. At the Look family summer place on Casco Bay, Maine, close by the nautical camp Dan had started, she spent hours alone in her motorboat—the more flying spray the better—edging in among spruce-wooded islands, landing to explore, ingeniously figuring out how to float her craft off half-hidden ledges when groundings occurred in lonely waters. All this when she was very young.

So the time came, inevitably, after years of saying good-by and hello at the dock, that Miriam's explorer-hero became her husband. Dan, long wed to the Arctic only, joked, "I waited for you to grow up."

Dan recently had purchased his boyhood home in Provincetown, Massachusetts, and there they went to live. Miriam immediately recognized its potential charm, a quality well hidden by mission furniture and quantities of stuffed arctic life and Eskimo equipment which she gradually had moved to the museum or the cellar, until today the house is delightful, with just enough of the Arctic remaining to look as if it were Dan MacMillan's and enough of the sea, indoors and out, to stamp it as the home of a sailor and a sailor's wife.

Because Dan never had been home long enough to straighten out his voluminous collection of arctic material and records, they set about the task together. They listed thousands of feet of motion-picture film, catalogued hundreds of books, negatives, and photographs, and in the process Miriam became vicariously, but effectively, acquainted with Etukasuk, Shooegingwah, and Akkommodingwah and the land in which they lived. She wanted to meet Mac's Eskimo friends, to sail north with him.

Miriam realized that the Arctic had to become her life, too, for it was his and nothing would change that. She knew that after persuading him to go to Europe the year in which they were married. His principal comment when they returned was that it wasn't exciting enough.

He was already planning another trip North, and he explained that he couldn't take her, that he had never taken a woman on the *Bowdoin*, and that if he should, the all-male crew undoubtedly would choose to throw her overboard as soon as the land had dropped out of sight astern.

People whose forebears come from Addison County, Maine, as did Miriam's, aren't stopped as easily as that. She got him to promise that if she went as far as Hopedale, Labrador, he would take her on the schooner as far as Nain, where she would stay, and pick her up on the way back south. He said yes dubiously, adding that he would not be able to wait for her and hoped she made it on time; otherwise she would have to spend the summer at Hopedale.

She took the train from Boston to Sydney, Nova Scotia, the steamer *Caribou* from Nova Scotia to Newfoundland, the train from Port Aux Basques to St. John's, and the mailboat *Kyle* (leaving biweekly) which reached Hopedale after making ninety stops.

Miriam not only beat Mac into Hopedale, but she was wearing Eskimo clothing, furnished by the natives. They accepted her immediately because they respected him.

The Eskimos sang out, "Seekoonah [Schooner]! Mac-Millanekut [Belongs to MacMillan]! Fren [Friend]!" And she was in the overloaded motorboat, jammed with Eskimos, that went out to meet him, shouting more loudly than any the only words she had had time to learn: "Aksunai! Aksuse! Aksutik! Illitarnamek! Nakomek!" which is to say, "Hello to one, hello to two, hello to three or more! May you be well, may you be strong! Thank you!"

After he finally discovered her among the fur-clad throng, he said slowly, "Great heavens, Miriam! Where'd you get that rigging, and how'd you ever get here so soon?"

She got off the schooner at Nain that time, but not on the next trip North. Her husband was adamant; he said explorer's wives upset expeditions and he was going to put her ashore. But at chow the night before she was to be taken off, the crew presented a petition, watching in silence while she—and Mac—read it. They wanted her to stay aboard, to go north with them; they respectfully urged the captain to allow this, because she was an asset to the expedition. Mac did so then, and thereafter, and she stood her trick at the wheel with all the rest. She also stood her watch for'ard and did scullion duty, as with all of them. She did not have to be called but was always on deck when it was her turn to relieve the man on watch; she weathered gales in Baffin Bay and Davis Strait with the best of them, and has known what it is like to face tough going through ice packs, towering bergs, and uncharted ledges, with the outcome uncertain. Miriam is a sailor, in good weather and bad, and asked no special treatment because of her sex.

As fond of the Eskimos as is Mac, she has helped many times in preparations for arctic trips, became interested in photography, and eventually took most of the thousands of feet of color film her husband uses in lectures.

Another arctic bond between Mac and Miriam has been the MacMillan-Moravian School for Eskimo children at Nain. With civilization working in on the Labrador coast, Mac felt the children needed an education and clean, healthful living. He admired the work of the Moravians, with whom he had been friendly for years, and wanted to help them in their care of the young ones of northern Labrador. Thus, in 1929, he built the school.

On the *Bowdoin* he carried all things needed to start it: lumber for the building, desks, small chairs, blackboards, chalk, erasers, an organ, a radio. There was an electric-light plant, too, and a stove, sleeping bags, blankets, dishes for kitchen utensils and the dining table, as well as towels, soap, food, and hundreds of books. All these he transported from the United States. Each year that he went North he landed provisions at their dock, and from 1935 on Miriam, too, continued this work and became a basic part of the program.

What these people of Labrador think of the name Mac-Millan was best illustrated the first time that Miriam saw the gray huts of the Eskimos at Nain as she went into the harbor on her initial trip with Mac. "Look, Miriam," Dan said, pointing at a building to the left of the village, "you can just see it in among those trees. That's our school."

Suddenly over the still waters came a cry, "Seekoonah! MacMillanekut! Seekoonah!" In the darkness there came a flash of light, then another and another, as the whole village lighted up.

Presently there sounded the chug-chugging of motor-boats, the incessant chattering of mingled Eskimo and English. The reception committee—that is, the entire population—was on its way. In the lead power boat, jammed to precarious capacity, was the Eskimo band, playing, "Now, Thank We Our Lord," and round and round they went, followed by every type of boat, all filled to the brim and then some with people, all yelling affectionately, "Aksunai! Illitarnamek!"

Here at the wheel of the *Bowdoin* was the man who had brought electric lights powered by windchargers for their church and school.

It was he who first brought to the Labrador the airplane, radio, snowmobile, canoe, victrola, motion pictures, and the amazing wire recorder, on which they had heard their own voices.

And it was MacMillan who gave the church its organ and bell, presented the school with a 28-foot cabin cruiser, and provided these Labrador Eskimos with food, clothing, radios, a dental clinic, and an education for their children.

# 18

EARLY IN 1941 the U. S. Army offered to charter the *Bowdoin* for $1,000 a month. To MacMillan, who never had made a nickel on any of his trips North—nor had he sought to—it sounded like quite a lot of money, but as a Reserve lieutenant commander, he thought he ought to talk to the Navy about it.

In Washington he sat across the desk from an admiral and told him the Army wanted the schooner. What should he do about it?

"You can do better than charter her," said the admiral. "You can sell her to the Navy."

"Sell her? Sir, I could no more sell her—she's part of my life——"

"Suppose I said to you that you could sell her to the Navy with the idea that she would be returned to you in the same condition in which we received her?"

"Who would decide that?"

"You would, MacMillan—you would be the skipper."

"But I've been retired for ten years . . ."

"The way things are going, there's no such thing as retirement from the Navy. What do you say?"

"Well, sir . . ."

"How much would you say the *Bowdoin* is worth?"

"I couldn't replace her for $50,000, Admiral."

"That's what I've been told. We sent two officers to Boothbay to survey her, and they came up with exactly the same figure. Suppose I write you out a check for $50,000?"

"No, sir. All I want is $35,000. That's what she cost me, and if I get that, I can pay back all of the boys who raised the money to build her. They never expected to get it back; it'll be a great surprise to them, and I'd like to do it."

The admiral wrote out the check, then looked at Mac-Millan. He said, "You know, I'm glad you went along on this. I have instructions on my desk to take over the *Bowdoin* as of tomorrow, and I would have had to do it anyway. Furthermore, your orders to report for active duty were mailed yesterday, and you'll find them waiting for you when you get home."

When the *Bowdoin* went North in forty-one, this time with a crew of bluejackets, her orders were to assist in the establishment of two airfields on the West Greenland coast, one at Narssaq and the other at Sondrestrom. Narssaqsuah (Big Level Place) is up a deep fjord and close by the place where the foundation stones of Eric the Red's farmhouse can still be found. Sondrestrom, farther north, is cut through precisely by the Arctic Circle and it is a place continuously plagued by the foehn, or warm wind, which comes down off the icecap. Bernt Balchen was working on the Sondrestrom project, and here Mac prepared the first survey ever made of this area for the Navy Hydrographic Office.

But by fall of 1941 Mac felt that he wasn't doing much more than "sit in the cabin" and that he ought to be able to contribute something else; as far as he was concerned, his job here was done. There was a big Navy transport anchored across the fjord, and he discussed the matter with its officers. Dan said, "I've finished here, and I'm going home." They looked at him and laughed. "Going home? You've got orders from the Secretary of the Navy?" Obviously they thought it was ridiculous.

Dan said, "I'm going to send a radiogram to the Secretary of the Navy. I'm going to say that the job is done and that if I don't hear from him in three days, I'm going to take the *Bowdoin* home. I've been retired ten years anyway, so I guess there isn't much they can do to me."

He sent the radiogram. On the third day there had been no reply. "What're you going to do now?" his fellow officers teased him.

"Going home," said Mac.

"They'll court-martial you," they warned.

"Maybe so," he said, and got up his anchor and steamed down the fjord.

The *Bowdoin* arrived at the sea about midnight; offshore there was a heavy snowstorm, black against the horizon. They received a message from Sondrestrom that a ship was outside, asking for assistance, and would MacMillan do what he could? He contacted the ship offshore. Yes, they needed directions. Visibility was zero; they were unsure of their position and didn't dare come toward the land for fear of grounding. Mac gave them their position and "talked" them in through the snowstorm to the coast, eventually leading this "big white steamer" safely up the fjord, past the islands to port and ledges to starboard to a sheltered anchorage. Then he started for home again, and early that next day the *Bowdoin* received a message from Washington: "Come on home. [Admiral] Sherman."

Working his way down the coast, he was warned by the natives: "Watch out for German submarines in the Straits of Belle Isle." At Battle Harbor the fishermen said, "You're goin' out? Those subs out there are driving steamers ashore," and they pointed to the wreck of a freighter on the beach. "Well," said Mac, "I'll just put a spotlight on the mainsail after dark and they can see I'm just another fisherman. They wouldn't want a little schooner for anything . . ."

Outside Battle Harbor a big Navy cruiser steamed up over the horizon, the blinker on her bridge flicking out: "What ship are you?"

"Schooner *Bowdoin*, American, bound from Greenland, going home."

The cruiser didn't even come in for a closer look; it was satisfied and steamed off on other business.

Under sail and power off Cape Sable at night, the watch tapped Dan on the shoulder, pointed off to starboard. "What island is that, sir?"

It was a small, low-lying object, a deeper black against the black of the night. "There is no island there," Dan said thoughtfully. A week later the President of the United States announced there were German submarines off the northeast coast.

Back home in the States, the schooner was ordered to

a Boston yard. "You're going back to Greenland in the spring," the Navy told Mac. "Get her fixed up. See that she has whatever she needs." With his accumulated mail there were several letters from the Secretary of the Navy wanting to know such things as: "When does the ice go out of Smith Sound?" and "What time does Hebron freeze up?" He sat down to answer the letters as the yard started to make his ship once more "ready in all respects for sea."

There came the day, however, when young Lieutenant Stuart Hotchkiss, a graduate of Yale who had done some ocean racing, came up the gangplank and said, "I have been ordered to relieve you, sir, and to assume command of the *Bowdoin*." Sentimentally it was unthinkable, yet the machinery of war is not administered on a sentimental basis. The young man was eminently qualified; in fact, he sailed the schooner all the way to Greenland and never used her power once. Moreover, the Navy had some more unanswered questions about the North and they needed Mac in Washington as a member of the Hydrographic Office to make charts of the North, serve as consultant to all expeditions going into the Arctic, and to compile a dictionary of the Eskimo language, a project on which he had long been working.

In the spring of forty-two they sent him to the Massachusetts Institute of Technology to learn about the new Loran (long-range navigation) equipment so that he could command a northern party assigned to select six secret sites for this increasingly important method of determining latitude and longitude. By 1943 he had a new assignment in the North: "Take charge of a party, fly the east and west coasts of Greenland, and take photos at 20,000 feet, enough photos so that navigational charts can be made from them for there are no charts of this area now available to us."

With Commander L. W. Parrish, the senior aviation officer, the party took twelve thousand photos, not entirely uneventfully. They had flown south on Baffin Island to go to the head of Frobisher Bay when it came in thick one day. Parrish went down low, looking for Resolution Island, and it didn't show up. Mac suggested they go back to the Franklin Islands off Frobisher Bay, get their bearings, and start over.

Parrish checked the fuel supply. He doubted that there was enough gas to go back to the Franklins and still get to Sondrestrom, their destination. But if that was the best way to locate themselves, he would go back and then fly as far as the fuel supply permitted. Meanwhile he suggested everyone put on parachutes.

Dan did not put on a parachute. "I knew nobody could live in that ice water." He went aft, curled up, and fell asleep.

After a short doze he awakened, looked out the window, and recognized a place where he had anchored the *Bowdoin* the year before. He went forward to see Parrish, saying, "I know where we are."

"You sure?" Parrish asked him.

"Yes. I anchored here. Go left; it will take you back to Greenland. Follow the fjord up to the head, and there is Sondrestrom."

They slowed down both engines to save gasoline, flew up between the mountains, and "flopped into the fjord airfield with barely a gallon of gas left."

Soon after Mac received a telegram from Miriam. Jerry Look was dead; he had failed to rally after an operation. Mac flew to Boston to be with her a few days, then went back to Washington to make more maps.

At the request of the Navy Hydrographic Office he placed between two and three hundred names on the new charts of North Labrador, to aid in the compiling of a new *Coast Pilot,* the coastal mariner's guidebook, of that area. The names he selected were principally those of persons who had spent their lives on that coast and had contributed to the knowledge of it and to the betterment and welfare of its natives.

Also while there, he completed an Eskimo-English conversational dictionary, entitled *Eskimo Place Names and Aid to Conversation, for use by the Armed Forces.*

Then came the war's end. True to its promise, the Navy sent MacMillan a telegram: "Are you interested in the *Bowdoin?*"

He was. Guy Abbate, who had sailed on her in prewar days with Dan, and who also had been assigned to her as a pharmacist mate when the Navy had her, knew where she was. Abbate called the MacMillans in Provincetown; he was obviously distressed. Yes, he had seen her in a Boston boatyard. She had been stripped. He understood she had been condemned and they were going to burn her.

Miriam and Mac went to Boston the next day. They stood on the cap log and looked at what lay there.

It is difficult to find an idiom or an image to convey what they felt. Sailors consider a wooden vessel, which came from living fibers, to be a living thing itself and are very mindful of the swelling and shrinking of planks, the creaking of timbers, the movement of this living hull, whether it is boiling buoyantly, crest and trough to leeward, or shuddering in a laborious thresh to windward. The old-timers did not talk about sailing "on" a vessel, which suggests the same impersonal relationship as that of a commuter on a bus; they sailed "in" vessels, and all of this close partnership between a man and what he goes to sea aboard has an inner quality about it. Somehow the one must understand the other, and once a sailor understands his ship, he takes it for granted that the ship understands him and she will do for him things that she will do for no one else. As with all love affairs, this one is cumulative; it is broader, deeper, more inviolate with each ledge escaped, each gale defeated.

The *Bowdoin* had been reduced to a derelict. If it was difficult to look at what she was, it was virtually unbearable to think of the assault upon her by the unfeeling and the alien. They also must have seen her when her Oregon pine was bright, her decks scoured, brass gleaming, and white paint fresh as the breeze of a May morning. Miriam wept as they stood there together, grieving for what had been and appalled at the wantonness of man.

The yard operator said laconically, "I don't care what happens to her. I got mine out of her."

A lot of people had. Her booms, anchors, chain, sails, binnacle, wheel, fuel and water tanks, most of her blocks, and, of all things, her engine—were gone. Her decks were black and grimy, her masts the same way; her standing rigging hung slack in the deadeyes, her paint was filthy.

Down below, in addition to the dirt and junk that was everywhere, someone had taken an ax to her cabin partitions; they were smashed and splintered.

Mac was over seventy. He had no great amount of money; materials were scarce and costly, and there was no labor for hire at any price he could afford to pay.

But he went to the telegraph office and offered the Navy their asking price for her: $4,000, on condition that the bill of sale would include everything he could find in the boatyard that belonged to her. The Navy agreed, and the first thing he found was her once-varnished wheel, stashed away in the grass; someone had been going to make a chandelier of it. The Navy even sent a gang of men over from its yard to help him search—and eventually they found the booms, sails, some of the running rigging, the anchors, binnacle, and chains. But no engine. That never did come to light. They found the windlass, though, and remounted it.

All that summer he worked on her, more than a hundred miles to and from his home in Provincetown. He came home tired and silent many times in the first few weeks; scraping the masts and booms of the *Bowdoin* is no job for one man. Once he sustained first- and second-degree burns on his arm up to the elbow with an acetylene torch; he wrapped it up with a piece of his shirt and worked for the remainder of the day just the same.

He heard about a company in Cambridge that had the kind of engine he wanted—a Cummins diesel—and he towed her over there on the Charles River to have it installed. When the one-hundred-horsepower engine was all

293

hooked up and ready to go, Mac received a receipted bill from the head of the company, saying, "We have long been interested in your work and hope you will continue it. Accept this engine as a gift."

Mac felt that the tide had turned. The *Bowdoin* would go to the Arctic again, and he would go with her, the ravages of war notwithstanding.

# 19

THE POSTWAR PERIOD, through the 1940s and '50s, was a time of coming to fruition, when all that had been started so long ago approached, not completion—for such matters as these never are finished—but an era of measurable result from the long effort.

Some of these results were personal, others professional, and still others broad enough in their social application as to be in neither category.

It also was a time when the legend that is MacMillan came to the full, and if you go where he has been, you will hear them say:

"The hat he likes best, far better than the cap with the admiral's scrambled eggs, is a white-visored thing that he gives a coat of paint now and then until it's so stiff he can hardly get it on. When he's fitting out to go North, he wears it, and there he is, slung aloft in a bos'un's chair, varnishing the mast or painting the ice barrel and looking like just another forem'st hand. He's always relaxed when he's fitting out; everybody else may be charged up, but not Mac—he has time to talk. One day a lady came down to the dock and saw him all covered with paint and having the time of his life. She assumed he was a painter from the boatyard. "Do you think they'll take you North when they go?" she asked him. He smiled. "Sure hope so."

And one of his crew will say, "High and dry on a ledge off Greenland, half under in a Labrador gale, Captain Mac doesn't swear, he doesn't get rattled. He just paces the deck and hums, making the best of a bad situation." "Sing when you're worried," he says.

In some ways he is like an Eskimo. MacMillan has always said, "If an Eskimo doesn't smile, there's something wrong with him." Mac likes the bright side. He doesn't want to hear about troubles; he doesn't want to hear anything bad about anyone. What he loves above all is to tell stories about the Arctic, and for many reasons his audiences find him a crackerjack yarn spinner. What's more, if any of them have seen him start off on a northern voyage, have heard him say quietly, "Start your engine. Let go for'ard. Let go aft!" they don't forget the emotional stir in the dockside crowd that inevitably rises at the sight of such a small vessel, such a quiet man, going so far away with so little fuss.

The lack of fuss is, of course, not accidental or incidental. MacMillan looks easygoing; actually he plans an expedition as one might build a piano, with absolute precision. This is why none of his men ever starved to death or died of scurvy. This is why he never had mutiny in his expeditions—or cannibalism, for that matter. He may have made mistakes, but not twice, not many and not major.

MacMillan's trip North in 1949—he was making one virtually every year—was one of several devoted to work along the Labrador, Baffin Island, Ellesmere Island, and Greenland coasts, sounding fjords, correcting charts, and obtaining additional information for the Navy Hydrographic Office.

All the charts of North Labrador issued by the U. S. Government now bore the name MacMillan, and much of what once was uncharted sea and unnamed land now possessed definition and identity. The origins of some of the Labrador names on the chart were easily recognizable: Miriam Lake, Bowdoin Harbor, which Mac was the first to enter and sound for water depth, Hettasch Island (for Dr. Paul Hettasch, who administered to the Eskimos on the Labrador for a half century), and Jackson Island, for Captain Jackson of the Moravian mission steamer *Harmony*.

Arrived at Tinutsarvik, so named because it is a place on the Labrador where trout are caught by building dykes of rocks, they passed near the big waterfall Kolortoaluk a fishing schooner from Newfoundland, at anchor. The year before, she had taken five or six hundred barrels of trout; now she was back for another load. Her skipper, pipe clenched in teeth, leaned over the rail with a grin. "I followed yer track here, MacMillan!" He held the rolled-up coastal chart in his hand and nodded his head approvingly. Accurate charts of the Labrador were a wonderful innovation; previously they had been so far off that one skipper found himself theoretically anchored on top of the Kiglipait Mountains, ten miles inland.

Also on this trip Mac wrote in the log: "I find that the

fossils which we gathered at the Lower Savage Islands are of the Cambrian Period of the Paleozoic Era and are, therefore, representative of the marine life of about 350,000,000 years ago. These are the oldest things we have ever brought back. . . . Man did not appear until 2,250,000 years later."

Between trips in the late forties Helen Henley, staff correspondent of the *Christian Science Monitor,* who has followed the course of the MacMillans for some years, noted: "When he put out from Boothbay Harbor this year (1949) he had manned the *Bowdoin* with the youngest crew ever to sail North. Of fourteen aboard, six were prep-school boys —some with no knowledge of ships or the sea."

Miss Henley asked Mac the obvious question: Why had he ever begun years ago to choose college and prep-school boys to sail his ship into the Arctic, instead of a crew hardened and seasoned by long experience?

Mac gave her the same answer that he has expressed many times, because it is part of his basic philosophy. "Boys today are not being given a chance. I do not think boys need a rest when school is out. They are brim full of activity. They should not spend summers just lying around beaches and going swimming. Their activity should be turned in another direction to permit them to work off their energy.

"Schools should put a boy on the road to accomplishment. I like to think of it as leading him to the top of a hill where, like the four points of the compass, various activities in life are spread before him. He should have a chance to look them over and choose what he will be happy doing.

"Success is something accomplished by a man who loves

his work. No man can be successful without loving his work. I like to work with the boys and help them find the thing in life that they will love."

Sitting on the wheelbox of the *Bowdoin,* he looked off to sea, sparkling blue in the fall afternoon sun. "And if I had my life to do over," he added, "I would want to do just what I have done."

In part, his impact upon these several hundred young men can be assessed by recollections of two of them, both now married and fathers, as they sat in the forecastle of the schooner reminiscing.

"I was a spoiled kid," one of them said, "and I didn't have any guts either. Just before we sailed, Mac showed some of his arctic films to an audience at the Portsmouth Navy Yard, and we who were scheduled to sail North with him within the next day or two were along to see the pictures.

"I looked at those pictures. Cold, deep snow, miles and miles of frozen ice blocks, big bergs, fogs, and waves smashing right over the rail of the schooner, and I said to myself, 'Boy, what is this I'm getting into?' After I saw that film, I didn't want any part of it.

"I went to see Mac and I said, 'Look, you're making a big mistake taking me up there. I made a mistake asking to go. I don't want to go.'

"He looked at me, and he said, 'We need you. You know something about pharmacy.'

"I yelled, 'Me be a doctor? That's crazy. I don't know how to be a doctor. I can't even stand the sight of blood. I don't know anything about medicine.'

"He handed me a book. He said, 'Everything you will need to know is in here. Learn it. We're going to be counting on you if anything goes wrong.'

"Well, you know something, I did learn it. And one day I sewed up a man's arm and I thought after, 'Who would have figured I could do this? Who would ever have figured it?' "

The other said, "What I never have forgotten is the day when one of the boys was on deck and Mac said, 'It would be a good idea if you went over the side and bailed out the ship's boat.' And this kid said, 'I'm not bailing out any boat. I didn't come here to do that kind of stuff.' And Mac, who was seventy-five or better, said, 'All right, I'll bail it out.' He jumped over the rail and started bailing, and the young fellow couldn't stand it, and he got into the boat without a word and finished the job."

There were letters, too; these are samples of dozens:

Dear Captain Mac and Miriam:

It's a little bit like being hit on the head. Only now, as I settle down to the ordinary life again, do I realize fully how strange and fascinating the things we did this summer really were . . . I may not have become an arctic explorer, but I think I've discovered some of that wild beauty that makes men go North.

Another one of the many men who went North with Mac wrote:

*Bowdoin* to me is a monument of the finest adventure and richest experience I have ever known. She has existed to broaden man's knowledge and men's hearts,

300

and at the same time has been a worthy tool for her Captain's teachings.

A woman invited aboard the *Bowdoin* with her daughter wrote:

"Dear MacMillans:

You and your ship are as much a part of my New England heritage as Bunker Hill . . . by your gracious gesture last evening this heritage now has become my daughter's. She may never make a trip to the Arctic, but within the pleasant walls of your cabin she has glimpsed the warmth and richness that comes of doing what one believes in for the good and benefit of others; a world where man discovers his own proud integrity by functioning as one small efficient part of the whole. The impact of such an experience—however brief—can last a life time. Thank you."

The MacMillan mail, up to and including today, is voluminous and from all over. It includes everything from the penciled scrawlings of the little midwestern boy who heard Mac lecture the other night and comments, "Thank you, now I understand all about icebergs," to the erudite members of scientific organizations who want to know something about glaciers.

Personal honors began to accumulate too.

As long ago as 1909 Provincetown had recognized its native son when the selectmen, C. Austin Cook and A. P. Hannum, had written him, commenting: "The people of Provincetown have followed your career with great interest and pleasure and now, as you return to your native town

301

[after the North Pole trip with Peary], we offer the congratulations of our people and ourselves for the great success that has crowned your labors and brought honor and fame to you and to the town of your birth . . ." Now, in these later years, the town has named a highway and a principal pier for him. When Mac observed his eightieth birthday Harry Kemp, Provincetown's nationally known "Poet of the Dunes," wrote:

Each day's bright event
Came on him as without a precedent;
Such new and vigorous strife was his delight,
How could he fail to find the hero's height,
This man to whom years are youth's measurement?—
Long may he walk like sunrise into new intent!

A committee consisting of the presidents of Harvard and Yale and the Chief Justice of the Supreme Judicial Court of Maine selected him to receive the Bowdoin Prize, awarded "once in each five years to that graduate or former member of Bowdoin College, . . . who shall have made during the period the most distinctive contribution in any field of human endeavor."

In 1944, on the occasion of the thirty-fifth anniversary of Peary's discovery of the Pole, he (and Bob Bartlett, too) was awarded a special congressional medal for his participation in that expedition, an award titled the Peary Polar Expedition Medal, "for outstanding service to the Government of the United States . . ." He received a special gold medal in 1949 from the Chicago Geographic Society for geographical and scientific achievement, and he was elected to the Florence Nightingale Institute of Honorables because "he has given special service to humanity by long and successful endeavors to improve the physical and mental condition of the Eskimo."

In 1953, for outstanding arctic explorations from 1908 to 1952, and for "valuable service to geographic education and science," the National Geographic Society awarded him its highest honor, the Hubbard Gold Medal.

The presentation was made by Dr. Gilbert Grosvenor, president of the society and editor of its magazine, at Constitution Hall in Washington. More than 4,700 members and friends of the society witnessed the ceremony, which preceded afternoon and evening lectures by MacMillan. Sharing the platform with MacMillan were Miriam, who by then had participated in eight trips North, and two of his colleagues of arctic explorations twenty-eight years before—Rear Admiral Richard E. Byrd and former Navy Lieutenant Commander Eugene F. McDonald, Jr.

In presenting the medal, Dr. Grosvenor emphasized that MacMillan's achievements north of the Arctic Circle "have been outstanding and continuous for forty-four years. I can find in history no explorer whose active devotion to solving the geographic secrets of the Arctic has continued for so long . . ."

Mac also is a distinguished medallist of the Explorers Club and received its scroll of honor for "accomplishments in the field of science and exploration . . ." He was further honored by receiving the Elisha Kent Kane Gold Medal for "daring exploration and scientific research."

In due course Senator Payne of Maine, with the support

of Senators Saltonstall and Kennedy (later President of the United States), Republican and Democrat respectively, and the late Senator Bridges of New Hampshire, obtained congressional approval of a measure authorizing the President to advance MacMillan to the grade of Rear Admiral. This was done, "in recognition of your lifelong and invaluable services on behalf of the United States and the United States Navy through outstanding contributions to the sciences of hydrography, meteorology, and geography in the polar areas."

Even the weather, which had shown MacMillan about every side of itself in nearly a half century of sailing North, gave him enough special recognition so that he conceded, "The devil threw the book at us on this one."

It was at the tail end of the 1954 trip in September. That morning the *Bowdoin* was anchored in the harbor of Hopedale, bound home, and the sky was not just red, but blood red, from which the good sailor takes warning, according to the ancient maxim of the sea.

The skipper of a nearby fishing schooner watched Mac-Millan, to see what he was going to do. Mac, with a good ship under him and a sound hundred-horse-power engine, decided to sail, and the fisherman, deep-laden with codfish, immediately followed.

Late in the day Mac noted in the log: "Raining and blowing from the northeast. The barometer has fairly tumbled downhill and is now at 29.20." Astern, the fisherman, with little freeboard, was plunging into the heavy sea; Mac felt she was loaded too deep for such weather.

With the glass dropping and the wind increasing, the

*Bowdoin,* under shortened sail, foresail and jumbo, raced along the coast. It was getting dark rapidly; the sky was a mass of low black clouds, and the seas were building up enough so that they began to tumble. The *Bowdoin* staggered in the cross-grained roll, racing on the crests, dropping into the troughs, and swinging her crosstrees through widening arcs. They had to find a harbor.

Mac knew that if he went beyond Turnavik West the only harbor was Ailik, open to the northeast, in which no schooner could lie in safety during a heavy blow. To go out to sea was to court disaster before morning. He decided to run for Turnavik West, a snug little hole between two islands.

It was pitch black now. They steamed along the coast, which was a barely visible, solid-black unlighted mass. There are few navigational aids on the Labrador, neither buoys, nor bells—only three part-time lights on a six-hundred-mile stretch of coast, and no comforting gleam of illuminated cities upon the shore.

Still they steamed. The sea was worse. The wind was worse. To starboard they could see white water against the dark; that would be the sea breaking over rocks. It was nearly midnight.

Suddenly, ahead and offshore, there was more white water and more rocks! Wind and sea appeared to be sweeping them toward a cul de sac; if they were going to get out of this, they would have to put her about and butt into the gathering storm.

Mac was at the forward rigging, looking. The helmsman waited with mounting tension for some kind of a command.

All of the crew was topside now, silent and waiting. The white water was closer; the blackness of the Labrador loomed to starboard.

"Starboard a bit!" Mac yelled into the wind.

The helmsman, trained to the sea, did as he was told, personally convinced, however, that it was a major error.

Now they were hurtling through a cross sea toward the Labrador coast. On deck nobody spoke. There was no sound aboard but that of the *Bowdoin*'s steady engine, and even that nearly drowned in the roar of wind and sea. Now they had stationed a couple of the crew along the deck to pass his commands aft to the helm, for it was hard to hear.

"Hard starboard!"

This time there were several others aboard who winced when the helmsman winced. The *Bowdoin*'s bow was headed directly for a roll of broken surf that ran the length of the immediate horizon.

Suddenly it was over. The schooner coasted through a rocky slot so narrow that one could have touched the ledges on either side with a boat hook. Mac spun her wheel, jingled the engine-room telegraph, backed her down short, and they were in a harbor so tiny that there wasn't room to put out an anchor.

They got a boat over, and he sent one of the boys up ahead of the schooner to examine the rock wall of the harbor with a flashlight. "You'll find a ringbolt there," he called. "Make our line fast to it."

"Don't see it," said the boy.

"You're down too low." Up a little, and there it was, and they made her fast at bow and stern the same way, leaving her all snugged down for the night.

"How did you know this was here, Mac?" said one of the crew.

"This is where the Newfoundland steamers used to lie when they came up to get Bob Bartlett's father's codfish. The *Roosevelt* used to lie in here. I've known about it for forty years."

"How could you find it in the dark?"

"I was all right when I saw a patch of black against the lighter sky. That's Bob Bartlett's house. I just headed her straight for it."

That night every fishing schooner in Ailik's Cove was lost when the hurricane that had swept up the east coast of the United States struck the Labrador coast with winds in excess of a hundred miles an hour. The little fisherman who had followed them went down with all hands.

The harbor, Mac said later, was the smallest the *Bowdoin* ever was in, "a couple of lengths bigger than the vessel."

In 1957 four "pioneers of arctic exploration" were photographed with news commentator Lowell Thomas at Idlewild Airport before leaving on a "photography expedition to polar regions in connection with a television series being prepared by Mr. Thomas."

The four were MacMillan, the last surviving member of the Peary polar expedition, Sir Hubert Wilkins, Peter Freuchen, and Colonel Bernt Balchen. Their aim was to retrace their trails by air and to examine the changes, the "new techniques of living" in the North.

Nearly a half century after MacMillan hobbled back to the *Roosevelt* on frozen heels they flew over the North Pole, these four, in the enclosed cabin of a heated plane, each with his own thoughts. They did not have to miss a single, well-balanced meal; the risk they took was no greater than any New York-to-Boston commuter, and millions watched them on the television screen when they dropped the wreath over the Pole, dedicated to those who had sought it so valiantly, so long.

Truly times and men, too, were changing, and it was brought home forcefully to them, for on this northern trip one of their number, Lorenz Peter Elfred Freuchen, seventy-two, died and his ashes were dropped from a plane over Thule, which he had named.

In Provincetown, Miriam received a Western Union message sent from Thule by way of Durban, South Africa, showing, indeed, what a changed world it had become: BACK FROM POLE. WONDERFUL TRIP EXCEPT FOR PETER'S DEATH. DAN.

# 20

PEARY'S STEAMER, the *Roosevelt,* was abandoned on a Latin-American mudbank, her timbers sticking up like bare bones after she was no longer able to make a dollar for anybody. MacMillan fretted that the *Bowdoin,* which had sailed more than 200,000 miles in northern work would suffer a similar fate if eventually sold to commercial interests.

Over a period of four or five years he and Miriam, and a host of persons all over the United States who were "friends of the *Bowdoin,*" studied, planned, and contributed cash to see that the schooner would be preserved. That is how she came to be sailed in 1959 to Mystic, Connecticut, for enshrinement by the Marine Historical Association. It was her "twenty-seventh expedition"; her crew was comprised principally of those who had been North on her on more than one trip, and it was in all respects an extraordinary voyage.

This is how it was when MacMillan, at eighty-four, permitted his ship to become part of a museum.

It was at West Harbor, near the mouth of the Mystic

River, that the ovation for MacMillan and his *Bowdoin* began. Here the "marine parade" formed, consisting of about thirty big yachts, with the procession being led by the Historical Association's schooner *Brilliant,* colorful with blue-uniformed Girl Scout Mariners aboard.

Schooners, yawls, sloops, and ketches, all dressed up with flags and pennants, banners and signs of welcome, joined this flotilla moving slowly up the Mystic River.

As the river narrowed, getting up toward Noank, the intensity of the celebration accelerated. Even though it was overcast, hundreds of persons lined the water front. The fleet also grew, adding everything from small sailing craft decorated with yellow and blue crepe to the ocean-going cruiser *Terra Mar,* carrying aboard the whole band of the Connecticut Governor's Foot Guard, 2d Company, tall fur hats and all.

The marine parade, eventually more than a mile long, wound its way up the river. Gun salutes roared spasmodically from the shore; the *Bowdoin* answered with her little twelve-gauge cannon lashed to the rail. Outboard motorboats, rowboats, tugboats, canoes, dories, steamers, prams, and cutters swarmed over the river, their wakes weaving in and out like twisting threads upon the water. Thousands of camera shutters were clicking, flash bulbs popping, occasional sirens and foghorns sounding, and above all, bursts of cheering and applause from the banks as the crowds yelled, "Hi, Mac! Hi, Miriam!"

"Baffin Land," said the barefooted Frank Henderson, who went four trips to the Arctic with Mac, "was never like this!" And he shook his head in wonder.

Aboard the motor sailer *Manatuck* the bagpipes skirled

as the black-and-red kilted Manchester (Connecticut) pipe band struck up a tune. Ashore, an orange-uniformed girl band played, "Hail the Conquering Hero"; astern, the Foot Guard band aboard the *Northeaster* burst into "Anchors Aweigh."

A small boy with red hair rowed by in a blue boat about six feet away and looked at his sister, remarking, as the *Bowdoin* went by, "Who's that?"

But the earth had not yet begun to shake, nor the river either.

At Mystic Village they both did. As the *Bowdoin* neared the opened drawbridge, a continuous deafening roar of approving noises commenced. Locomotives blew their whistles; the bridge tender sounded his wailing clarion, and the fire whistle cut loose.

Abruptly the *Bowdoin* turned the bend and faced the basin where she was to lie at the dockside, berthed between the New Bedford whaleship *Charles W. Morgan* and the lofty-sparred square-rigger *Joseph Conrad*. Even as the roar of the crowd increased, anticipating the docking of the *Bowdoin*, the schooner demonstrated a certain individuality to the last by nudging the bottom mud and coming to a gradual halt.

A little towboat, the *Weir*, took a line from the *Bowdoin*'s quarter, snaked her off in about three minutes, and the schooner went into berth without incident by a newly cut channel.

At the dock the gangplank was lowered and the distinguished guests came aboard to greet Mac and Miriam.

Lieutenant Governor Dempsey read the gubernatorial order proclaiming June 27 as Bowdoin Day in Connecticut.

311

"The schooner," said the proclamation, is a "worthy addition" to the Mystic fleet, "well qualified to take her place alongside the *Conrad* and the *Morgan*." The Foot Guard band with white trousers, red coats crossed with white straps and embroidered with silver piping and epaulets, played "Bowdoin Alma Mater" and "The Star-Spangled Banner."

Clifford R. Mallory, president of the Marine Historical Association, said Mystic Seaport is "the work of hundreds of thousands who believe in the ideals we are trying to perpetuate today, and we all welcome with open hearts the schooner *Bowdoin*."

Mac, standing like a ramrod, was a small figure in a dark blue suit. "I am thoroughly and humbly pleased at the honor which has been bestowed upon the Bowdoin, my men, Miriam, and myself." He looked at the hundreds lining the dock and continued: "We haven't lost her; we haven't lost the *Bowdoin*. We can come here any time we want and go aboard. She will have a good home here, for a hundred years or more."

Miriam, in blue slacks and an Eskimo-decorated jacket, greeted them both in Eskimo and English, as "good and kind friends," and then there was music again, and everyone moved off for the reception to the MacMillans.

The *Bowdoin*'s last crew picked up its gear, took a look around, and walked up the dock, in ones and twos.

That is the way it was, and as the Yankee whalemen used to say in their logs, "So ends," for there will be no one else who will go sledging over the hard blue ice of the Polar Sea.

# RECORD OF
# ARCTIC VOYAGES

| DATE | NAME AND CHARACTER OF EXPEDITION | SPONSORS AND SCIENTIFIC PERSONALITIES | AREA COVERED |
|---|---|---|---|
| 1908–1909 | Peary North Pole Expedition | Peary Arctic Club. Led by Commander Robert E. Peary; assistants: Henson, Bartlett, Marvin, Borup, Goodsell, and MacMillan. | Northern Grant Land and interior, Northern coast of Greenland, Polar Sea north of Cape Columbia, Grant Land. Polar Sea north of Cape Morris Jesup, Greenland, North Pole. |
| 1910 | Cabot Labrador Expedition | William B. Cabot, leader; George Howe, Schofield Clark, MacMillan | Coast and interior of Labrador; Mailboat, Battle Harbor to Turnavik West; Trapboat, to Asawaban River; Canoe, interior to George River |
| 1911 | Canoe trip along Labrador coast | MacMillan solo | Davis Inlet to Hebron, by canal, Hebron to Cape Chidley aboard S. S. *Harmony*, canoe trip through McLelan Strait |

| DURATION | APPROXI-<br>MATE MILES<br>TRAVELED | NATURE OF WORK DONE,<br>ACCOMPLISHMENTS, DISCOVERIES |
|---|---|---|
| 14 months | 8,000; 1,500<br>by dog team | Peary discovered the North Pole. MacMillan accompanied main party to 84°20′ N before being forced to turn back on account of frozen feet. Mac-Millan sledged a total of 1,500 miles; established tidal station at Cape Columbia, most northern land in North America; conducted survey of Clements Markham Inlet, Grant Land; sledged to most northern point of Greenland and thence to 84° 17′5″ on the Polar Sea; sledged to Ward Hunt Island to establish food cache for Peary if he should be carried west by drift ice on return from Pole; sledged to Cape Morris Jesup to establish line of food caches for Peary if he should be carried east by drift ice as he was in 1906. Established tidal station at Fort Conger, headquarters of the Greely Expedition, abandoned 26 years before. As expedition ornithologist, compiled list of all northern birds observed during trip. |
| 3 months | 3,000 | First to explore Indian trail from Davis Inlet to George River. Studied geological formation of the Labrador interior, compiled lists of bird and animal life, and gathered anthropological and ethnological information concerning the little-known Nascapi Indians. |
| 3 months | 3,000 | Acquired intimate knowledge of one of the world's most dangerous coasts and recognized need for its charting. Studied inside runs of Labrador through which he later sailed his arctic schooner *Bowdoin*. During this trip, he lived with the Eskimos, acquired knowledge of the work of the Moravian missionaries, who since 1771 have worked with the Labrador Eskimos. Visited with the Moravians at Hopedale, Nain, Hebron, Okak and Killinek. Made complete listing of all birds, flowers and animals observed on the Labrador coast. |

315

| DATE | NAME AND CHARACTER OF EXPEDITION | SPONSORS AND SCIENTIFIC PERSONALITIES | AREA COVERED |
|---|---|---|---|
| 1912 | Motor boat trip (21'-power boat *George Borup*) from Boston to Hebron, North Labrador | MacMillan and one companion, Jonathan (Jot) Small of Provincetown. On part of journey accompanied by the eminent ornithologist, A. C. Bent. | Labrador coast |
| 1913– 1917 | Crocker Land Expedition | American Museum of Natural History, American Geographical Society, and University of Illinois. Led by MacMillan; assistants: Ensign Fitzhugh Green, USN; Elmer Ekblaw, geologist and botanist; Dr. Maurice Tanquary, zoologist; Dr. Harrison J. Hunt, physician; Jerome Allen, radio operator. | NW shores Axel Heiberg Island, Greely Fjord, King Christian Island, northern, eastern and certain southern shores of North Cornwall, eastern coast Ellesmere Island from Cape Sabine to Clarence Head, North Greenland coast from McCormick Bay to Foulke Fjord, Renssalaer Harbor, and Humboldt Glacier |
| 1920 | S. S. *Thetis* | MacMillan was second mate | Cruise to Hudson Bay |
| 1921– 1922 | First trip of *Bowdoin* | Department of Terrestrial Magnetism and Atmospheric Electricity of the Carnegie Institution of | Baffin Island, circumnavigation of Fox (Foxe) Channel or Fox Basin |

| DURATION | APPROXI-<br>MATE MILES<br>TRAVELED | NATURE OF WORK DONE,<br>ACCOMPLISHMENTS, DISCOVERIES |
|---|---|---|
| 5 months | 3,500 | Continued study of the Labrador, its coastal characteristics, settlers and Eskimos, flora and fauna. First power boat to go up the Labrador coast. Extensive work in ornithology by Arthur C. Bent. |
| 51 months | 9,000;<br>10,500 by<br>dog team | Disproved existence of "Crocker Land" which had been placed on contemporary maps 120 miles northwest of Axel Heiberg Island. Surveyed or explored areas listed in column 4. First to land on King Christian Island. Discovered coal deposits in Bay Fjord and Axel Heiberg Island. Recovered three records of Dr. Elisha Kent Kane of the Second Grinnell Expedition of 1853–55. Recovered two records and a portion of silk flag left by Peary and two records of Sir George Nares of the British North Pole Expedition of 1875–76. Recovered mail (three personal letters) left by Sir Allen Young at Cape Isabella in 1876 for the British Expedition under the command of Nares. Secured two sets of the rare eggs of the knot, *Tringa canutus*. Compiled three-month series of tidal observations at Etah, North Greenland. Compiled 3,000 words of the Smith Sound Eskimo language. Took 5,500 photographs and 10,000 feet of motion picture film. Conducted extensive work in geology, botany, ornithology, meteorology, ethnology, and anthropology. |
| 3 months | 6,000 | Work in ethnology and anthropology among Eskimos and Indians of area. |
| 1 year<br>(frozen in<br>for 10<br>months) | 5,000; 800<br>by dog team | First to circumnavigate Fox (Foxe) Channel or Fox Basin; "fix" salient points in this area for navigational charts; and discover the nesting ground of the blue goose, an ornithological question long |

| DATE | NAME AND CHARACTER OF EXPEDITION | SPONSORS AND SCIENTIFIC PERSONALITIES | AREA COVERED |
|---|---|---|---|
| | | Washington, D.C. Mac-Millan in command; Ralph Robinson, assistant; Richard Goddard (now Professor of Astronomy, Dartmouth College) and Dawson Howell, magnetic observers. | |
| 1923–1924 | *Bowdoin* "wintered in" and nearly lost in effort of getting out | Carnegie Institution and National Geographic Society. MacMillan in command; Richard Goddard, magnetic observer; Don Mix, radio operator; John Jaynes, engineer; Ralph Robinson, assistant. | North Greenland, Ellesmere Island, Bay Fjord and Eureka Sound |
| 1925 | Two-ship expedition *Bowdoin* and *Peary,* in charge of Mac-Millan now commissioned a Naval Lieutenant Commander to experiment with use of planes and short-wave radio in the Arctic. Captain of *Peary,* George Steele. | National Geographic Society, and U. S. Navy, which furnished planes and mechanics under the command of Lt. Commander Richard E. Byrd. Maynard Owen Williams and Jacob Gayer, correspondent and photographer, respectively, of the National Geographic So- | Headquarters at Etah, North Greenland |

318

| DURATION | APPROXI-MATE MILES TRAVELED | NATURE OF WORK DONE, ACCOMPLISHMENTS, DISCOVERIES |
|---|---|---|
| | | unsolved. Studied Baffin Island Eskimos. Established a magnetic station at what now is called Schooner Harbor (named for the *Bowdoin*) inside the Trinity Islands on the southwestern coast of Baffin Island. |
| 15 months (frozen in for 325 days) | 8,500 by ship; 3,000 by dog team | First survey of Refuge Harbor, North Greenland. Established a nonmagnetic scientific station and recorded continuous tidal and meteorological observations for one year. Performed extensive work in botany, geology, ornithology and anthropology. During the spring of 1924, Mac sledged across Smith Sound to Cape Sabine, Ellesmere Island, and put up Greely Memorial tablet near Starvation Camp, sent north by the National Geographic Society. The tablet reads: "To the Memory of the Dead Who Under Lieutenant A. W. Greely Here Gave Their Lives to Ensure the Final and Complete Success of the First Scientific Cooperation of the United States with Other Nations, 1881–1884." This expedition operated the first short-wave radio from the Arctic. |
| 3 months | 12,500 | This expedition proved conclusively that planes could be used to advantage far beyond the Arctic Circle. Made the first major use of short-wave radio in the Arctic by maintaining constant communication with civilization and by contacting U. S. Naval units halfway around the world. Established tidal observatory station at Etah. Brought back first color photographs ever taken in the Arctic (by Gayer of the National Geographic Society). Major ornithological studies. |

319

| DATE | NAME AND CHARACTER OF EXPEDITION | SPONSORS AND SCIENTIFIC PERSONALITIES | AREA COVERED |
|---|---|---|---|
| | | ciety; Lieutenant Benjamin Rigg, Coast and Geodetic Survey, magnetic and tidal observer; Dr. Walter N. Koelz, ornithologist; John Reinhartz, radio operator; Lt. Commander Eugene F. McDonald, Jr., second in command. | |
| 1926 | Two ships, *Bowdoin* and *Sachem* | Field Museum of Chicago. MacMillan's assistants: Dr. Alfred Weed and Charles Sewall. | Labrador, Baffin Island, Greenland |
| 1927– 1928 | Anetalak Bay Scientific Station, *Bowdoin* and *Radio*. *Radio* returned after 3 months, *Bowdoin* remained 12 months. | Field Museum of Chicago. Sharat K. Roy, fossiologist; Dr. Alfred Weed, icthyologist; Dr. Duncan K. Strong, anthropologist; Charles Sewall, botanist; Clifford Hymoe, radio operator; Frank Henderson, chief assistant; Dr. Earl K. Langford, physician and surgeon; Arthur Reuckert, artist; Novio Bertrand, taxidermist. | Labrador, Baffin Island |
| 1929 | *Bowdoin* voyage | Assistants, Dr. William C. Kendall, U. S. Bureau of Fisheries (world authority on *salmonidae*); Dr. Adelbert W. Fernald, orthodontist; Dr. Samuel Palmer, botanist (Swarthmore College). | Labrador, Baffin Island |

320

| DURATION | APPROXI-MATE MILES TRAVELED | NATURE OF WORK DONE, ACCOMPLISHMENTS, DISCOVERIES |
|---|---|---|
| 3 months | 8,000 | Marine life studies. Collections of plants of Labrador and of Greenland. |
| 12 months | 9,000 | Winter work done by snowmobile and dog team. Established scientific station at Anetalak Bay. Extensive studies of Silliman's Fossil Mount in Frobisher Bay. Studies of trout, wolf fish, rock cod, birds and wild life. Anthropological data on Nascapi Indians. Established MacMillan-Moravian Eskimo School at Nain. Extracted 1,800 Eskimo teeth. 28'-cabin cruiser *Seeko* taken north by Frank Henderson. *Seeko* later donated by MacMillan to Moravians for work with natives. |
| 3 months | 4,000 | Studies of plant life. Investigation of sea trout. Established free dental clinics for Eskimos and settlers in Hopedale and Nain, Labrador. Trained Moravian missionaries in dental work. Installed electric light plant at Hopedale and Nain. |

| DATE | NAME AND CHARACTER OF EXPEDITION | SPONSORS AND SCIENTIFIC PERSONALITIES | AREA COVERED |
|---|---|---|---|
| 1930 | *Bowdoin* voyage, historical research | Students | Newfoundland, Iceland, east coast of Greenland, Labrador, Baffin Island |
| 1931– 1933 | *Bowdoin* and airplane. Surveying Labrador coast adjacent to Nain in 1931 and compilation of data in Boston, 1932–1933. | Grenfell Association and British government. Charles Rocheville, pilot. Accompanied by *Bowdoin* under command of Jack Crowell. | Labrador Coast, Nain and approaches |
| 1934 | *Bowdoin* voyage | Bowdoin College and Clark University. Dr. Alfred Gross, ornithologist; Dr. David Potter, botanist. | Gulf of St. Lawrence, Labrador, Baffin Island |
| 1937 | Special study of the Grinnell Glacier and Icecap. *Gertrude Thebaud* chartered because she would accommodate more scientists and students than the *Bowdoin*. | Canadian ornithologist, Dr. V. C. Wynne-Edwards; U. S. Biological Survey, Washington, D.C., Harold S. Peters; Dr. David Potter, botanist (Professor of Botany, Clark University); Dr. Martin J. Buerger, Professor of Geology, Mass. Inst. of Technology. | Baffin Island |
| 1938 | *Bowdoin* voyage | MacMillan. Students: college, preparatory and high school. | Labrador, Baffin Island, Greenland |

| DURATION | APPROXI-<br>MATE MILES<br>TRAVELED | NATURE OF WORK DONE,<br>ACCOMPLISHMENTS, DISCOVERIES |
|---|---|---|
| 3 months | 8,000 | Followed the track of the Norsemen led by Erik the Red from Iceland to Greenland, Labrador, the Helluland of the Norsemen, Markland, the "woody land," and Vineland, "the land of the vine." |
| 3 months in Labrador | 2,500; 3,000 by plane | Surveyed Labrador coast adjacent to Moravian-Eskimo village of Nain in 1931. This information sent to the British Admiralty by Sir Wilfred T. Grenfell is now included in a map titled "Nain and Approaches." |
| 3 months | 4,500 | Studies of bird life. Main ornithological goal was the group of islands in the middle of Hudson Strait known as "The Buttons," to the Eskimos, the Putjak or "Stepping Stones." Studies of plants at Cape Mugford, Labrador. MacMillan discovered what is now named on charts Bowdoin Harbor in northern Labrador. |
| 3 months | 4,500 | Expedition conducted study of Grinnell Glacier and Icecap. Study of botany, geology, ornithology, and ichthyology. Marked beginning of Mac-Millan's long practice of taking youth North; many of his young sailors learned seamanship and navigation and a knowledge of the Arctic under his direction. |
| 3 months | 8,500 | Students instructed in seamanship and navigation. Work in ornithology, geology, and botany. |

323

| DATE | NAME AND CHARACTER OF EXPEDITION | SPONSORS AND SCIENTIFIC PERSONALITIES | AREA COVERED |
|---|---|---|---|
| 1939 | *Bowdoin* voyage | MacMillan. Students: college, preparatory and high school. | Labrador, Baffin Island, Greenland |
| 1941 | *Bowdoin* purchased by U. S. Navy: U. S. S. *Bowdoin.* MacMillan recalled to active duty. | U. S. Navy | West Coast of Greenland |
| 1942–1945 | MacMillan, consultant on Arctic work | U. S. Navy | Washington, D.C. |
| 1943 | Intelligence flights | U. S. Navy | Nova Scotia, Newfoundland, Labrador, Greenland |
| 1944 | Reconnaissance flights, four planes | U. S. Navy | Greenland, Frobisher Bay, Baffin Island, Ungava |

| DURATION | APPROXI-MATE MILES TRAVELED | NATURE OF WORK DONE, ACCOMPLISHMENTS, DISCOVERIES |
|---|---|---|
| 3 months | 9,000 | Exploration of deep fjords of Greenland and study of some of largest and fastest moving glaciers in the world, particularly the Rink and Umiamako in the Kangerdluk Fjord. Work in botany, ornithology, oceanography, glaciology. *Note:* Sealed bottle containing record giving ship's position thrown into sea above Arctic Circle by Miriam MacMillan was picked up nine months later on shores of Orkney Island, Ireland. |
| 5 months | 6,000 | Aided in construction of two airfields. Survey and sounding of Sondrestrom Fjord at Arctic Circle. |
| 3 years | 0 | Assigned to Hydrographic Office to assist in editing of northern charts. Furnished list to U. S. government of 10,000 books and periodicals containing information about the Arctic. Author of *Eskimo Place Names and Aid to Conversation* written for the armed forces. Compiled Eskimo-English and English-Eskimo list of 5,000 words as used by the Labrador, Baffin Island and Greenland Eskimos. MacMillan's arctic schooner *Bowdoin,* now U. S. S. *Bowdoin,* continued active war work in Arctic waters, 1942–1945, under Lieutenant Stuart Hotchkiss. |
| 3 months | 6,000 | Selected sites for six secret radar installations. |
| 3 months | 9,000 | Photographed east and west coasts of Greenland at 20,000 ft. altitude. Brought back 12,000 pictures of areas covered, to be used principally in preparation of military maps and charts. |

| DATE | NAME AND CHARACTER OF EXPEDITION | SPONSORS AND SCIENTIFIC PERSONALITIES | AREA COVERED |
|---|---|---|---|
| 1945 | Reconditioning of *Bowdoin* | Dr. Alfred Bailey, Colorado Museum; Robert Grayce, Audubon Society. | Labrador |
| 1946–1954 | Six trips north, *Bowdoin* voyages | Each expedition carried scientists and students. Bowdoin College, Chicago Geographic Society. Dr. William Powers, geologist; Rutherford Platt, botanist; Dr. Reinhard Korgen, Bowdoin College; Novio Bertrand, taxidermist. | Labrador, Newfoundland, Greenland, Baffin Island, Ellesmere Island |
| 1951 | Flight to Greenland | U. S. government | Greenland |
| 1957 | Flight to North Pole | Arranged by Lowell Thomas | Top of the world |

326

| DURATION | APPROXI- MATE MILES TRAVELED | NATURE OF WORK DONE, ACCOMPLISHMENTS, DISCOVERIES |
|---|---|---|
| 1 month | 4,000 | *Bowdoin,* repurchased from government after war, suffered neglect and plundering. Put back in shape for Arctic work. Bird work on Labrador. |
| Each trip averaged 3 months. | 69,000 | Doctor on each trip made study of Eskimos and natives and attended the sick en route. Taxidermist on each trip continued preparation of specimens for Bowdoin College Arctic Museum and other museum exhibits. Continued studies in botany, geology, ornithology, glaciology; work for Hydrographic Department in Washington; and study of seamanship and navigation. In 1947 for the first time in *Bowdoin* reached Cape Sabine, Ellesmere Island, Greely Starvation Camp and site of National Geographic Society's tablet placed there by MacMillan in 1924 when he sledged over from Greenland. Schooner nearly lost in ice pack here. On each trip carried supplies to MacMillan-Moravian Eskimo School. Kate Hettasch, faithful teacher, born on Labrador, daughter of Dr. and Mrs. Paul Hettasch (50 years on Labrador coast) continuing commendable work on Labrador. Revisited Refuge Harbor, North Greenland. Miriam, who made nine trips, found Mac's record here, left 25 years before. Recorded language and songs of primitive Eskimos with wire recorder. |
| 1 month | 5,000 | Consultant on a project for constructing radar stations on the summit of the Greenland Icecap. |
| 1 month | 12,000 | Commemorative flight in honor of Arctic explorers who had sought the Pole over three centuries. Broadcast on television. MacMillan present as only surviving member of Peary 1909 North Pole Expedition. |

327

*ARCTIC ODYSSEY*

| DATE | NAME AND CHARACTER OF EXPEDITION | SPONSORS AND SCIENTIFIC PERSONALITIES | AREA COVERED |
|------|------|------|------|
| 1957 | Homeward bound | Rear Admiral Donald B. MacMillan, USNR, and Marine Historical Association, Mystic, Conn. | Buzzards Bay to Fishers Island Sound to Mystic, Conn. |

| DURATION | APPROXI-MATE MILES TRAVELED | NATURE OF WORK DONE, ACCOMPLISHMENTS, DISCOVERIES |
|---|---|---|
| 3 days | 120 | Last anchorage *Bowdoin* in Mystic Seaport. After sailing over 200,000 miles in the interests of contributing to man's knowledge of the world, the schooner *Bowdoin* was enshrined at Mystic Seaport, where she now is visited by thousands each year. |

Space limits listing names of all "alumni" of the schooner *Bowdoin* whom Mac and Miriam affectionately refer to as "their *Bowdoin* family." With pride they have followed these boys and men on sea, land, and air in fields of education, science and exploration, many steering praiseworthy life courses stimulated by *Bowdoin* trips and Mac's leadership.

329

# INDEX

# INDEX

333

# INDEX

335

## INDEX

*George B. Cluett* (schooner), 200, 201, 202, 218
*George Borup* (power boat), 151, 155, 158-164
George River, 131
Gilbert, Sir Humphrey, 61
*Gjoa* (ship), 228
*Gleam* (launch), 59
Goddard, Richard, 246, 252
Godthaab, 265
Godthaab Fjord, 265
Goode Point, 90
Goodsell, J. W., 84, 89, 92, 98, 111, 112, 121, 128
*Gracie Parker* (schooner), 29, 30
Grand Banks, 2, 6-8
Grand Manan, 151
Grant Land, 54, 100, 112, 113, 115, 148
Gready, 155, 163
Greely, Adolphus W., 50, 70, 111, 112, 114, 124, 202, 217, 246
Greely Expedition, 45, 113, 220
Green, Fitzhugh, 167, 172, 175-185, 199
Greenland, 86, 99, 100, 102, 122, 123, 174, 183, 185, 186, 196, 241, 259, 265, 290, 297
Grenfell, Dr., 160
Grenfell Association, 200
Grenfell Mission, 131
Grosvenor, Gilbert, 220, 303
Gushue, Mr., 100, 120

Hakluyt's Island, 209
Hall, Charles Francis, 50, 70, 102, 202
Hampton Roads, Virginia, 219
Hand, William H., 223, 239
Hannum, A. P., 301
Hansen, Captain, 215
Hantzsch, Bernhard, 224
Harlow, Lieutenant Commander, 45, 46
*Harmony*, S.S., 138, 143-144, 147, 297
Harris, Dr. R. A., 165

Harriseeket River, 34
Hattersley-Smith, Geoffrey, 100
Hawke's Harbor, 62
Hawthorne, Nathaniel, 35
Hayes, Isaac Israel, 50, 202, 222
Hayes Expedition, 211
Hayes Sound, 170, 172
Hazen, Lake, 112, 113
Hebron, Labrador, 143, 159, 289
Henderson, Frank, 272, 274, 310
Hendrik, Hans, 189-190, 203
Hendriksen Sound, 208
Henley, Helen, 298
Henson, Matthew, 58, 84, 88, 92, 94, 96, 98, 99, 106, 110, 111, 127-128, 174
Hettasch, Paul, 144, 297
Hettasch Island, 297
Hodgdon brothers, 223
Holsteinsborg, Greenland, 9, 44
Hopedale, Labrador, 156, 281, 304
Hotchkiss, Stuart, 289
Hovey, Edmund Otis, 200, 202, 215
Howe, George, 131, 132, 137
Howell, Dawson, 226
Hubbard, Thomas, 59
Hudson Bay, 144, 191, 221
Hudson Strait, 143
Hudson's Bay Company, 220-221, 229, 234, 240
Humboldt Glacier, 196, 209
Hunt, Harrison J., 167, 194, 197-198, 199, 200
Hvitberget (White Mountain), 172, 182
Hyde, President (Bowdoin), 42

Igloodahouny, 264
Illinois, University of, 165, 166
Inahloo (Eskimo), 211, 216
Inglefield Bay, 262
Inugeeto (Eskimo), 76, 81, 100, 263, 277, 278
*Invermore*, S. S., 131
Isachsen, G. J., 166
Ittibloo, 209

336

# INDEX

Peary, Robert, 44, 48, 49-51, 52-56, 58-59, 61, 67, 69, 70, 73, 74, 76, 85-86, 88-100, 104-108, 165, 166, 172-175, 177-179, 184, 199, 202, 209, 221, 223, 228, 258, 264, 272, 302, 309
Peary, Mrs. Robert, 123, 129
Peary, Robert, Jr., 44, 129
Peary Arctic Club, 59, 91, 111, 122, 128
Peeawahto (Eskimo), 170, 176, 179, 180-182, 184-185
*Pennsylvania* (ocean liner), 45-46
Percy, Charlie, 57, 105
Peteravik, 192, 193, 244
*Phantom* (steamer), 34
Polar Sea, 68, 87, 88, 92, 93, 100, 105, 108, 148, 165, 166, 173, 174, 177, 178, 179, 257
Polaris North Pole Expedition, 202
Port Manvers Run, 275
Porter, George, 73
Porter Bay, 73, 88
Portland, Maine, 32, 33, 34, 49
Proteus Point, 111
Provincetown, Massachusetts, 1-6, 25-27, 29, 33, 36, 43, 64, 142, 240, 280, 301-302
Provision Point, 168, 209, 216

*Radio* (schooner), 270
Rasmussen, Knud, 105, 175, 186
Ready, George Washington, 27
Redcliffe Peninsula, 264
Refuge Harbor, 241, 242, 249
Reid Glacier, 260
Rensselaer Harbor, 196, 197
Repulse Harbor, 102
Resolution Island, 290
Reuchert, Arthur, 270
Reuter's, 125
Rice Strait, 183
Richardson, Mayor (Sydney, Nova Scotia), 129
Rief Island, 103
Rigg, Benjamin H., 257
Rink Glacier, 269
Robeson Channel, 63, 102

Robinson, Ralph, 225, 230, 246, 247, 252, 253
Rogers, Henry Huttleston, 122
*Rogers*, U.S.S., 228
*Roosevelt* (steamer), 49-50, 56-72, 76, 83, 97, 100, 102, 103, 105, 107, 110, 117, 118, 119, 122-124, 128-129, 132, 221, 223, 228, 277, 307, 308, 309
Roosevelt, Archie, 59
Roosevelt, Kermit, 59
Roosevelt, Theodore, 52, 59-60, 76
Roosevelt, Mrs. Theodore, 59
Ross, James, 206
Ross, John, 65
Ross, Neil, 24
*Rowena* (yacht), 258
Roy, Sharat K., 270

*Sachem* (schooner), 275
St. John's, Newfoundland, 147
St. Paul's Island, 128-129, 152, 153
Saltonstall, Senator, 304
Saunders Island, 215
Schei's Island, 171
Schley, Winfield S., 45, 220
Schnell, Fred, 263
Schooner Harbor, 228, 236, 237, 238
*Seattle*, U.S.S., 263
Seeglo (Eskimo), 110
Shackleton, Sir Ernest, 122
*Sheelah* (yacht), 129
Shetland Islands, 124
Shooegingwah (Eskimo), 280
Silliman's Fossil Mount, 270
Simony, Governor, 265
Skraelingodden, 171
Small, Jonathan (Jot) Cook, 149-164, 168, 194, 195, 200, 202, 203, 208, 210, 225, 230
Smith Sound, 98, 119, 168, 174, 181, 184, 193, 214, 246, 259, 260, 262, 289
Smokey Tickle, 123
Sondrestrom, Greenland, 286, 287, 290
Soule, Dillingham Company, 40

339

ICELAND

Mt. Hekla + 4-47

Reykjavik ★

Angmagssalik •

Denmark Strait

Gunbjorns Field 12139 +

Mt. Forel + 11024

Sondrestrom Fiord →

Holsteinsborg •

Jakobshavn •

Greenland Sea

Jan Mayen (NORWAY)

GREENLAND (DENMARK)

Umiamako Glacier →

Rink Glacier →

Disko I.

Godhavn •

Da

Cape

Upernavik •

SPITSBERGEN (NORWAY)

MacMillan May 14, 1909 + Cape Morris Jesup

20°

0°

20°

40°

60°

80°

100°

120°

140°

North Pole ★

Cape Hecla Channel

Cape Sheridan Channel

Robeson Channel

Lady Franklin Bay

Bellot Island

Kennedy Channel

Humboldt Glacier

Refuge Harbor

Crystal Palace Glacier

Littleton Island

Nerke

Umanak (Thule)

Cape Alexander

Kane Basin

Grant Land

Fort Conger

Cape Columbia

Ellesmere Island

Beitstad Fiord

Bay

Glacier

Etah

Smith Sound

Cape York

Melville Bay

Baffin Bay

Markham Inlet

MacMillan April 22, 1914 + +

Crocker Land ?

Cape Thomas Hubbard

Axel Heiberg Island

Ellef Ringnes Island

Amund Ringnes Island

Cape Sabine

Clarence Head

Cornwall Island

Devon I.

Eureka Sound

King Christian I.

Cape Nothorst

Melville Island

Prince Patrick Island

Banks Island

Victoria Island

Northwest Passage

Northwest Passage

B a f f i n   I s l a

Pond Inlet •

Foxe Basin

Spicer Islands

Arctic Circle

Fury and Hecla Strait

75°

65

NORTHWEST TERRITORIES

Coppe

Northwest Passage